Visions of Canada

Visions of Canada

Searching for our Future

KNOWLTON NASH

M&S

Canadian Cataloguing in Publication Data

Nash, Knowlton
    Visions of Canada

ISBN 0-7710-6708-9

1. Canada – Politics and government – 1984–   .*
2. Canada – Civilization – 20th century.
3. Canada – Forecasting. I. Title.

FC630.N37 1991   971.064'7   C91-094447-4
F1034.2.N37 1991

Printed and bound in Canada. The paper used in this book is
acid-free.

McClelland & Stewart Inc.
The Canadian Publishers
481 University Avenue
Toronto, Ontario
M5G 2E9

To all of us

CONTENTS

PREFACE

You simply can't help falling in love with the sheer, sweeping beauty of Canada. Nowhere in the world can you experience such majesty in one place and tranquility in another. For 70,000 miles through skyways and on highways in the past year, I've searched for a vision of Canada and seen the dazzling physical glory of the nation in the snow-capped Rockies, shiny white in the setting sun; the softly ebbing tides of the Bay of Fundy lapping at dusk onto Evangeline Beach at Grand Pré, Nova Scotia; the swirling hurly-burly of the downtown streets of Montreal, Toronto, or Vancouver; the stabbing forty-below frigidity of Lac La Biche in northern Alberta.

But while our national physique boldly flourishes its self-confidence, in dramatic contrast our national psyche is fraught with agonizing uncertainty as we face the clash of our old values and new realities. Canada is a profoundly different country from the one Sir John A. Macdonald brought forth. He was midwife to a nation dual in theory and predominantly British in fact. Today, the children of Britain are a shrinking minority, duality is in question, and multiculturalism is astride our city streets.

Cyclonic arguments swirl through the country over diluted federalism, stronger provincialism, and a wretched economy. Above all this, there is a storm of angst over whether Canada should, could, or can survive as a united nation. Our differences confront and convulse us as never before. The Quebec sovereignty debate has focussed the minds of Canadians on our constitutional conflicts as nothing else has in our 124 years of national life. It has produced an agonizing self-examination, and that is what this book is about. It is my own search for a vision of this country through conversations with forty-five Canadians, who told me what their visions are. These forty-five people were chosen arbitrarily, not to be a scientifically representative sample of our national state of mind, but to reflect various attitudes and to provide a flavour of Canada as we work our way through the alternatives for survival. Their provocative and sometimes colliding visions of this country vividly illustrate the challenge of reconciliation, but still have immeasurably enriched my own sense of Canada. I shall be forever grateful to every one of them.

Their thoughts, whether iconoclastic or orthodox, may help readers in their own evaluation of the nature of the country and the task of building a new Canada. The order in which the interviews appear was designed to produce a kind of intellectual synergy, in some cases providing reinforcing ideas, in other cases contrasting contentions.

A book like this always is a product of many minds and hands, and my thanks first go to McClelland & Stewart President Avie Bennett, Publisher Doug Gibson, and their colleagues, whose ideas gave birth to the book. And to Dinah Forbes, whose sensitive editing skills, advice, and patience were invaluable. I owe a special thank you to Diana Massiah, without whom the book would not have been possible. Her tireless efforts in arranging the interviews across the country and in preparation of the transcripts provided the foundation on which *Visions of Canada* rests. And thanks are by no means enough for my wife, Lorraine, who, with her creative encouragement, personal inspiration, and pragmatic tolerance, is my rock of stability.

JEANNE SAUVÉ

The Right Honourable Jeanne Sauvé was Governor General of Canada from 1984 to 1990. Born in Saskatchewan, Madame Sauvé attended the University of Ottawa and the Université de Paris. She was assistant to the director of the Youth Department of UNESCO in 1951 and in 1952 returned to Canada to embark on a twenty-year career as a broadcaster and journalist. She began her political career in 1972 and has variously served as Minister of State of Science, Minister of Environment, and Minister of Communications. She became Speaker of the House of Commons in 1980, and four years later, was named the twenty-third Governor General of Canada.

"One of the greatest crises in our history."

Nash: You must be pained by the current debate on the constitution and the possibility that Quebec will leave.
Sauvé: Indeed, I think we are living through one of the greatest crises of our history. To begin with there is a great proportion of Quebeckers who, as they put it, have had enough of negotiating with the other element of Canada, and they have been disappointed and traumatized by the failure of Meech Lake. I think that is overdramatized, as a matter of fact. And then in the English-speaking part of Canada, there is a growing impatience with Quebec because it always wants something more, and they have a feeling it will never

stop. And I don't think it will stop. If we are going to live side by side, new situations will create circumstances where you will want to negotiate new arrangements. I think we are too impatient with that.

Nash: This time a deadline has been proposed with a Quebec referendum for October 1992. That tends to concentrate the debate.

Sauvé: Certainly it is going to concentrate it, but it is a dangerous deadline because it is not certain that we will be able to reach an agreement in that short time since we are looking at great changes in the Canadian structure, and it's not only Quebec that wants changes. From the attitudes of the premiers you've got to conclude that they are not happy with current arrangements. There is constant bickering and confrontation between the federal government and provincial authorities. It has been a political game, but it has gone beyond what is reasonable. That bickering simply has to stop.

Nash: As Governor General you were at the very pinnacle of Canada. Now that you are an observer looking at the way Canada is run, how would you change it?

Sauvé: We should get out of joint programs. The division between what the provinces will do and what the federal government will do is not always well thought out. As well, there is a lot of costly overlapping because we keep civil servants to watch the provincial civil services to see whether they are doing what we want. It's a mess. We should decide who should do what and let that authority do it. We should settle these questions once and for all, get out of the joint programs, and allow one authority to do what it can do best and where it can best serve the citizens of Canada.

Nash: Would that lead to a net transfer of power from the federal government to the provinces?

Sauvé: In some cases it wouldn't be a transfer of powers. The power was taken by the federal government, and they just have to let it go back where it was before. Since about 1940 the federal government has created all of these social security programs, which are one of the good things that we have in Canada, but perhaps the time has come now to settle the matter of jurisdictions. Maybe some programs will come to the federal government and some go back to the provincial governments.

Nash: What do you estimate the chances are of Quebec separating?

Sauvé: I think we have never been so close to proposing that option to the Quebec people. But I don't think it will happen.

Nash: What gives you that optimism?

Sauvé: I think that most Quebeckers are comfortable enough within the Canadian framework, and that they will see that it's better to be part of a bigger entity than a smaller one. I think they finally understand that their language and culture has been able not only to survive but to develop within Canada. They might want more powers in order to ensure that and to ensure growth, but I think they will recognize in the end that the final results are not as negative as some would like to put it.

Nash: If there is a split, would it be amicable, or do you think it would turn sour?

Sauvé: I don't think it would be sour for a long time, if it turned that way. There would be a reconciliation in time.

Nash: What would you do if there were separation?

Sauvé: I would stay here in Quebec. This is my home, and I would live with it.

Nash: You would find it pretty uncomfortable from what you are saying.

Sauvé: I don't think so. I am close to a lot of the prominent separatists; they were former friends and they remain friends. I wouldn't like the situation, but I would work very hard to try to solve some of the problems.

Nash: And try to bring about a reconciliation?

Sauvé: Yes, I think that would be the only thing to do.

Nash: If there were painful economic consequences to separation, would that accelerate conversations about reconciliation?

Sauvé: I am sure it would, but the damage would be done, wouldn't it? It would take years and years to reestablish the prosperity of Quebec.

Nash: Aside from the economics, what would the rest of Canada lose?

Sauvé: Politically we would have less clout. We are part of G7* now, and I don't know what it would mean in such international forums to amputate six million people. I think we would lose our reputation as a peaceful, prosperous, happy country. We seem to be the only ones who don't know how many benefits we draw from our Canadian citizenship.

Nash: Do we need within this country to build a more evident sense of pride?

Sauvé: We don't believe enough in ourselves, and patriotism is not very strong in Canada. When I was Governor General I made a few speeches on patriotism because I do feel that it is not strong enough in Canada. We are not proud enough of what we are. We don't seem to have that faith in ourselves that would allow us to grow even more as a country.

Nash: In many ways there has never been a time when the political leadership of the country has been looked upon with such disdain by Canadians. Do we have the political leadership today to get us out of our crisis and into an agreeable arrangement?

Sauvé: I've talked with many people from different areas – young people, older people – and I am really surprised that they believe that politicians have no credibility. Politicians have to change their way of addressing problems. I think people do not like the fact that politicians do not explain things as they are. This was the success of René Lévesque. He took the population into his confidence, and he could tell them that he wasn't going to do something that they really wanted, but he explained it to them in terms that were credible. His sincerity came through because he was a very sincere man. But this crisis for politicians not only exists in Canada, it's universal.

---

*The group of the world's leading industralized nations.

Nash: Aside from what you hope will happen, what do you think will happen in Canada over the next three or four years?

Sauvé: I hope that we will stick together and that we will have the courage and the imagination to restructure our country and satisfy all those who are part of it. There is a malaise within Canada. It is not only in Quebec. I think we should be bold enough to take a fresh look at our country and do whatever is required in order to allow this country to fulfill its role.

Nash: Is there time?

Sauvé: Deadlines can be changed.

Nash: What do you think is good about Canada today and what is bad?

Sauvé: What's good about Canada is that it has been working as it is now for about 124 years, and I don't think that you should simply scrap an experience of 124 years without thinking about it seriously. What's good about Canada is the temperament of Canadians. Canadians are, in general, tolerant people, although they have their bouts of intolerance once in a while. But they come back to being quite reasonable. What's good about our country is the land we occupy which is vast, our resources which are many and which we could exploit even better. Everybody thinks Canada is a country of the future, except ourselves. We are so traumatized by our powerful neighbour that we never think of ourselves as a country that could make it, and make it in a big way. Canadians are awakening to the fact that they can initiate growth and progress and works of art of their own, which are valuable to themselves and which would be valuable to the rest of the world as well. Those are some of the good things.

The bad things are, we haven't got enough population, and in trying to augment our population we are creating problems for ourselves which are going to increase. The diversity of the Canadian population is going to cause problems because we haven't seen it coming and we haven't thought about it enough. Our policy of multiculturalism cannot possibly lead to a united country. I am not disposed to abandon the idea that two great cultures, the French and the English cultures, founded this country and live side by side and produce something unique. That is what's unique about Canada. We have to try to integrate the new Canadians into one or the other group and work at it without asking them to forget where they come from. But we cannot accent multiculturalism, otherwise Canada will become a country that has no core, no centre, no strength from which to build its patriotism.

Nash: You talk about being traumatized by living next door to the American giant. But is there a trauma, too, in the basic French-English conflict?

Sauvé: Some people still think that it would be more practical to have only one language, to have only one culture, and don't see the advantage of the diversity. It's not a trauma, it's lack of acceptance, and with it goes a bit of hostility in some quarters of the Canadian population. I speak the other language of this country. I am familiar with its literature, with its creativity, and with the culture that flows from the language. It has enriched my life, and I am not prepared to abandon that. I think it is a great asset.

LISE PAYETTE

Lise Payette is a long-time broadcaster, writer, and politician who played a central role in the Parti Québécois government of René Lévesque. Born in Montreal, she began her radio career in Rouyn-Noranda and Trois-Rivières. Her popularity in Quebec zoomed in a network radio morning program in the 1960s, and she added to her prominence with a late-night television talk show, "Appelez-moi Lise." She was elected to the Quebec National Assembly in 1976 and was appointed to the cabinet of the Lévesque government. In the early 1980s she withdrew from politics to return to writing and now devotes her time to writing television screenplays.

"We are not like you."

Nash: You are a strong sovereigntist, why?

Payette: I am, and I always will be, because I am convinced that it is the only solution for Quebec. If we don't do it this time, even if we don't talk about it for a hundred years, it will come. We simply are different.

Nash: How do you define that difference, other than the difference in language, between a Québécois and an English-speaking Canadian?

Payette: We don't want to be special, we just want to be ourselves. We are not like you: We don't eat what you eat, we live differently, we love differently. You may laugh when I say that, but that is very important in a culture. We have felt for a long, long time that we cannot be totally ourselves inside Canada. It is impossible.

Nash: You use the word "separate" and most people use the word "sovereignty." What's the difference?

Payette: I use the word "separate" like we do for a marriage. Let's separate. It means that you take your things and you walk out of a relationship. We are not going to run away with the country under our arms. That's impossible. We are still neighbours, and I hope we will be good neighbours instead of a bad couple.

Nash: Do you think that is possible after a divorce?

Payette: I think so. It will depend on the way we do it and if we are mature enough.

Nash: Is there anything that English-speaking Canada could do to avoid a split?

Payette: I hope that they don't do a thing. I hope they let us do what we want to do. I hope they don't change the way they want to live themselves. It is too much to ask. And I hope they don't feel that that is what we are asking for. I just hope they will be strong enough to let us go and make our own country.

Nash: The referendum proposed for October 1992 seems to have focussed the minds of English-speaking Canadians on what we can counter-offer to the Allaire report's twenty-two conditions.*

Payette: I don't think that kind of a negotiation will be going on. You are like a husband who has just been told that it is over. Then you realize that we are serious, so you get together with the boys and you try to find a solution. Well, it's too late. I don't think it would have worked out anyway.

---

*The Allaire report, published last spring, outlined twenty-two constitutional demands of the Quebec Government. It would shift power from Ottawa to Quebec in a wide range of areas, essentially leaving the federal government fully in charge of only defence, customs and tariffs, currency and the common debt, and equalization payments.

Nash: How do you foresee negotiations over separation taking place?

Payette: I think it will be humiliating for us and for you to start negotiating piece by piece. You take your ties, I'll take the dishes; you take this and I will take that. I hope we won't come to that.

Nash: Was the idea of a duality – a bilingual, bicultural nation – doomed from the beginning?

Payette: I think so. From the beginning it was silly. Why should you speak French in Toronto and Vancouver?

Nash: What's your feeling about English Canadians?

Payette: Some of my best friends are Anglo-Canadians. My sister lives in Vancouver. She is married to an English-speaking person.

Nash: What does she think?

Payette: She feels integrated into the Anglo-Saxon world in Canada. Sometimes she finds it difficult in Vancouver because, being French Canadian, she is not welcomed everywhere. She feels that and knows that, but that's the way she wanted to live.

Nash: If Canada is divisible, is Quebec divisible? I am thinking of the Crees in the North and other similar situations.

Payette: This is an instance where you in English Canada don't get all the truth. In fact it has been going quite well with Native people in Quebec. We are the only province to have a contract with them for the use of their land. It has been negotiated, and they were happy at the time.

Nash: Do you think that separation would have worrisome consequences in terms of economic problems for Quebec as well as for the rest of Canada?

Payette: I don't think so. I think we can manage on our side and you on your side, but it is a change.

Nash: What would have to change? Do you envision separate currency, separate everything?

Payette: Whatever. To me, these matters are not that important because I know there is a solution somewhere. What's important to me is that we stop spending our lives talking about possible arrangements, that we stop spending all the energies we have on that question. There are so many things to do in this world, life is so short. Some people have spent all their lives talking about the constitution and federalism. I am fed up with it.

Nash: You spent a lot of your own life talking about it, too.

Payette: Well, four and a half years in politics and then I stopped. When I am asked, I say I have already given. My life is short. I want to do something else before I die. It's terrible to feel that my children will have to do the same thing.

Nash: It is another year or so before a referendum. Do you make the assumption that the referendum will pass?

Payette: I don't know. Who can say? It is a difficult decision to take. I feel that the younger people will not change their minds. Maybe some of the older people will still be scared because we were pretty scared in 1980. Some of you people came over here to say things that were horrible.

Nash: Would that not perhaps happen again in 1992?

Payette: Yes, it will happen again, but some of us won't be scared again. We were scared once and we realized that it was silly. I hope the outcome will be for the sovereignty of Quebec.

Nash: Do you think the question posed in the referendum should be very clear; that is, simply: "Do you want to be part of Canada or separate?"

Payette: That's what I would like to have, but I am not sure that is what we are going to have. That's what I wanted in 1980. I didn't agree with the question at all. A short and clear question, and let's find out what we mean.

Nash: What caused the change within the Quebec business community to make them so supportive of sovereignty today?

Payette: Self-assurance. They realized they were able to do it. This change happened quite fast after the 1980 referendum.

Nash: What do you think Premier Bourassa might do?

Payette: When I went to the funeral for René Lévesque, I saw Bourassa coming in. When he walked down the aisle he was crying, and I thought, he will do it now. I felt maybe he realizes now he is the only one for a while at least. He is there. He has the means to do it.

Nash: Do you mean that in his heart he is at least partly sovereigntist?

Payette: I think so. He almost left the Liberal party with Lévesque when Lévesque founded the Parti Québécois. But then he probably thought it would be easier for him to make a career in the Liberal party, which is fair, and that's why he didn't leave. In his heart, there is a longing for our country.

Nash: You are quite emotional about this.

Payette: I am not angry, but I am emotional. I have three children, I am a grandmother of a girl who is three. I hope we will separate for her sake and that she is able to grow up in a country she knows very well, in a language she knows very well, and she is able to travel around the world with her own national identity. And when she says something, I hope that she won't have to do what I did and say, "I think this, but Canada thinks something else."

Nash: How much did the failure of Meech Lake stimulate sovereigntist support in Quebec?

Payette: Anything that goes wrong will stimulate support, that's for sure. In fact, we don't have to do anything, we just have to let you do it for us. Maybe I should feel ashamed about that, because I would be very proud if we made our own decision, but if we don't, you will throw us out.

Nash: Almost certainly something specific will come back from the rest of Canada. The whole process is geared to that. It will be given to Bourassa, and he'll be asked, can you live with this?

Payette: If I were Bourassa I would say to Canada, "No thank you, we will try to make it on our own." But he is not like that, and I guess most people in Quebec are not, either. They want to keep everything that is possible to keep. They will negotiate to the last moment.

Nash: There is the old joke about a free and independent Quebec within a unified Canada.

Payette: That is very reassuring because then you have

everything. I think it is asking too much from Canada. I would like things to be much clearer and stronger. It's like having an extra-marital affair. Coming back home, you are forgiven, but you don't forget, so what is the use?

Nash: In this case, who is the injured party?

Payette: I think Quebec will be. I think you will make us pay for our "foolish" attitude. I hope we are all intelligent enough on both sides to go through this like adults, that we are able to discuss the issues and stay calm. I hope some of the English people are not serious when they talk about violence. I hope we don't come to that. But if we do, it will be your fault, not ours.

Nash: Your heart and soul clearly is in separation.

Payette: It will be done one day. I just don't know for sure when.

ELSIE WAYNE

Elsie Wayne has been mayor of Saint John, New Brunswick, since 1983 and was the first woman mayor in Canada's first incorporated city. She is one of Canada's most active civic leaders and a tireless promoter for Saint John, which she labels "The Greatest Little City in the East." From 1990 to 1991 she was also a commissioner on the Citizens' Forum on Canada's Future (The Spicer Commission) and is a council member of the Children's Educational Foundation of Canada. Among many other honours, Mrs. Wayne is an honorary colonel in the Honourable Order of Kentucky Colonels. She was born in Shediac, New Brunswick.

"They are asking too much."

Nash: Quebec has now said what it wants, how do you think the rest of Canada should respond?

Wayne: I think the rest of Canada will respond to Quebec by saying, "We want you to be a part of Canada, but let's sit down and talk. The majority of you are francophone. You are a distinct society. " I really believe that the majority of Canadians feel this way about Quebec, but they don't want them to have all kinds of special powers and have more than everyone else in the country. You can't expect people in New Brunswick to want that. There is just no way.

Nash: A Quebecker would say the country was founded on duality, which means the French and the English are equal.

That, in turn, would mean Quebec is equal to the English-speaking part of Canada.

Wayne: They say there are two founding nations, but if you talk to the aboriginal people, they will say they were here first. So what can we do? Do we tear the country apart because some are afraid of assimilation? I spend a lot of time thinking about this, and I say to myself, they are going to have to give, too.

Nash: How would you accommodate what Quebec is seeking?

Wayne: To me, you don't dismantle the federal government. I honestly believe they will not separate. They will see that this is a mistake. Just think about it. If they signed on the dotted line, all those federal jobs come out of Hull, Quebec City, Montreal, wherever they are, the very next day. A lot of people are saying, "If Quebec goes, we are not going to do business with Quebec, they are another country. Instead we will do business with the other provinces." As well, Quebec would have to pay its fair share of the national debt.

There are certain programs that perhaps should be down at the level of the provinces, not just in Quebec but straight across Canada. Culture and language should be at the provincial level anyway, and the federal government shouldn't be involved. You may see a change, but it will be done straight across the board, because there isn't a government which does that for one province that will ever stay in power.

Nash: There is such emotion about this in Quebec and in the country as a whole. What are your citizens of Saint John telling you?

Wayne: In my province, the anglophones are saying they will allow that Quebec is a distinct society, but that doesn't mean it will get special status, or special rights and privileges. The Acadian people are worried what will it mean to them if Quebec goes. We all worry that if Quebec were to separate, what it would mean, not only to New Brunswick, but Nova Scotia, P.E.I., and Newfoundland.

Nash: You would be isolated.

Wayne: That's right, and we are saying they can't do that. They have to leave a corridor between Ontario and New

Brunswick. And they also can't take all the land they think is theirs, because if you look back in history, they don't own all the land. They built on land that they don't own at all.

We have a job to do in the rest of Canada to let Quebeckers know that we want them to stay, but we also don't want them to hold us up for ransom. But I still say, if there is a referendum, they will not go. People at the grassroots are going to rise and they are going to say, "No way are we going to do this." People don't want hyphenated Canadians in our country. They want you to be a Canadian.

Nash: You just spoke of a corridor. How would you get a corridor?

Wayne: There isn't any way that the federal government could possibly allow Quebec to separate without that corridor being there. That would have to be part and parcel of the negotiations. Even so, you are going to see us in the Maritime provinces become more Americanized.

Nash: Closer links to New England?

Wayne: I really don't want to become Americanized, but that's where we would have to turn. We are the ones who would get hurt.

Nash: Do you mean the Atlantic provinces would get hurt because you would be forced to look south not west?

Wayne: Yes. We would be cut off even with a corridor. It's not the same. The fact is that there are barriers up even now. Our workers can't go into Quebec, but we accept Quebec companies into New Brunswick.

Nash: If there was a decision to split by the government of Quebec, do you think that the negotiations would be tough?

Wayne: If Quebec thinks this is going to be easy, they're wrong. It won't be easy. It will be the hardest thing they have ever seen on the table before them.

Nash: It wouldn't be an amiable divorce?

Wayne: If you have one province that's talking about tearing the heart out of the country – and that is what they are doing – and saying, "Okay, I don't care about you, I am just going to go my way," well, then you are not going to sit down with a smile on your face and say, "You can have it all." No way.

Nash: It seems that most of the business, cultural, media, and academic élites in Quebec are sovereigntists. Why is that do you think?

Wayne: Because there is a lack of understanding. I don't think they understand how the rest of this country feels. If Bourassa would only go on the road, and enough Quebeckers would get out of Quebec and into other parts of Canada, they would find out that we are not that different. We are not different at all. Nobody hates anybody. But there is absolutely nowhere in Canada where they want sovereignty association. Either they are in or they are out. You can't have it both ways. Yes, maybe some of the rules can be changed to keep them in, but not all the rules and certainly not all that they are asking for.

Nash: What about the basic question of duality? Was it an idea that was wrong from the beginning, or is it an idea that somehow we have gone astray in trying to apply over the years?

Wayne: It has not been applied properly. That is what caused this divisiveness within our country. You can't legislate language and culture. But you can promote it to a point where everybody wants it.

Nash: You don't think we should legislate bilingualism?

Wayne: That's the problem. If it continues this way, then this is going to continue to divide us, and we will continue to fight. If we are going to have official bilingualism in our country then we have to look at the way it is being applied to the educational system.

Nash: You come from a somewhat Tory city with fond ties to the monarchy, but what about the monarchy in a renewed federalism? What role do you think it should play?

Wayne: I know that Quebeckers have had influence on a lot of Acadians in that they don't want to sing the royal anthem any more. To the rest of us, that's insulting. That's part of our history and we don't intend to change it. The majority of people are proud of it. She is our Queen. We love to stand at attention for her and we will fight any movement to change that. We haven't said much yet, but it is coming.

Nash: How important is it to you that Quebec stay as a part of Canada?

Wayne: If they left, it would be a tremendous loss to this country. I know people get angry and say, "If they want to go, let them go," but down deep in their hearts, they don't want to see that happen. We are a family. I know there comes a time in life when the children leave home, but Quebec isn't one of the children. We are all equal. We are a family.

Nash: But you wouldn't go as far as the Quebec politicians are asking the rest of Canada to go?

Wayne: No, because they are asking for too much. We can't dismantle everything. If we weaken the powers of the federal government, then all of us are going to suffer across the country. And you can't do that. I have a feeling that they only want part of their demands, and when we sit down to negotiate we can get to what they want. I would have to see those last three or four things that they really want.

ALLAN BLAKENEY

A former premier of Saskatchewan, Allan Blakeney was born in Bridgewater, Nova Scotia, and later became a Rhodes Scholar. He worked closely with Saskatchewan Premier Tommy Douglas both as a civil servant and later as an elected politician who played a key role in the development of medicare in Saskatchewan. Blakeney became premier in 1971 and was reelected in 1975 and 1978 but was defeated in 1982. He stepped down as NDP leader in Saskatchewan in 1987. Blakeney was a central participant in many First Ministers' conferences on the Constitution. He now teaches at the University of Saskatchewan in Saskatoon.

"Something has snapped."

Nash: There are so many things to do before any accommodation can be reached by the deadline Quebec is talking about of October 1992. Is there time to reach one?
Blakeney: No. There is no time and I would suggest there is not meant to be time. Many who are cynical believe that the proposal was put forward either to be passed in its total form or to result in a magnificent failure. Nobody can believe realistically that it is possible for the rest of Canada to come forward with a proposal that will be satisfactory to Quebec in that period of time.
Nash: Then what do we do?
Blakeney: So, what happens?

Nash: You have U.D.I. (a unilateral declaration of independence), I suppose, if Quebec votes for sovereignty.

Blakeney: And then the bargaining starts.

Nash: What are you bargaining over then? Are you bargaining over the terms of the divorce or are you bargaining over a reshaping of Canada?

Blakeney: You are bargaining over both. I think it's important for Canadians outside of Quebec not to accept implicitly the idea that the geographic area now known as Quebec has any right to declare U.D.I. There is no legal right, we all know that. There is no right in international law. There is no moral right. Whatever right there is inheres in the Québécois as a people. They may well have a right to self-determination, and the United Nations has said something like that. Suppose we fully concede that, and suppose we fully concede that there is a moral right for peoples to have self-determination. Let's assume all those to be true. We have to find out which groups of people, wherever they may be in Canada, would wish to be citizens of a separate state centred in Quebec and which groups would wish to be citizens of the old Canada. And we would have to draw some boundaries.

Nash: Are you talking about geographic boundaries?

Blakeney: Yes.

Nash: You don't accept that Quebec as it geographically is now would be able to take that land mass out of Canada?

Blakeney: No. On what conceivable grounds? On domestic law? On international law? Surely not. Morals? On what conceivable grounds? The right of self-determination of peoples is all you can say.

Nash: Wouldn't the Quebec government argue that when they hold a referendum, they are finding out what the people want? Supposing the people came back saying they want a form of separation or sovereignty. Doesn't that give the Quebec government a legitimacy to pursue that because it is coming from the people in a vote?

Blakeney: Why don't we have a referendum in Canada then? Or in Ontario and Quebec?

Nash: So it's not the Quebec referendum itself you object to?

You're saying that the whole country should have that referendum?

Blakeney: First, we are Canadians. If a group of Canadians wish to exercise a presumed right to self-determination of peoples and withdraw from Canada, and if we as Canadians accept that proposition, then the task is to define the group of people who are asserting the right to self-determination. And that group of people is in no sense to be defined by provincial boundaries which were drawn for a whole lot of other purposes.

Nash: Where would you draw that line? Obviously the heavy French-speaking population is in the southern part of the province, and the gigantic geographic area to the north has mostly Native people.

Blakeney: You would have a referendum which would ask, "Do you wish to be a citizen of old Canada or new Francophone? And do you wish the area where you live to be part of the old state or the new state?" This would be a national referendum and let's do it on the basis of federal constituencies. Northern New Brunswick people may wish to be part of the new state. The Native people in northern Quebec may want to stay with the old state. We've got to keep in mind we are talking about partitioning Canada and the withdrawal of a people, presumably the Francophone people of Quebec and surrounding areas, and they have to define whether they want to be a part of the old state of the nation.

Nash: So you envision the possibility of having a nationwide referendum based on federal constituencies to find out who wants to stay and who wants to go. Surely that would be unacceptable to the present government of Quebec?

Blakeney: Oh sure, because they wish their majority to govern the minority in Quebec, but they do not wish the Canadian majority to govern the Canadian minority.

Nash: Presuming there is no deal, and then there is a Quebec vote in favour of sovereignty, are you suggesting that the federal government should respond, "I hear what you are saying, but we are not proceeding that way," and then proceed to a national referendum of the kind you suggest?

Blakeney: If we are going to have separate nations, surely we owe it to everybody to draw the boundaries to leave as few minorities on each side as we can. Can any federal government really accept the proposition that they are going to force people who wish to be Canadians to be citizens of another state?

Nash: What do you think is going to happen, as distinct from what you would like to see?

Blakeney: It is quite unlikely that any response from the rest of Canada will be formulated and accepted before 1992. I don't see very much moving. There is a possibility that someone could come up with a proposal for a significantly decentralized Canada, which would be acceptable to Canadians because of their current dissatisfaction with the Ottawa government. That's a possibility. Failing that, I see a referendum in Quebec.

Nash: How would you see the referendum going?

Blakeney: I expect it would pass.

Nash: But then, wouldn't you expect a declaration of independence?

Blakeney: Not for a while. I think the negotiations would start.

Nash: It would be like a union strike vote?

Blakeney: I don't mean to suggest that it would not be for real. But it would not be assumed to be the last act in the drama any more than the 1980 referendum was going to be. It was going to be an act in the drama, one which says, "We are serious, we want you to be serious, and if you are not serious then we are gone." Then I would expect negotiations to start in earnest, and I would anticipate that the negotiations would be very difficult indeed.

Nash: And go on for a long time?

Blakeney: Yes, for a couple of years anyway.

Nash: Would it be resolved by the dawn of the twenty-first century do you think?

Blakeney: Something will be resolved. Canada doesn't work all that badly. There is hardly a country in the world that wouldn't trade its problems for ours. It's not impossible for the country to operate. What is clearly necessary is for the federal government to get hold of the reins of fiscal, monetary, and economic power. That being done, I think quite a few things might happen.

Nash: What do you say to those who say that, in effect, all of this discussion on the Constitution is a waste of time and we should be concentrating now solely on working out the terms of divorce? A number of people are saying that.

Blakeney: Sure, because when the bases of discussion seem to be so far apart, it doesn't seem worthwhile to attempt to arrive at any settlement. But I don't hold that view.

Nash: Many would say that your perspective, in terms of the kind of referendum you were talking about, is a policy of defying the current statements by the leaders of Quebec.

Blakeney: I think it would be sharpening them and saying that they can't have it both ways. They can't say they are relying on the international law and then deny that the international law is talking about the self-determination of peoples. They get around that by saying people who live in this geographic area of Quebec are a people, some of them are French, and some of them are Native, and some of them are English, but they are all a people. The way to find out whether that is true or not is to ask them. You can't assume that because there is a geographic area and there is a provincial government, this makes them a people. A people is defined as a people with a common language, common heroes.

Nash: You've been a principal player in so many of these constitutional confrontations, what are your feelings about this one?

Blakeney: I think this is a very disturbing one, because I see a goodly number of people thinking that these negotiations are unlikely to succeed since we are starting from such sharply different sets of premises.

Nash: There is also a kind of sourness across the land these days, a sourness toward politicians.

Blakeney: Indeed. I've heard people who are certainly not looking for confrontation say that something has snapped in

Quebec. I heard someone else say that something has snapped in western Canada. The snapping means we have been tolerant long enough. If it is true that Québécois feel that they have turned the other cheek often enough, and if western Canadians feel that they have turned the other cheek often enough, then it's clearly going to be more difficult to get some sort of *rapprochement*.

Nash: You hear the question all the time, "What does Quebec want?" But what does the West want in a new Canada?

Blakeney: The West is not a coherent unit with respect to the Constitution. To oversimplify, there are two views of the Canadian federation: one view held persistently by Quebec and Alberta, for very different reasons, is the good old states' rights view. Quebec's reason is almost wholly cultural, while Alberta's is both economic and cultural. Alberta's political culture is that of an outsider looking in, and they've always felt that they have been outsiders even when they were rich. This comes from the fact that their political culture came up from the United States. Then you have the view of the four Atlantic provinces, Manitoba, and Saskatchewan that you need a strong central government to iron out their economic problems, the ups and downs of their economies.

Nash: The equalization payments.

Blakeney: The equalization payments. Not only that, but in the case of Saskatchewan and, to a lesser extent, Manitoba, the system of selling their products on the world markets, and looking after transportation, and all the things that are vital to the economy on the Prairies, are essentially federal. Ontario and British Columbia are a little harder to explain. B.C., of course, is always harder to explain, partly because some of it is like Alberta and some of it isn't. B.C. governments year in and year out are never as hot for provincial rights as the Alberta and Quebec people are. For the most part, the commitment to decentralization is much stronger in Alberta than in Saskatchewan or Manitoba and, by and large, B.C.

Nash: What's your sense of what level of decentralization there should be?

Blakeney: I would like to think that we could move to a model where more administration was done by provincial and municipal governments, for example, the German model, where most major issues are decided by the German federal parliament, but the programs are delivered by the provincial Länder governments. I'd like to see a bit more of that. But in terms of the significant transfer of legislative jurisdiction to provinces, I don't see any particular need for it, and no particular benefit for Canadians from it.

Nash: Rather than a general transfer of federal powers to the provinces, what areas do you think would be appropriate to transfer only to Quebec?

Blakeney: Culture is no problem. Education is no problem, although there are some difficulties associated with it. Canada needs a good deal more spent on post-graduate education-cum-research. However, I think we have to maintain some level of institutional bilingualism or else the divisive forces would keep growing, and we would just be two linguistic solitudes totally. So, language with that qualification. Another area they might well handle is unemployment insurance, because they seem to feel that it is important in manpower policy. But that, too, has real problems. Immigration is half federal and half provincial now, as is agriculture. They talk about transferring social policies, and I don't see too many problems with that.

Nash: Medicare?

Blakeney: I wouldn't quarrel with medicare if portability were guaranteed. We now have asymmetry with respect to the Quebec pension plan and, in effect, with family allowances and with the Canada Assistance Plan, where they get tax points instead. We can continue that for a while. There comes a point when the position of Quebec MPs in Parliament becomes difficult.

Nash: Should Quebec MPs or members of the Senate from Quebec have the ability to vote on matters that don't apply to Quebec?

Blakeney: There are two main problems: One, should they vote on matters that don't apply to Quebec? Two, should they vote in order to decide which is the government? Are they going to be part of any confidence vote?

Nash: If a number of these areas, such as culture, were transferred to Quebec, would you then take the vote away from the MPs in those areas?

Blakeney: I would think that, with respect to the specific items, the answer is yes, I would. I haven't fully analyzed that because they might say, "Well, you're affecting the extent to which we will get compensation," because all of this level of asymmetry assumes that where the federal government delivers a service in nine provinces, Quebec will get an amount of money to compensate.

Nash: The amount of money being roughly what the federal government would have put into the federal program in Quebec.

Blakeney: And if you say, "Well, they can't vote on whether the program is dismantled," then you say they can't vote on whether they are going to have a program and whether they are going to get their money for it. So it's not without its difficulties.

Nash: If you were reshaping Canada, what would you do with the Senate? Would you have a Triple-E Senate – elected, equal, and effective?

Blakeney: I think that an elected Senate is not all that appropriate for Canada. I would much prefer to see an upper chamber which was effectively appointed, probably by provincial legislators. Prince Edward Island might have a third the number that Ontario does. It wouldn't be equal, but it would provide some measure of protection for the small provinces.

PHILIPPE DE GASPÉ BEAUBIEN

Philippe de Gaspé Beaubien is chairman and chief executive officer of Telemedia Corporation, a major communications company based in Montreal. It has interests in twenty-seven radio stations in Quebec and Ontario, a news network in Quebec, a radio syndication company in Ontario, twenty-five regional newspapers in Quebec and five in Ontario, as well as fifteen magazines, including TV Guide, Canadian Living, Harrowsmith, Western Living, *and* City *magazines in Edmonton, Vancouver, and Calgary. The company also owns three magazines in Vermont and Massachusetts. De Gaspé Beaubien was director of operations for Expo 67 in Montreal and was known as "The Mayor of Expo." The Montreal-born executive has deep family roots in Quebec.*

"Tell me that I am equal."

Nash: You have deep roots in Quebec, you have businesses in Quebec, you have businesses elsewhere in Canada, and you have very strong feelings for Quebec and for Canada. Where does that leave your heart in this debate?

Beaubien: Between my stomach and my head, and it's being tugged by both. I am in both communities and I have a great many good friends in both. I am torn because they are being torn. It's not an easy time, but I think we have a chance to come out a stronger country, if we can lick this one.

Nash: How do we go about licking it?

Beaubien: The first condition for any partnership is knowledge of one partner by the other. If you have that then you can probably grow to the next step, which is respect, and then if you are lucky, it can grow further to trust, where you can talk to each other openly and frankly. If you are even luckier, you get some care, which enlarges the circle of people who mean something to you, and then you can share. You can share your views, your ideals, a common view of a nation. But the basic component on which all of this is built is knowledge, and frankly our biggest problem is that we have so little knowledge about the other. If we could get back to honouring our understood commitment that it would be a bicultural nation, that we were two equal partners going into the deal; if Quebec was reassured of that – in a sense giving them what they call their sense of identity, control of their own destiny, acknowledging the fact that they are a separate community – that would go a long way to resolving our problems. I don't know if that is possible now because a lot of new Canadians have come in and we didn't bother explaining the original deal between us, and because of that they say, "Wait a minute. This is a separate status you are giving the other co-founding element. What about us?"

Nash: Can we achieve the kind of knowledge and understanding you seek?

Beaubien: I don't know. It is very serious this time because the train is really on the tracks and rolling down at a fairly fast speed in Quebec, and they were very deeply, emotionally hurt by the Meech Lake breakdown. People in Ontario don't realize that when I talk to them, but to the people of Quebec that was the ultimate rejection. It's a problem that has been there for a great long time. My great, great grandfather on my mother's side was Honoré Mercier. He was the prime minister of Quebec and caused more problems for Laurier than Lévesque ever caused for Trudeau.

Nash: Is it a matter of power, or is it a matter of pride?

Beaubien: It's a matter of survival of the French fact that has been here for four hundred years. In that time they've licked all the odds. Just licking the winters is something, and then being able to hold on to this land, to hold on to your culture, your traditions, despite the threat from the Indians in the beginning. Now, all of a sudden they are finding that their numbers are not increasing, that the birth rate is going down, and they are asking, "Is this the end for us?"

Nash: Would that situation change if Quebec were separate?

Beaubien: At least they would have a chance to say, if it's happening, it's because of what we do, not what other people do. There is so much opportunity here for Canada. Europe doesn't believe what we are doing to each other. Asia can't fathom it, although they are still investing because they don't believe separation is going to happen.

Nash: What is your educated guess about what will happen?

Beaubien: I am an optimist, and I am spending some of my time trying to get people together, keeping doors and windows open, getting people to talk to one another. So I am optimistic that we are going to find a solution. But I am afraid that it will depend on whether my English-speaking friends signal that they really want us to be together.

Nash: In terms of specific powers, what could English-speaking Canada suggest that would give the kind of signal you are seeking for Quebec? What would indicate English-speaking Canada does understand and is prepared for some movement? The Allaire report gave twenty-two conditions.

Beaubien: I think all those are negotiable. If the people of Quebec have an opportunity to find that they can still speak their language, have a place in the community, control those vital elements that affect their own destiny, then I think all the ancillary requests are negotiable. If they feel that they are equal partners, they would relax.

Nash: One of the interesting things about this moment in our constitutional debate is that the Quebec business community, for the most part, supports the sovereigntists, whereas it didn't during the referendum debate in 1980. What happened to change that?

Beaubien: Meech Lake.

Nash: But isn't there also a new and growing confidence, an entrepreneurial confidence, as well?

Beaubien: For a long time people were scared about the possibility of going on their own. I think they have grown accustomed to the fact that separation is not ideal, and there is going to be some suffering. But from what I hear, we can do it on our own. Even if we don't do it as well, we will do it on our own. I think that's bad, because as a country we are better because of each other. We brought the French temperament and the English temperament closer together in this society than it has ever been anywhere else in the world.

Nash: If it did come to a question of separation, how would you view the negotiations for the divorce? Would they be acrimonious?

Beaubien: On the French side, I think they would be pretty peaceful. They are practical people. They know they have to have the rest of Canada as a market. But I hope it doesn't have to come to that. But we have to have an offer from the remainder of Canada. Most of the people I talk to are happy that there is a deadline on this. They see it as being very positive because it is going to force a decision. It is going to force us to move. These issues have been gnawing at Quebec for two hundred years. If we could find a way to satisfy each other, I feel there would be a tremendous growth potential for Canada. If we could just get our English-speaking friends to understand that we had a deal.

Nash: The duality of the French and English nation.

Beaubien: Yes. Honour that deal and we will find a way. If you can come back to the original deal, we will find a way. The big problem is, are we going to stick by the deal that we made originally, or are we going to say, "Well, Canada's changed a great deal since that time. It is no longer a duality"? At that point, Quebec will say, "Look we are not too sure we want to be one of ten. We want to be one of two."

Nash: But there is a big challenge to overcome the apprehensions of Quebec and other parts of Canada about, among other things, bilingualism and biculturalism.

Beaubien: I don't think you will find that Quebec is

interested in making the country bilingual. You have never heard Quebec insisting on that. Their orientation at the present time is mainly here within the province.

Nash: You were speaking earlier of the need for more public involvement now, more people talking together about the issues.

Beaubien: I have spent most of my life trying to be an interpreter to both sides. As such, sometimes you belong to neither. You spend time telling how it is on the other side, trying to encourage patience and understanding and putting water in your wine. It's as if I am in the last moments of the throes of a divorce where I like both parties. I know they are well-suited. I think they are going to have a hell of a time finding a better match. I think way down deep they love one another. But emotion is playing such a strong role right now, and we don't make good decisions when they are based on emotion.

Nash: It must be particularly hard for you given your personal roots and your family roots, which go back to the very beginnings of this country.

Beaubien: My family helped found Detroit and Chicago. The first settlers in Chicago were Beaubiens; the name of the street is still there. One of my ancestors was the largest landholder in all the United States. He owned half the state of New Mexico. Another one of my ancestors went to Vancouver.

Nash: If we split, would we be inevitably worse off in dealing with Asia, with Europe?

Beaubien: If we split, we will be significantly weaker. Canada would suffer and Quebec would suffer. But I have not despaired. I am still hoping there is a way.

Nash: Is the biggest problem now the response from the rest of Canada?

Beaubien: Yes. People in Quebec are waiting to hear if there is a deal. They are on the receiving end. They are not planning to make any offer to make anything else work. They are exhausted with the number of times they have done that, and they have said, "Now we wait and see."

Nash: So if the rest of Canada came back and said they had a framework of an arrangement . . .

Beaubien: If they came back and said, "We will honour the original commitment about dual partnership that we made at the beginning of the settlement. I know it's not going to be easy because Canada has changed, but if that's what keeps you, we will go back to that base and build from there." If that was said, I think that we would resolve this issue. The goodwill is there. The more I talk to my friends in other parts of Canada, the more I find that they, too, desire to continue, not to start all over again. We have been together a long time, and we have the respect of many places in the world.

Nash: Is there a danger that in establishing Allaire's twenty-two points, in establishing so tough a negotiating position, if you achieve anything less it might seem to the people of Quebec to be a defeat?

Beaubien: I have been trying to define in my own mind what a distinct society means, and I come back to the business terms of being able to run my own company, but in alliance with you. I can run the aspects that matter to my survival – survival of my language and of my culture, what makes me what I am and not you, and that is a very distinct and enriching thing. If that can be assured, I have no doubts that the majority of those twenty-two points can be addressed because the basis is there. You still want me. I am still part of the family. I still belong to something, and nobody is going to take that away from me. If I have that, then we will have to compromise.

Nash: It sounds like a cry for recognition.

Beaubien: Tell me that I am equal. Tell me that I am your equal. Then I think we can make it work. I desperately hope that happens for the sake of my children, my grandchildren. In my mind we have no right to sacrifice what we have spent so much time in building. We have no right to leave our grandchildren with a mess.

GORDON ROBERTSON

Born in Davidson, Saskatchewan, Gordon Robertson was, until his retirement, a top civil servant and an expert on the complexities of constitutional matters. He joined the Department of External Affairs in 1941, and two years later became secretary to the Office of the Prime Minister. He was deputy minister of Northern Affairs and Commissioner of the Northwest Territories for ten years before becoming clerk of the Privy Council and then secretary to the cabinet, where he served between 1963 and 1975. In 1975 he became secretary to the cabinet for federal-provincial relations. He has been involved in Canada's constitutional problems since 1947 and was at every conference of First Ministers on the Constitution between 1950 and 1979. After retirement in 1979 he became president of the Institute for Research on Public Policy in Ottawa.

"The prospects [of unity] are well below fifty-fifty."

Nash: You know personally most of the players in this constitutional drama. Do you sense a real will among them to make a deal?

Robertson: I am not sure that I do, quite honestly. I have been in the game a long, long time, probably longer than even you realize. I started in 1949 with Mr. St. Laurent, and my assistant was Pierre Trudeau. He was with me for a couple of years. I have been at it on and off ever since then, and I have never seen a situation anything like the present one, where I detect so little capacity of one side to understand the other side, and so little apparent willingness to meet at some point in the middle. The kind of thing that distresses me on the Quebec side is that the most federalist positions in the province are reflected in the Allaire report. Yet the Allaire report as a recipe for Canada is an utter disaster. The Canada modelled after the Allaire report would, in my judgement, be much worse than separation. I would far sooner see separation than have a Canada of that kind, because a Canada of that kind would not be workable. I would rather see two countries that could work than one country that can't.

Nash: What about the rest of Canada?

Robertson: On the other side, there are people like Clyde Wells, who is highly respected, and others saying that a principle of federalism is that all provinces are equal. It is not a principle of federalism. It's a dogmatic statement. If you make a dogmatic statement like that, and believe that is true, there is no basis for compromise. So how do you get a compromise between what Quebec wants and what people who believe that all provinces must be treated equal want, and still have a workable country? That's the problem. The only solution that I can see is for both sides to put a bit of water in their wine, and for English-speaking Canadians to accept that it is *not* a principle of federalism that all provinces must be treated equally, and for the Quebec side to realize that they don't have to dismantle the federal government in order to protect their language and their culture and the things they regard as vital. But how do you get them both to that point?

Nash: What about the idea of giving all the provinces, not all of the twenty-two jurisdictional areas in the Allaire report, but certain areas that some of the provinces can choose to delegate back to the federal government? That would make them all equal in a sense. Is that a viable proposition?

Robertson: I don't think it is, quite honestly. It is a very interesting idea, but if there is one thing that my long association with federal-provincial relations has told me, it is that if there are powers available for provinces, they will want them. It won't be possible to have a smorgasbord like that without all the provinces wanting to have the same things on their plates. So I am sceptical that it is a workable plan.

Nash: Looking at it from another way, what in your judgement would be the minimum federal jurisdictional areas?

Robertson: Beyond question the federal government must have control over economic policy and over monetary policy. It has to have control over nearly all, but not absolutely all, transportation. And communications; there too, the federal government has to have virtually all control, because communication is almost an indivisible matter. It must have control over foreign affairs and foreign policy. I don't see how it's possible to do as Allaire has proposed and have external policy as a shared jurisdiction. So I think there are at least eight or nine or possibly ten fields that one could identify as being minimal requirements for an effective federal government.

Now there are a number of things that I think could be shared jurisdictionally. Agriculture is shared, immigration is shared, social security measures could be shared, maybe regional development could be shared. The environment obviously has to be shared, and there must be a substantial federal power there for matters that extend beyond the provinces.

Nash: In those shared jurisdictional areas, could you maintain national standards effectively?

Robertson: I am not quite sure that we need to have national standards in most areas of social policy.

Nash: Medicare?

Robertson: I can't quite see why it wouldn't be possible for provinces to work out, as they do now, most aspects of medicare and leave them to handle arrangements regarding portability and that kind of thing. I am not quite sure that you need Big Brother to impose the standards there. And again, in connection with the environment, I don't know that you need to have national standards as long as you have a federal government with jurisdiction over issues that extend beyond the boundaries of a province. I am not altogether seized with the importance of having national standards in shared areas imposed from the centre. I think they could work on the basis of interprovincial agreement.

Nash: What about some of these other areas of contention now? The Senate, for instance.

Robertson: For a long time I have believed that one of the most important things lacking in our federal system is an effective Senate that gives much better representation and weight to the small provinces than we have now.

Nash: That's only one E – elected. There are two others that are talked about – effective and equal.

Robertson: I give them two Es. It seems to me that, assuming Quebec is still a part of Canada, equal representation is just not on. You can't expect Quebec to be content with a 10 per cent representation in the Senate. That just isn't real. It has to be a two-E Senate: elected and effective. Now the question becomes, what does effective mean? It can't mean that the Senate would have the power to defeat the Government of Canada. It has to be effective in the sense of a suspensive veto. There might be one or two areas in which the Senate could have an absolute veto, but very few. I would think for most things it has to be a suspensive veto, which could be a pretty effective tool if you had good, credible representation in the Senate. That is elected representation.

Nash: What about the monarchy? Should the monarchy play the same role in a new Canada as it does today?

Robertson: That is one of the most difficult questions of all. I don't think English-speaking Canada is yet ready to do away with the monarchial tradition, but if we were to totally redraw our Constitution with a constituent assembly, as some have advocated, I can't imagine that Quebec, if it was a participant in a constituent assembly, would agree to a brand-new constitution that included the monarchy.

Nash: Given your sense of the minimal needs for federal government, are those conditions acceptable to Quebec?

Robertson: I doubt that they are, quite honestly. The only hope I see is that, at the end of the day, perhaps in the autumn of 1992, both the people of Quebec and the people of the rest of Canada will have a better appreciation of what I think will be the horror story if we do try to split up. Its consequences would be devastating for quite a prolonged period of adjustment. For a period of five years, maybe even ten years, there would be economic and financial uncertainty that would bring about a reduction in gross national product, a reduction in employment, a difficulty in securing foreign investment, and all kinds of other consequences that would really hurt both sides. If these things can be understood by both sides, which they are not at the present time, then I think people might look more seriously at how to avoid splitting up. But I don't see any tendency or propensity at the present time to make the necessary compromises.

Nash: What are some of those horror stories of which you speak? How would our everyday lives be affected?

Robertson: I think we would start off by negotiating the basic terms of separation, and this would raise the question of the national debt. What share of the national debt should be assumed by Quebec? A study for the Bélanger-Campeau report says 18.5 per cent would be appropriate. Another percentage that has been suggested is related to the population, which is about 25 per cent or 26 per cent. One has to realize that every percentage point represents roughly $4 billion. There is going to be an awful wrangle over every percentage point as to how much Quebec can take on. English-speaking Canada has to recognize that, as things now stand, 100 per cent of the debt is the obligation of the Government of Canada. None of it is the obligation of the Government of Quebec. So the bargaining position from which the rest of us start is weak. Quebec does not legally have to take on ten cents of the debt, and they won't unless it's in their interest to do so. So we might get into the situation where, in order to get Quebec up from saying 18 per cent to 25 per cent of the debt, English-speaking Canada would threaten all sorts of horror stories about trading arrangements and about maintaining ownership and control of the St. Lawrence Seaway, and about referendum in Quebec to see whether this section or that section wanted to remain with

Canada. One can carry on these imaginings about negotiations into a situation where tempers are very, very frayed on both sides, and people do foolish things. And if people did foolish things, you could have consequences that would shatter international confidence. People wouldn't want to invest. If the Japanese, the Germans, won't want to invest, investment will only come at higher rates of interest, and our trade suffers.

Nash: You are talking about these consequences happening both for Quebec and the rest of Canada?

Robertson: Both. It is very hard to get a good analysis of this kind of situation without sounding as if one is engaging in terrorism. What I have said now probably will sound like terrorism, but I think it's realistic as a possibility.

Nash: You don't, I gather, see negotiations over separation as being a fairly amicable discussion?

Robertson: It is very hard to be amicable, or to be sure of remaining amicable, if every percentage point you are dealing with is worth $4 billion. That's very, very difficult.

Nash: Do you think that any kind of sovereignty association would be possible?

Robertson: I think the only options are renewed federalism or independence for Quebec.

Nash: Total independence?

Robertson: Yes, total independence. After Quebec is independent one can negotiate an arrangement, or as part of the process of becoming independent, arrangements can be made. But I don't think it can be anything less than independence either for Quebec or for us.

Nash: It is hard to judge at this point whether Quebec is negotiating, and what is movable and what is bottom-line. What's your judgement?

Robertson: For the Parti Québécois there is only one satisfactory answer, and that is separation. As far as Mr. Bourassa and the Quebec government are concerned, I suspect that Allaire is not the bottom line, but a negotiating position. But the trouble is that they have set the negotiating position at such an extreme level that it is going to be very difficult to arrive at a satisfactory point between that extreme level on the one hand and what's essential for an effective federal government on the other hand.

Nash: If the worst comes to the worst, and there is a separation, how do you envision the rest of Canada: as it is now, minus Quebec, or broken down into regions?

Robertson: I think it probably would stay, at least for a substantial time, as a single country with an independent Quebec in the middle, looking a bit like Pakistan used to. I don't think that one would, for quite a long time, see provincial identities disappear and Canada simply become regions. I could be quite wrong on that, but my own view is that the rest of Canada would retain its provincial characteristics, and retain the essence of a federal system, and would be a reasonably effective country. It would be a much diminished country pyschologically, politically, economically, but quite possibly a reasonably successful country.

Nash: What about internationally?

Robertson: Oh, we would be much diminished, of course. I think that part of our role and its importance has been in the success of making it possible here for two cultures, different in language, different in history, to live together successfully. We are a living example of what can be done. If we become a living example of what doesn't work, then we are not going to be very influential. And of course, the saddest thing would be that both English Canada and Quebec would be so much more dependent on the United States.

Nash: How much dependence, how much pull, would the U.S.A. exert especially on areas that are far from the centre and close to the U.S.A., such as British Columbia?

Robertson: It would be a great pull. A genuine question is whether I am right that we would stick together as a diminished country of nine provinces, or whether we would split further. I still think we would stick together, but those pulls would be greater.

Nash: Do we have the passion and the will-power among the leaders, the players, and among the people to keep the country together?

Robertson: That's a good question. It used to be there. I like to think that it still is there. Perhaps we may get out of adversity and out of a terrible, terrible crisis if there is a sense that there is still a common identity, a common will to be together rather than to be chips and pieces solely focussed on a narrow interest.

Nash: There has been a lot of focus on that narrow interest. There's been evidence of it that almost every provincial-federal meeting. Have we, in a way, been too regionally or provincially selfish?

Robertson: Oh yes, I think we have. And I think one has to recognize that the Charter of Rights has, on the whole, made the thing worse. The Charter has not exacerbated regional interests, but it has exacerbated the focus on the individual interest. It's done a lot of good, I am not denying that. I am still in favour of the Charter of Rights, but one has to recognize, I think, some of the problems it has created. One of the problems is an increased intensity of focus on individual or group interests, as opposed to the general interest, so that we really rather have made things worse in the last few years.

Nash: Do you see any modification, any sign at all, of that changing?

Robertson: Yes, I do. It's quite interesting in the last little while how many people have suggested that there is an important downside to multiculturalism. Multiculturalism is one aspect of the focus on a particular interest instead of the general interst. I think that there is going to be, and perhaps we are already seeing, a gradual increase in appreciation that the focus on individual or group interest can go too far, and that there has to be greater weight given to the total social interest of the whole country.

Nash: Now you sound as if you are talking about altering the thing we have talked about for decades, generations, in this country: the mosaic of Canada, and how much better it is than the melting pot of the United States. Are you suggesting that we have gone too far with the mosaic and we should be doing more melting?

Robertson: Yes, yes I am. I think we have carried it to the point of mosaic madness. And, as I mentioned, I think there is a growing appreciation that this can have deleterious effects.

Nash: Are you a pessimist or an optimist about the future of Canada as a united country?

Robertson: I would put the prospects somewhere below fifty-fifty. I can't see that they will be better than fifty-fifty and I think, on the whole, unless there is a change in attitude on both sides, it's well below fifty-fifty.

Nash: And at the moment you don't discern those changes?

Robertson: No. No, I don't discern them at all. Only the perception of a really disastrous crisis would produce them.

ALLAN GREGG

Allan Gregg, one of Canada's foremost researchers into public attitudes, is chairman of Hill & Knowlton (Canada) Ltd., and chairman of Decima Research. Gregg began his career as a university teacher before joining the Progressive Conservative Party as executive assistant to the president and as national campaign secretary. He founded Decima Research in 1979 and has become a much sought after public speaker on social and political trends in Canada. An author and commentator, Gregg is also a director of the Canadian Academy of Recording Arts and Sciences, and chairman of the Toronto Festival of Festivals.

"Rootless and rudderless."

Nash: As much as anybody in the country, you have your finger on the pulse of what Canadians are thinking. What is our state of mind in both English-speaking Canada and Quebec?

Gregg: Well, English-speaking Canadians are easier to describe because they are more unanimous in their confusion, whereas the Quebeckers are far more decided. You wonder if that is going to shift. I would use two words to describe the population lately, and they are rootless and rudderless. The rootless part is because they have grown up with values that, increasingly, experience is telling them aren't worth clinging to any more. We were always told that things were going to be better. People are saying today, "Well maybe that is not the case. " We have always had this vision that we are very tolerant and fair, and those were the rules by which the game of being a Canadian was played. Increasingly, there is a view that the rules are either unworkable or they have been breached. The conclusion on the part of English Canadians in unprecedented numbers is, why be fair and tolerant? And they're also of the view, increasingly, that maybe there isn't a national interest. They are saying, "Let's forget about it and pursue my own interest." So there is a distemper, a real anxiousness and minginess out there. This is happening against a background of Canadians thinking that they are so generous-minded, so charitable, so tolerant, so peaceable.

Nash: That's what we would like to think rather than what in fact we are becoming?

Gregg: The reason that the second word is rudderless is that there has been no replacement ethos. People know increasingly what they don't want, but there has been no kind of congealment or consensus as to what we do want. That's happening now over the constitutional issue.

Nash: Is that also reflected in our attitude toward governments?

Gregg: Today the population says that governments can't organize a two-hole outhouse. There is just no faith. The loss of confidence in government as an agency or an initiator of the public good is without precedent.

Nash: If we have that attitude throughout English-speaking Canada, surely it bodes ill in terms of making a deal with Quebec.

Gregg: Very difficult. If public opinion doesn't change in English Canada between now and the referendum there will be no reconciliation.

Nash: How can it change?

Gregg: I don't know. I sat in stunned disbelief throughout the entire Meech Lake process and studied public opinion weekly, and in many instances, daily. I have never seen élites in this country more unanimous. All three political party leaders on the same side, the business community all on the same side, the media, by and large. But English Canada was completely and utterly unmoved by the exhortations of their leadership. I had never seen that before.

English Canada, first of all, does not understand that there has been a fundamental change in the province of Quebec. The fundamental change is a tremendous kind of confidence and optimism and outward orientation, which has never before been witnessed in that province. The hallmark of that province has always been an acute awareness of minority status and fear that hostile English people will steal their culture and steal their language. Quebeckers today believe they have to be very vigilant about language and culture, but quite frankly, they think they have crossed that particular Rubicon. They think they are on to bigger and better things, and they think English Canada is holding them back, dragging them down.

Nash: Dragging them down from an economic point of view?

Gregg: That's right. Economics is driving this right now. It is the reason why you see 84 per cent of the members of the Quebec City Chamber of Commerce voting in favour of sovereignty association. Sovereignty association is no longer only for the academics and the radical left. It is now a very legitimate posture put forward in the boardrooms of Quebec because they say in the same breath, "English Canada is bankrupt, they are timorous, they are afraid, they don't know their place in the world, they don't want to trade, the financial institutions are moribund, they think government is the enemy as opposed to a willing and cooperative partner in commerce." They are saying, "The world is our oyster and we don't need you guys. In fact, you are probably holding us back." English Canada doesn't recognize that there has been this profound change and, whether it's merited or not, it's real. They think Quebec is just bargaining for another wharf. Quebec is saying, "If push comes to shove, I am going to go, and you are shoving me. And in the end, we'll do quite nicely thank you, and you guys will be in big trouble." I think both of those postures are wildly unrealistic.

Nash: Is there a gap between these attitudes, which are held by

the élites of Quebec, and those held by the people of Quebec?
Gregg: You raise an interesting point. As much as English
Canada can be accused of naïvety for not understanding the
tremendous risks at stake over the prospect of national dis-
integration, which would be the inevitable consequence of
Quebec leaving or even of sovereignty assocation, Quebeckers are equally naïve in their view that they are God's
gift to small and medium business. You take away those CIDA
grants from Bombardier and Lavalin and just see how great
their commerce would be. If Quebec Hydro couldn't float
another bond, which I am sure would happen for a year after
any kind of significant political dislocation, then you would
have a whole different perspective on James Bay expansion
and Quebec's ability to export electricity.

Nash: There is much discussion about the transfer of power
from Ottawa to the provinces. How much of a transference
do you think English Canadians are prepared to accept?

Gregg: The population wants a hell of a lot more decentralization than they have right now. They see the federal government as unresponsive, aloof, and completely and utterly
inefficient, unable to deliver the kind of things they have
historically expected from government. They believe their
provincial governments are far more responsive, far more
efficient, than the federal government, and therefore they are
prepared to accept a tremendous devolution of jurisdiction
to the provinces. But they want national standards. If you
ask, "Who should be in control of education?" 85 per cent of
English Canadians and 95 per cent of Quebeckers will say,
"Provincial government." If you ask, "Should there be one
standard of education that applies throughout the entire
nation, below which no government should ever be allowed
to fall, or should standards of education be established in
different ways in different provinces?" then 75 per cent of
Canadians, including 65 per cent of Quebeckers, will say,
"One standard."

Nash: What about bilingualism? How popular is it today?

Gregg: If you ask, "Given the choice, would you have your
children become fully bilingual?" there is virtually no

Canadian who would say no. If you say, "Given the opportunity, would you personally become bilingual?" about three-quarters of Canadians would jump at the chance. When you get beyond that to the government deciding for you whether your next job, whether your remuneration, is going to be contingent upon your ability to speak two languages, the levels of support go right into the dumper, and you are down to about 35 per cent of English Canadians.

Nash: Do English Canadians accept a duality in Canada today?

Gregg: Yes, by and large. If you put it on that basis, people will nod their heads in agreement. Where it gets confused and muddy is when you bring in the issue of multiculturalism. The Ukranians have made every bit as big a contribution to the city of Winnipeg as the francophones have to St. Boniface, and the notion that somehow Quebec and the francophones stand alone in the country as the only recognized culture after the English, insults sensibilities. When push comes to shove, the recognition that there are only two founding people starts to break down in the face of other arguments.

Nash: If you said in English-speaking Canada that you only have to speak English and in French-speaking Canada you only have to speak French, would that be perceived by Quebeckers that the rest of the country isn't much concerned about bilinguality?

Gregg: Quebeckers are really over that hurdle. They believe that there is virtually nothing English Canada could do, or North America could do, to extinguish their language and culture, whereas ten years ago, that was the absolute core of Lévesque's argument for sovereignty association.

Nash: Some people suggest we are facing the choice of an eviscerated Canada or a truncated Canada. That's a pretty hard choice.

Gregg: The prospect of significant decentralization and devolution of powers in the context of some strong standards doesn't scare me that much. I think in getting to that point we, as Canadians, would be forced to go through a process

that would ask us, "Why do you want the federal government?" and we would come up with some answers. Right now,
there is no answer. Ask, "Why do we have a federal government?" and the first response the average Canadian makes is,
"They are no good for anything, they are hopeless, they are
useless." That absence of legitimacy is what makes the country ungovernable.

Nash: What about the argument for the special status for
Quebec?

Gregg: The whole notion of asymmetrical federalism has no
chance, just none whatsoever. I can't see English Canadian
public opinion changing sufficiently to make the prospect of
giving Quebec anything that is special, unique, different,
politically viable. If it was asymmetrical federalism or no
Quebec, right now they would probably choose no Quebec.

Nash: How do you think Canada will look by the year 2000?

Gregg: I am a bit of an optimist. If I learned one thing study-
ing Canadian attitudes, it is that we are remarkably resilient
and pragmatic people. We might not be very well-informed,
but we are eminently reasonable. Quebeckers, especially, are
nothing if not pragmatic.

There are only three options being discussed in Quebec
right now. One is status quo, which is unacceptable to 85 per
cent of Quebeckers. The second is outright independence,
nothing to do with English Canda, which is unacceptable to
85 per cent of Quebeckers. So you are left with this thing
called sovereignty association, which right now is defined by
Quebeckers as having my cake and eating it too. They think
there is no downside to sovereignty association.

Nash: Somewhat like getting a divorce and having a joint
checking account.

Gregg: Checking account, conjugal rights, and everything
else. But I think that within the province of Quebec there
will be increasing acknowledgement that sovereignty association, however it is defined, has got a downside to it, and they
will not want to deal with that downside.

Nash: What percentage of Quebeckers would you estimate
are floating on the whole issue – are soft sovereigntists?

Gregg: It's big. If you say that upwards of 65 per cent support an option termed sovereignty association, half of those could potentially switch their support.

Nash: Is it your sense that, if the decision is going to be made by that group in the middle, it will essentially be made on the grounds of the pocket-book not emotion?

Gregg: The emotional battle has already been waged. It has been won by the sovereigntists. Emotionally, Quebeckers have turned a page. On just strictly an emotional level they are more than prepared to, if not go it alone, certainly take far more control of their destiny. We are moving now to the economic arguments, and they will not be made credibly by anyone from outside that province. They will have to be made by the people in the province themselves.

Nash: Which is to say by the business community. The labour élite in Quebec is very sovereigntist.

Gregg: Sure, and Bourassa is going to be extremely important in this. I have not seen in the last ten years anyone who can read his constituency and play his constituency better than Bourassa. He has got very strong credentials and an image as a good manager, a good negotiator, and a good administrator.

Nash: So your feeling is that he is probably the best person there insofar as the federalist option is concerned?

Gregg: No question. I think, in a perverse way, his interests and Mulroney's interests on this issue are utterly aligned, and that both of them know it. You will see a fascinating cat-and-mouse game over the next little while as Mulroney tries to demonstrate to English Canada that he is not selling out the store for Quebec and as Bourassa tries to continue to strengthen his nationalist bona fides as a strong Quebec nationalist, while at the same time they both try to move together.

JANE JACOBS

An internationally acclaimed writer and thinker, Jane Jacobs revolutionized urban planning with her books Death and Life of Great American Cities, The Economy of Cities, *and other works on city living. Her books have become standard textbooks for urban studies. She was born in Scranton, Pennsylvania, where she became a reporter for the local newspaper before moving to New York near the end of the Second World War. She began writing on urban affairs in New York, and moved to Toronto with her architect husband in 1967. An activist advocate of a "people" approach to city planning, she urges mixed development, conservation, nature in the city, and ivy on the walls.*

"Quebec will be separate."

Nash: Do you think Canada has a future as a single nation?
Jacobs: As a single nation, no, I don't think so. I think this is going to go on and on and on until it's settled that there has to be a division. The reason I think this is because of the fundamental difference we call duality. The French really believe in Canada as two founding peoples on an equal basis, and that all the immigrants who have come into the rest of Canada are part of the other founding nation, even though they aren't basically English, Scots, and so on. The rest of Canada obviously can't see it that way. They think of Quebec

as a province like the other provinces. This is an old, old, different vision of what the country is.

Nash: And you think those different visions will inevitably lead to a separation?

Jacobs: It can't be resolved. It is irreconcilable. But this could be lived with and sustained as long as it wasn't confronted.

Nash: Now we confront it.

Jacobs: When I first came here in 1968, I was amazed at constitutional conventions that couldn't arrive at anything, and I gradually began to understand why. The sticking point always was what you do about Quebec's veto. All the ingenious devices that we thought up to solve this just couldn't satisfy the other notion that Quebec has to be a province like any other province.

Nash: Could you resolve that difficulty, if there was the will to do so, by simply granting many of the same powers to all the provinces, not just to one?

Jacobs: Well, that has been suggested too – that any province can have a veto on any addition or amendment to the Constitution. But on the face of it this simply isn't practical. Nothing will ever get done.

Nash: If you delegate all federal powers, or most of them, we will have a kind of boneless wonder as a country.

Jacobs: That's right. You would have, in effect, ten nations. It would not only be a boneless wonder, it would be a dog-eat-dog situation. For instance, Newfoundland, to take an extreme example, but Saskatchewan is another, simply can't exist on its own resources. It needs those transfer payments from the richer provinces. And you can't have sovereignty and live on the largesse of another nation without being a puppet or a satellite.

Nash: If a split is inevitable, what happens to Quebec? What happens to the future of Canada?

Jacobs: I think it could work very well, as the Norway and Sweden separation did, for instance. It could work very smoothly, but what happens depends to a great extent on how long this takes. The longer it takes, the more acrimony there will be and the more obstructions there will arise to doing it in a sensible and kindly way, with each party wishing well to the other.

Nash: Would you have to negotiate the details before there was a formal separation, or do you envision an announcement of separation prior to any negotiations?

Jacobs: You begin with the arrangement. That's the way it was done with Norway and Sweden, which I keep bringing up because they separated without a war and without aftermath of war.

Nash: Tell me about that, because I'm not that familiar with the details.

Jacobs: Norway, in effect, had no sovereignty. First it came under the sway of foreign merchants, and finally Denmark took it over as a kind of protectorate. Then, after the Napoleonic Wars, the winners arranged that Norway should go to Sweden because Denmark had not sided with the victors. Part of its punishment was to have Norway taken away and given to Sweden. This was in the early nineteenth century. Norway at this point decided it wanted to be a country on its own. It waged a very long struggle, and it won little bits of things at a time. At first it won only symbolic things, such as a flag that it could show on its ships in certain waters. They had a governor general, and they had representatives from Norway who were in the cabinet in Sweden. But they were stooges of the Swedes. But the Norwegians kept at it, getting a little bit, and a little bit, and sometimes not getting what they wanted, but just postponing it. It got more and more bitter as time went on and various irreconcilable things came up.

Nash: When did the break finally come?

Jacobs: The break finally came in 1905. It came because the Norwegians wanted a real prime minister from their own parliament. They didn't want a governor general sent in from Sweden in place of a prime minister. Finally, Sweden acceded to this. But the Swedish people became more and more angry at Norway because Norway was forever asking for more and never seemed to be satisfied, no matter how much Sweden tried to placate it. The two populations just got more and more outraged. The Swedish king and his government were sympathetic to Norway's demands and willing to give in, but because of the popular feeling, they reached a point where they couldn't. When it looked as if Norway would go to war over one of these issues, the Swedish government would back down and give them a little more. When it looked as if the Swedes were really going to war against the Norwegians, the Norwegians would back down. In 1905 they had another one of these to-dos. Then the Norwegian parliament declared their independence. By this time, the Swedes were willing to let Norway go.

Nash: In Canada now, especially in western Canada, a lot of people are saying, "Well, if that is what Quebec wants, let them go."

Jacobs: That is exactly what happened in Norway and Sweden, and once the decision was made, it made an amazing difference to the negotiations. There had been attempts at negotiations, but they never really worked out because the two positions were irreconcilable. But once the decision was made that Norway was a separate country, then the negotiations went on in good faith and amazingly fast. Here in Canada, I think the country won't know exactly what it wants or how it should be different until after the separation is made.

Nash: In practical terms, assuming a deadline of October 1992 for the Quebec referendum, what should English-speaking Canadians do?

Jacobs: They should get to work with Quebec on the negotiations to make it a separation with as few exacerbating details left dangling in the air as possible.

Nash: Do you think that, in the end, separation will be better for both sides?

Jacobs: It will be much better.

Nash: Why?

Jacobs: For one thing, the longer this goes on, the more acrimonious it's going to be. It does have a parallel to divorce cases. Very often the outside observers see their friends who are divorcing, cutting off their noses to spite their faces.

They get so angry at each other that they do things that are against their own interest, and this is what I see happening in Canada. Much of what the non-French part of Canada thinks it wants now is to foil Quebec or to spite Quebec or to get even or to have as much power in the provinces as Quebec does as a province or as a separate country.

There are two points I would like to make. One is that, unless both parts have their own money, their own currency, it is going to be a mess, and this has not been faced either in Quebec or in English Canada. It hasn't been faced in Quebec because they don't feel quite that responsible, and they are scared of it. They don't have quite that much confidence in themselves. The second point is about Canada and the world. Canada has prided itself, and quite rightly so in many ways, on being an honest broker where it is needed.

Nash: Won't the ability to be an honest broker be lessened if there is a split?

Jacobs: No. I think it would be increased. Let me put it this way. The problem Canada is facing is not unknown in the rest of the world, to make an understatement. It is one of the great historical themes of our times. At the beginning of this century there were only fifty sovereignties in the world. There are now more than 150. People keep talking as if consolidation of sovereignties were the trend. It is quite the opposite. Multiplication of sovereignties has been the trend. There are more than three times as many now as there were at the turn of the century, and that is very largely because of the breakup of great empires into independent nations.

Nash: You see us as a part of that trend.

Jacobs: We are part of that now. Mostly that only happens as a result of wars and insurrections, when territories get taken away. The remarkable aspect of the Norway-Sweden breakup was that it did not involve a civil war, armed insurrection, or a lost war. This is a model for how these separations should happen: for the resulting sovereign nations to be as friendly as Norway and Sweden are, be helpful to one another, be good neighbours and get along well, and yet each be master in his own house.

Nash: Why would that split enhance Canada's international role?

Jacobs: It will. I think it's a great pity that this did not happen in 1980 when the referendum occurred in Quebec because there was not nearly the acrimony then between the two parts. It's grown enormously in this decade. If it had occurred then and been accepted with good will on both sides, it would have been a modern example of how these things can be done in a civilized fashion and with no harm. I think that model would have been a rather stunning and electrifying one for the rest of the world. The longer this goes on, the less and less it looks as if Canada will be a model. We won't get into a war, but it could become nasty and gratuitous, just because the divorcing parties are so angry.

Nash: But wouldn't a split mean Canada would be less influential in things like the G7, the leading-nation economic body, or GATT or NORAD or the UN?

Jacobs: No, I don't see why it would if the two parts work together. A lot of these things like G7 don't really amount to a hill of beans. They are public relations exercises. On NORAD, and on other defence matters, Canada and Quebec can and should cooperate. Those alliances don't depend on a consolidated sovereignty, and you could just as well make an argument that, there being two of us, we would be twice as influential as just the one of us is. I think though, where influence comes into these matters is how wise and sensible the countries involved are in the joint arrangements, not how big they are.

Nash: There is still a feeling among a lot of people in Canada that we should try to preserve our unity.

Jacobs: Of course there is. There always is. Look at the Soviets with Lithuania, Latvia, and Estonia. They've got the same emotion. And in Georgia and so on. Many there feel it is terribly important to preserve the whole. We think they are absurd.

Nash: Do you really feel that the effort and the emotion being spent to find ways to retain national unity is a wasted effort?

Jacobs: It is a wasted effort. It is worse than wasted, because it only leads to recriminations, hatred, spite.

Nash: Supposing there is a split in Canada, there has been some suggestion that we might then reconstruct the country so that, in addition to the existing provinces, you might make Toronto a province or Vancouver a province, simply because these cities are strong entities. Do you think that's a good idea?

Jacobs: I think these things should be taken a step at a time. The first thing to do is make the separation. Negotiate with Quebec first, then look and see whether the Atlantic provinces would do better combined as one province. That might be so, it might not. There are arguments both ways, but it is something that should be considered in its own terms and for its own good, not just because of Quebec. As for city states like Toronto and Vancouver, maybe you might add Winnipeg to that and Calgary or Edmonton. I don't know whether that would be a good thing or not. Emotionally I am inclined to want it, but thinking of it rationally, I can see reasons against it. If the province of Ontario did not have the tax revenues from Toronto, both business and personal revenues, it would have virtually nothing. We would have an exaggerated form of what the western and the Atlantic provinces already complain of when they talk about how rich Ontario is. What they really mean is how rich Toronto is. The reason people want to have the city states is that they are irked over having too little local government in important ways and over the provinces having too much power, say, over Vancouver or over Toronto. Why should the province decide on the local property tax? It is much better to solve these problems not by making Toronto or Vancouver separate provinces, but by the provinces giving the cities more control over certain items.

Nash: What about the question of Native rights?

Jacobs: At least in the beginning, I think that is much better handled by delegating more government, more powers, to the Native people in their territories, than it is by saying right off these are separate nations. There has been much too little power devolved to them and that, I think, we are all beginning to recognize.

Nash: You have said what you would like to see happening, what should happen. But what's your best educated guess of what, in fact, will happen by the year 2000? What is Canada going to look like, this territory north of the American border?

Jacobs: I would guess that by the year 2000, Quebec will be separate. I think the whole thing can be a mess or the whole thing can be a very orderly, constructive thing in the way that Norway and Sweden was.

Nash: Your answer to making a split come amicably is to forget about trying to find ways to satisfy Quebec within a restructured Canada and simply concentrate all attention on how we best determine the terms of divorce.

Jacobs: Yes, as amicably and as constructively as possible, and as soon as possible.

Don Perdue, New York

ROBERT MACNEIL

Robert MacNeil is executive editor and co-anchor of the PBS program "The MacNeil/Lehrer NewsHour," as well as being a best-selling author, commentator, and lecturer. Born in Montreal and brought up in Halifax, MacNeil began his broadcasting career in Halifax, moving a few years later to the CBC in Ottawa. He later worked with Reuters and was a correspondent for the BBC and NBC, covering, among other things, the assassination of President John F. Kennedy. He became senior correspondent for PBS in 1971. He has won numerous major awards for his broadcast journalism. Currently he is writing a book exploring his Canadian roots.

"A kinder, gentler America."

Nash: You have lived in England for a long time, as well as in the United States, yet you've never given up your Canadian citizenship. Why?

MacNeil: When George Bush campaigned and said he wanted to create a "kinder, gentler America," thirteen seconds after those words were out of his mouth, I said, "But there is one, and it is north of the forty-ninth parallel." In everything George Bush was saying – a country which is compassionate and decent to people in its social services, which believes in a gentler way of organizing the relationships of people in their civic and other affairs, which hates violence, which will not tolerate a one-hundredth of the violence that is part of the American identity – Canada is that country. The civility Canadians have for each other, strained as it is now by the political dialogue, I greatly admire and value and really attach myself to quite strongly. I believe the United States would be better if it had more of those Canadian values, but it wouldn't be the United States if it did. The idea of a social democracy that is not afraid of borrowing from socialism and is not afraid of capitalism either, but has found some fairly happy compromise between the two to create a decent life for the maximum number of people, I think is something to be admired, and I value that.

Nash: Are there also some intangible reasons for your wanting to remain a Canadian?

MacNeil: I find myself with a real sense of pride in the fact that Canada is a country of two cultures and two languages. I think that is something valuable. I feel that the Quebec contribution to Canada as a culture, as a distinct place in the world, is very real and very important.

Nash: What does our constitutional crisis look like to you, not only from your Nova Scotian background, but also from where you are now in New York?

MacNeil: It coincides in me with a late-middle-aged sort of renaissance of my own Canadianism and my own Nova Scotianism, and I am having difficulty discovering what Canada is for myself. Up to the time of Confederation and certainly from Confederation onwards, there has been a series of fits of trying to describe whatever the Canadian ideal is, the thing that, in a phrase, explains the Canadian improbability against all the logic of geography and economics and communications and everything else. There's always been a glue of the moment that kept the country together, a sort of generational glue that the current generation now conspicuously lacks. The failure of Meech Lake has made it even more apparent that there are a lot of people who don't see the sense of the country any more.

Nash: Why don't we have that glue?

MacNeil: Look at some of the gods that have failed. Anti-Americanism, which is always a god of Canadian unity,

worked for a while in the economic nationalism of the Trudeau years. But the Canadian standard of living is dependent
upon a very close relationship with the United States. There
also was the unifying force of Canada as a moral force in the
world that came out of the Second World War, and through
Canada's burgeoning new independence in diplomacy and
carving out for itself a different role in the world. It seems to
me that this has foundered again. The kind of moral weight
that Canada used to have in the councils of the world isn't
there any more, and therefore it isn't listened to.

Nash: What would happen then if Canada did split, would
that voice become almost totally indistinguishable?

MacNeil: First, of all, I am not sure it is going to split and I
don't know anybody who is sure. Majorities of Québécois say
this or say that according to opinion polls, but opinion polls
do not tell you what is going to happen when there is actually a referendum. Every Québécois nationalist, from the
most fierce and determined down to the least fierce and the
most lukewarm, also has, in his psyche, some piece of Canadianism. He has some piece of the moderation of Canada, and
the gradualism of Canada, and the dislike for revolutionary
and violent ruptures and dramatic solutions. But your question was, "Will the voice of Canada be heard or become indistinguishable?" Certainly the Quebec voice will be heard,
because it would be a new national voice in the world. It
therefore would get a lot of attention and would be listened
to because it would be a phenomenon. Then it will be up to
the Quebec government to come up with policies which are
interesting and distinct and which do not alienate the financial community in New York that floats their bond issues
and rates their Quebec Hydro bonds.

Nash: What about Washington? When President Bush was in
Canada he said that he would prefer to deal with a single unit
called Canada.

MacNeil: That has been the dogma and the ideology of the
State Department for a long time, but it probably applies to
almost any country. I think all governments with many

responsibilities in the world like to deal with known national entities. The last thing they want to contemplate is having to deal with splintering entities. But I am sure they have all kinds of plans of how to accommodate themselves gracefully to two Canadas, if that came about.

Nash: One of the things that distinguishes Canadians from Americans is that we are less visibly expressive in our patriotism. We don't wave flags as much as Americans do.

MacNeil: So far, it's not been in our nature to do that. Although I have a great affection for this country, I was never more reminded of why I am not an American than I was with all the display of American patriotism that followed the Iraq war. It seemed to be me quite disproportionate to what had been achieved. But there is a great hunger here for that kind of thing. Canadians have very seldom felt that need. When Canada defeated the Soviet Union at hockey that first time there was one of those moments, but they are relatively few, and it's been the absence of nationalistic spirit in the Canadian psyche which many people have applauded. Canada has never made a religion of its nationality. There is in the United States a kind of secular religion of democracy, and people believe in it passionately. I found myself thinking that the other day when I was on the shuttle going into Washington and the plane settled gently down along the Potomac to land at National Airport, and there on the left were all the shrines and temples of American democracy: the Lincoln Memorial and the Jefferson Memorial. I don't know whether you, Knowlton, have had this experience, but in the four or five years that I lived in Washington I found myself taking visitors to these landmarks late at night, and I had moments of being moved, aroused, emotionally involved with a sort of quasi-religious kind of reaction. I've never had that experience in Canada. I've never had it for any of the shrines of Canadian democracy, because they don't evoke that kind of response. You can't stand in front of a statue of Sir John A. and get the hair rising on the back of your neck because, although he said marvellous things about the need to unify the country, nothing came out of his mouth with the kind of crystallizing and inspiring eloquence of a Jefferson or of a Lincoln.

Nash: In Canada serious thought is being given to the devolution of power from the centre to the provinces, and much of the argument focusses around how much is too much.

MacNeil: If you are in Newfoundland, with a tiny population and very small resources and very little power to raise taxation on your own, you obviously want the shelter of Confederation to fulfill the promise of the Constitution that the country as a whole will maintain a certain standard of living for its least fortunate members. There is much more willingness in the United States morally and socially to let the devil take the hindmost. This is part of this kindler, gentler stuff that we are talking about. Now, is Canada going to abandon that? Clearly, though, there is nothing sacred about the nature of the Canadian Confederation. Nobody is going to go to war over it. There isn't going to be a civil war in Canada to preserve the union.

Nash: No one has talked about that.

MacNeil: There is no Abraham Lincoln saying you've got to fight to preserve it and there is no fundamental moral principle at stake here. But there is another point to be made. The Canada you and I grew up in had a sort of Anglo-Scottish ascendency. It's changed now with immigration. This country, the United States, changed enormously after the great waves of immigration up to the First World War, and it was really those immigrants, the Germans and the northern Europeans and the southern Europeans, who built the United States that we know today. The United States is the creation of those immigrants who went through Ellis Island.

Nash: Those immigrants became the melting pot.

MacNeil: And Canada is going to be recreated by its new ethnic *mélange*. Whether it will continue to be a mosaic, or whether it will become more of a melting pot, who can say? In a city like Toronto, which is so fascinating now and used to be so boring, how do we know that all those groups are going to continue to keep their identity two generations from now, and that there won't be enormous numbers of increased marriages across ethnic lines, which Canadians never liked as much as Americans did? Who knows what new Canadian reality and society is going to be created now with the ethnic mix and its different birth rates and different views of the world? It was very convenient for the Anglo-Scottish ascendancy in Canada, and all the values that it imposed on the society, that the immigrant groups at first were docile and would willingly bend themselves to the mores that obtained at the time. They were decent, and as long as the dominant groups didn't interfere with their ethnic identity and left them alone to do their thing, by and large they got on with it, and the others got on with running the country and making the money and setting the moral tone for the country and creating ideas of Canadianism. But what are all these new Canadians going to subscribe to in terms of values? How many more of them are going to say, "Oh, I don't like this climate, it's a lot better down south," or, "If I go across the border and shop and the values are so much better, why won't my whole standard of living be better? Why don't we become more American all the time?" There is also the phenomenon in various parts of Canada where their cross-border identity with the region closest to them in the United States is becoming a lot more evident, more naked. Also, under the subtle and not-so-subtle influences of the Free Trade Agreement, do not the economic ties begin to have a kind of psychic resonance?

Things are happening to Americanize the Canadian way of doing things all the time. Knowlton, you have covered American politics, and you have covered Canadian politics, and you know damn well the Prime Minister's Office in Canada is now like a mini-American presidency in the way it behaves and the way it treats itself. And all kinds of other things are happening. For instance, the new Charter of Rights and Freedoms has in its essence a resort to court decisions and ratification of laws that never before had the same weight in the Canadian, and certainly not in the British, tradition. Now all kinds of things are being tested in the courts, which is very much the American way, so that the sovereignty of Parliament is to some degree lessened. The courts will play a larger role in the way they have done in the United States. American ways of doing things are gradually eating in.

Nash: If that kind of Americanization is eating its way into Canada, are we not in danger of losing that distinctive quality that you were talking about earlier, of a "kinder, gentler" society?

MacNeil: Maybe. A lot of people raised that at the time of the Free Trade Agreement. They were the cultural sovereignty people who said, "Look, part of our culture is this 'kinder, gentler' nation with more generous social services and a willingness to tax ourselves more heavily in order to pay for them, and a social contract rather different from the American social contract, and inevitably under the forces of the marketplace, that will be eroded." And they may be right. It's going to take some very strong-minded Canadian politicians, and very strong-minded voters, to continue to say, "We want to be a high-taxed nation, because we value the services we get for it."

JIM PATTISON

As chairman and president of The Jim Pattison Group, Jim Pattison is one of Canada's most active entrepreneurs. He began as a used-car dealer in Vancouver in 1952 and today heads the fourth largest privately held company in Canada. It operates firms in Canada, the United States, the Caribbean, and Europe, with interests in the fields of broadcasting, magazines, advertising, airlines, groceries, soft drinks, finance, among others. The annual sales of his companies are over $2.5 billion. Pattison was in charge of Vancouver's Expo 86 and is largely credited with its success.

"People are resigned to Quebec leaving."

Nash: As a westerner and a businessman, what's your personal sense of what Quebec is asking for?
Pattison: I don't see any problem, frankly. If the people of Quebec want to have their own country and don't like the way it's been all these years, then I don't see anything wrong with that.
Nash: You don't have any sense that the country itself would be diminished by the loss of Quebec?
Pattison: I don't think there is any question that, from an economic point of view, that to break the country up, we certainly would suffer. But we are not planning on abandoning Quebec, although we do expect there will be some changes. We are adjusting our whole thinking to a country

that, if it stays together, fine, but if it doesn't, then we are going to work with whatever happens. I live in western Canada, and in my company we have 13,000 employees. We have employees also in eastern Canada, and then we have some in the States, of course, as well as a small number in Europe.

Nash: When you say "we," do you mean your company is making contingency plans?

Pattison: We are absolutely putting our mind to the fact that Quebec may well leave. We think that Quebec will survive okay, although both entities may not wind up as good as they were before for a while. But the world will go on.

Nash: What kinds of differences would it make to you in your business if there were a split?

Pattison: I don't think it would make much difference. There will be a loss of confidence from outside, but that's a reality, so you work with it.

Nash: What's your sense of western Canadian feelings about this?

Pattison: I think people accept Quebec leaving. That doesn't mean to say that they wouldn't prefer to have the country stay together. But today they are totally resigned to seeing Quebec go. They have accepted that possibility.

Nash: Do you think it is worthwhile seriously looking at some of the things that Quebec wants to have – the devolution of powers from the centre to the provinces?

Pattison: If they are going to give Quebec certain concessions, I think at least British Columbia and the West are going to want pretty well the same things.

Nash: So you don't think the idea of special status for Quebec, special arrangements for Quebec but for nobody else, would work as far as the West is concerned?

Pattison: No. But you have to be realistic. Language is special in Quebec, you can't take that away.

Nash: What do you think might happen to the rest of the country if there were a split? Would B.C., for instance, begin to meld into the U.S. Pacific Northwest?

Pattison: Our focus now is north and south, not east and west. If you go down to the Canadian border now, the ordinary person probably has an hour and forty-five minute wait to go across to buy gas, food, clothes. They are going down to Bellingham and Seattle. Things are significantly cheaper thirty miles south of here. Food and clothes are sharply lower. The selection is greater.

Nash: I suppose part of the difference is that we pay more here in taxes, which is reflected in the cost of goods here, in order to have a bigger social safety net than the Americans have.

Pattison: Our real estate costs are higher, our interest costs are higher, the fundamentals of the country are all higher, which makes us basically non-competitive.

Nash: If you look down the road fifty years from now, do you think that economic attractiveness of the U.S. might result in political union?

Pattison: I think so. It is a high probability.

Nash: A good thing, do you think?

Pattison: Strictly business, absolutely. We would be much better off. Rates would be lower, our ability to grow faster, our pool of capital would grow. This is very important. If you take the circumstances of today and project fifty years from now, the answer is yes. But it never works that way.

Nash: Should we try to persuade Quebec to stay?

Pattison: They have been doing that for years. The chance of pacifying Quebec is less than at any time that I have seen. We have plants in Granby, Laval, Hawkesbury, right across the border, and I have to tell you right now that the people up here do not understand what is happening down with the real people in Quebec. That's why I said, if the people want to leave, I accept it. Let's make it as easy as possible, and let's get on with it.

Nash: You think we should really start with the divorce proceedings?

Pattison: I don't consider it divorce. If the people want to leave, what's wrong with it? The issue is what's fair for Quebec and what's fair for the rest of the country. But we have got to understand that the people don't want to stay right now. It's just when like your wife says, "I don't want to stay here any more. I want to leave." You say, "We can fight or we can try to make this thing work." But you can't change your wife once she has made up her mind she wants out. We have been struggling with trying to make peace for years, so okay, let's do the best and still be friends.

Nash: You still want to be friends with Quebec even after a split?

Pattison: Absolutely. My goodness, I have no plans of getting out of any of our plants in Quebec today because of this. I may have to get out because I can manufacture cheaper in Mexico or Texas.

Nash: So you would be watching very closely the competitive environment for your plants in Quebec and the rest of Canada.

Pattison: I don't care about the political side. That is not an issue for me. The issue for me is when I've got somebody sitting in Toronto who I am paying $18 an hour to, and I can produce exactly the same thing for $12 in Longview, Texas, or $1.50 in Nogales, Mexico, and it's not a freight-sensitive product. That's what I'm focussing on. I am not worried about the political environment of Quebec. I am not worried about the political environment of the States. I am not worried about the political environment of Canada, whatever it is. You tell me I am going to go to Iraq, then I am worried about the political environment. The big probem in this country today is that we have not had good management over a long period of years, and one of these days our currency is going to reflect it.

Nash: What have we done wrong?

Pattison: The bottom line is that we have priced ourselves out of many markets.

Nash: Can you tell me what you think a Canadian is, what comes to your mind, especially since you are out of the country a lot?

Pattison: I feel good that I am a Canadian. Canadians are well-respected. I am always proud to have a Canadian passport. I think that we look like the Americans and talk like the Americans, but we do not think like the Americans in many ways.

Nash: What are some of those ways that we are different?

Pattison: We don't work as hard. In my opinion, Canadian management doesn't work as hard. We don't cause any waves anywhere. When you are a leader like the United States is or Britain was, you have to make hard calls. Leaders have everybody shooting at them, and when you are an American you obviously have people who like you and dislike you. I don't know anybody who doesn't like a Canadian when you are out travelling.

P. K. PAGE

One of Canada's most distinguished poets, P. K. Page is also a noted visual artist. She lives in Victoria with her husband, retired ambassador and editor, Arthur Irwin. She was born in England, came as a child to Canada to settle in Red Deer, Alberta, and was educated in Calgary and Winnipeg. She worked in Montreal with the National Film Board and travelled with her husband when he was Canada's High Commissioner to Australia and Ambassador to Brazil and Mexico. She studied art in New York and Brazil. She has lived in Victoria since 1964.

"If Quebec left, it would break my heart."

Nash: We aren't an overly passionate people when it comes to expressing our patriotism, but do you feel any sense of passion about the present challenge facing Canada?

Page: All passion's spent. My age isn't the age of passion. You become more philosophical as you grow older. But do I care about my country? Of course I care. Should I care about my country? That I am not sure about.

Nash: Why not?

Page: Because I think that we're moving towards something bigger than nationalism.

Nash: Internationalism?

Page: I don't know. I am not sure that nationalism isn't at the heart of much of our trouble. At the same time I do feel strongly about my country. There is a great dichotomy in me about this.

Nash: I suppose there is a great dichotomy in a lot of people about that. And we certainly don't very often, as Canadians, articulate our patriotic emotions, unlike Americans, who do much more flag-waving.

Page: I think that is ugly. I would hate us to become that kind of people. If I boast about myself, I think it is ugly. If I boast about my country, I think it's ugly. I think Americans are too boastful, and I don't want to see us emulate them.

Nash: You may remember Keith Spicer spoke early on, when he was beginning his work with his commission, about our need for more poets to write about Canada. Do we need more poets?

Page: The poet originally was a prophet, a seer, and if what Spicer meant was more people with vision, then I think he is right. But where are they? We don't seem to be producing that kind of poet any more than we are producing politicians of vision.

Nash: We are forever looking for our Canadian identity. What do we have that unites us, that makes us uniquely Canadian?

Page: We must have something otherwise there wouldn't have been a Canada. I grew up on the Prairies, and then I went to the Maritimes, where I knew Miller Brittain and Jack Humphrey as painters, and I thought they were fine painters. Then God put me down in British Columbia where nobody had ever heard of Miller Brittain or Jack Humphrey. Here they were all talking about Jack Shadbolt and Emily Carr. How can you have a sense of country when the parts don't know about each other? That's not so true today, however. We have at least got to a point where we do know something about each other. In B.C. we know about Mary Pratt.

Nash: Are you a Nova Scotian or a Prairie citizen, or a B.C.er first and Canadian second?

Page: I am not. I am definitely not. Out here most people seem to be B.C.ers, but I'm not. I have lived in Alberta,

Manitoba, the Maritimes, Ontario, Quebec – in fact there are only two provinces I haven't lived in – Prince Edward Island and Saskatchewan.

Nash: You also have travelled enormously both within the country and outside. Given that background, what's your sense of the possibility of Quebec leaving?

Page: If Quebec left it would utterly break my heart. My eyes fill with tears as I think about it. When we were in Latin America, I discovered I was a Latin. People laughed, were demonstrative, they embraced each other, kissed each other, and it was easy for me to fall into their ways. When I came back to Canada and I put my arms around friends or kissed them when I saw them, they drew away. They said they didn't know what had happened to me abroad. And I felt, what valuable luggage to have had to leave at the border. Shortly after we returned, my husband was asked to a conference of some kind in the Laurentians, and I went too and sat in on the discussions, and I remember saying, "If Quebec separates, I go with Quebec. I understand these people. They have passion, imagination. I understand these people."

Nash: You are saying that if Quebec left, we would lose part of our soul?

Page: Yes we would.

Nash: Right now, in the make-up of Canada, the white Anglo-Saxons are a minority. In a way we are a nation of minorities.

Page: That's right, and this may in the long run help us all. There'll be less polarity.

It strikes me that we have got ourselves backwards. We think of the self first. We have lost our God, so why shouldn't we be God? We think of our country second. Conceivably it could be useful to us, I suppose. And we think of our planet last. But if we loved our planet first, our country second, and ourselves last, I think the problems the country faces would be easier to handle. . . . It's like being in a small group of people who are warring with each other. When faced with something bigger than themselves they are forced to focus on it. There is no unified focus as long as we are thinking only about "me."

Nash: If Quebec left, there are some who suggest we might be drawn by the force of economics into close alignment with the United States.

Page: I don't want to become part of the United States. I hate their politics, their war-mongering politicians.

Nash: But the dominant economic pull through history has been north-south across the border, and is increasingly so these days because it costs more to trade east-west and to be a Canadian.

Page: What is this cost? Dollars and cents. How did we get our heads so full of dollars and cents? I grew up in a family that had very little money. My father was in the army. I don't know what the pay was but it was small. He was keeping his mother as well as a wife and child – me – and then he had another child. I don't remember it hurting me. I don't even remember money being discussed. It was considered *déclassé*.

Nash: Many French Canadians feel their pride and their rights have been insulted by English-speaking Canada through the rejection of Meech and other things in the past.

Page: I am not as sympathetic to that as you might think. I am very pro-French, but if we and they could just for once forget our rights! And just for once live in the present. We've only got now, we haven't got the past. That's gone. We haven't even got the future – we may all be dead tomorrow.

One of the things I loved about Brazil was just that capacity to live in the now. When Brazilians met you they were completely unreserved with you and expected the same behaviour in return. At that the moment you were friends – good friends. It made for wonderful meetings. I think that is the way we should live.

Nash: As you said earlier, it is a Latin trait, something that perhaps exists within French-speaking Canada, but doesn't exist to anything like that degree in English-speaking Canada.

Page: That's true, except the French are going on with *"Je me souviens."* I can understand that, but I am not sympathetic to it. We have such wonderful possibilities here, and to destroy them because of my memories or theirs when we could be struggling on towards that greater bigness! We've only got to look at the stars.

ELIJAH HARPER

Elijah Harper, a forty-one-year-old Cree-Ojibway, skyrocketed to prominence in mid-1990 through his resolute opposition to the Meech Lake accord in the Manitoba legislature because it excluded Native rights. He used the rules of the legislature to disallow debate on Meech, thus barring Manitoba's approval before the time limit and effectively killing the accord. Harper studied anthropology at university and later became chief of the Red Sucker Lake Band. A quiet, self-effacing, but deeply committed Native leader, he spent two years in the NDP cabinet in Manitoba.

"We have never been part of this country."

Nash: What does Canada as a nation mean to you?

Harper: We have never been part of this country. We've never been really recognized for who we are and what we have done in this country. I feel that to be complete, we need to formally recognize the aboriginal people.

Nash: When you say formally recognize, in what tangible ways would that be done?

Harper: We were here prior to the arrival of the Europeans, so some sense of that has to be recognized within the Constitution. I think your Constitution would want to do that to show the true history, the true reality of this country.

Nash: So at present, you don't feel part of Canada.

Harper: Not really. It totally ignores aboriginal peoples even as the first citizens, the first inhabitants, and the kind of contribution that we have made. That needs to be corrected.

Nash: In what ways would you correct that?

Harper: Start by saying within the Constitution that aboriginal people do have the inherent right of self-government. It existed for thousands of years prior to the arrival of anybody. We had communities, we had political structures, we traded among ourselves, among the First Nations in this country.

Nash: You speak of self-government. What precisely do you mean by that?

Harper: It means the ability to make our own decisions. Basically, to be able to manage our own affairs and be able to determine our future and our destiny. We have to develop our own institutions in our language, our own cultural institutions, our own administrations, our own justice system within our reserves.

Nash: You mean a justice system different from that in the rest of Canada?

Harper: The values are quite different, and our system will be more sensitive to our needs. As a matter of fact, the Canadian Bar Association supports a separate justice system for aboriginal people.

Nash: Have you felt a sense of discrimination against yourself, against Native peoples?

Harper: I have experienced it, it's there. It still exists. It's a colonial policy, and it hasn't changed over hundreds of years.

Nash: Do you think that today there's a greater sense of awareness of the issues of Native peoples and perhaps even a sense of guilt in some parts of Canada?

Harper: I sense that, but it doesn't really mean anything. People may sympathize with aboriginal people, but it doesn't really mean anything until you start to see concrete changes in what's happening. There needs to be a greater change. You need the governments to start dealing with aboriginal people more sincerely. There is a lack of political will to do that today.

Nash: Do you have any apprehension that in the concentration on the problems between Quebec and the rest of

Canada, your concerns may get overlooked in a rush to meet a deadine to resolve those problems?

Harper: When I hear comments being made in the papers and on TV, it's always about the English and French and never about aboriginal people. We have never had the recognition that aboriginal people are going to play an important role in the future of Canada. Politicians in general underestimate the kind of influence that we aboriginal people will have, even in Quebec. When Bourassa talks about sovereignty and rights for that province, he says he will speak to the prime minister, but he ignores aboriginal people. That's one fundamental mistake he is making. When you look at history of that province in terms of Indian lands, 85 per cent of the land base of Quebec has never been ceded. It's never been formally negotiated nor a treaty signed, so how can Quebec claim Indian land?

Nash: Why is it that in dealing with the provinces, you have more difficulty than with the federal government?

Harper: It's about power and politics. The provinces don't want to give up what they have. We never signed treaties with the provincial governments. So it is the federal government that has to provide the leadership, take action, and be sure that our rights are implemented or recognized. We have lots of time. We have waited for over a hundred years as aboriginal people. I don't see why we should be in a rush. One of the reasons why Meech failed was because of the time-frame.

Nash: But there is the deadline of the referendum in Quebec.

Harper: Who is imposing it?

Nash: Quebec has set the deadline.

Harper: So? We should stand up and say, "Take more time." We are responding to political agendas, to the time-frames of elections, and often when you do that you don't make the right decisions. We should have learned something from the Meech Lake fiasco.

Nash: What's your sense of the demands of Quebec?

Harper: As aboriginal peoples, when we said no to Meech, we weren't saying no to Quebec at all. We never said no. As a matter of fact, we support them in their quest to maintain their language and their culture. We have always felt that Quebec is a province that would be more sympathetic, more supportive, and understanding of us. But the federal government hasn't provided any leadership to uphold aboriginal rights in that province.

Nash: What do you think the new Canada should look like? How should it be constructed, or reconstructed?

Harper: We obviously have to deal with the aboriginal question. It hasn't been settled from day one, so it has to be addressed and cleared and settled once and for all so that aboriginal people will be equal participants in this country. Even at constitutional conferences we were just invitees at the pleasure of the prime minister.

Nash: You want to be more than an invitee?

Harper: Definitely. We want full representation as equal partners.

Nash: Apart from what you think Canada should do, let me ask you to look into a crystal ball and tell me what you think Canada will be like in the year 2000?

Harper: I sense that aboriginal rights will be addressed. I think Canada will be strong, will be united, and I don't think Quebec will separate.

Nash: So you are basically an optimist about the future?

Harper: As an aboriginal person and as a leader for aboriginal people, I can't afford to think otherwise. I feel that some of those areas that I am talking about will take time to develop, but others will come about by the year 2000. We need to address the development of areas in our own backyards, because a lot of the land is being exploited by outside people without our input, and resources have been extracted without any kind of benefit to us.

Nash: Why is the environment so important to you?

Harper: It's us. We're part of the environment. We are part of it because of who we are and how we relate to the environment. A lot of that has to do with our spirituality, our values, our traditions. It's a way of life. How we treat the environment will affect us eventually because when we assault Mother Earth, we assault ourselves.

Nash: You speak of spirituality and traditions, is that something that most Canadians really don't quite understand? What does it mean, spirituality?

Harper: Spirituality is how we relate to ourselves, how we relate to other people, how we relate to the environment. It's how we relate to our Creator, how we conduct ourselves, how we play. Basically, it's respect for other people, that's part of spirituality. How we live with one another. Look at our relationship with the environment, with the planet, with Mother Earth. As aboriginal people we never owned the land, and it couldn't be given, not in terms of the European concept of land tenure, where you bought and sold the land.

Nash: You mean the land belongs to everybody.

Harper: Definitely, and all the resources should benefit everyone. That's why when you look at treaties from an aboriginal or Indian point of view, it was never theirs to give away. We could only share our land and resources with the people. We feel we are here as caretakers to provide protection for the land and environment or to provide stewardship of the resources of the land. The governments think they own everything. They want to regulate everything. How can you own that bird that was given to me by the Creator? We have the feeling that the government wants to own everything, wants to have a say in everything.

Nash: How do you negotiate that? You are dealing with fundamentally different philosophies.

Harper: The resources that we extract from Canada should benefit everyone. The water, the minerals, the oil, should help our people, help other Canadian people. They should benefit everyone, not just big companies.

RAYMOND MORIYAMA

One of Canada's outstanding architects, Raymond Moriyama was born in Vancouver and educated at the universities of Toronto and McGill. He began his practice of architecture in Toronto in 1958, and his work includes the Ontario Science Centre, the Scarborough Civic Centre, the Metropolitan Toronto Library, the Canadian embassy in Tokyo, the North York City Centre, and the headquarters for the Regional Municipality of Ottawa-Carleton. He won the Governor General's Award for Architecture in 1982, 1986, and 1990, the Massey Medal for Architecture in 1961 and 1975, and was given a Lifetime Achievement Award by the Toronto Arts Foundation in 1990, and the Civic Award of Merit by the City of Scarborough in 1977 and by the City of Toronto in 1980.

"Maybe unification . . . after separation."

Nash: What does Canada mean to you?

Moriyama: To me, Canada is the future. It has areas where no man has walked. There aren't too many other countries where you could say that. We have a much gentler situation in the urban centres than in most countries. I tend to see a positive future and, in a funny way, I relate it to the geology of the country. When I was working on the Tokyo embassy I was trying to think, how do I represent Canada? I feel that Canadians are really vital people, but at the same time, there is a kind of northern openness. By and large, we are a well-mannered people. I wondered, how do I represent this in the embassy? Rather than being architecturally aggressive, I thought we will lean back and be a little more relaxed and well-mannered, and I thought in many ways that reflected our character.

Nash: What are some of the areas that you think can make us come together as a nation? Or is it in our character to do so?

Moriyama: I like to think so. Right now, it seems fashionable to be cynical. You don't hear people talking positively about Canada. Everybody is talking about the negative side. I find myself waving the Canadian flag more and more, and I find that not only satisfying, but much more a reality for me than to be nit-picking about the negative conditions. Look a little more into the future and convey an attitude of positiveness, so that it does help to bring us together to create a shared ambience about ourselves.

Nash: Do we have those shared values in this country?

Moriyama: This is really naïve, but we are sharing a piece of land, sharing climatic conditions, but I think we tend to look at what separates us rather than at the positive things that bring us together. I keep asking myself, why can't we talk about the things we share rather than the things that we don't share?

Nash: How do we deal with the particular issue we have with Quebec's insistence on having more powers? How does the rest of Canada respond to the kind of requests that Quebec is making?

Moriyama: Sometimes I stand back and say, objectively, let them separate. Maybe that's the only way it's going to work, and maybe that's the way it should be. Then maybe the unification will come after a separation.

Nash: You take that point of view objectively you say, but what does your emotion tell you?

Moriyama: Because I tend to be a Canadian nationalist, I would like to see us together. That part of me says we've got to keep it.

Nash: If Quebec went, would there be a chipping away at the soul of Canada, do you think?

Moriyama: I tend to believe the scenario that we will stay together, but at the same time I think it is too romantic. Globally, it doesn't matter. As much as I would like to see it as a unified country, internationally I don't think it really matters whether we are one or two countries.

Nash: French-speaking Canadians would argue that they are in a special position, being one of the founding nations of the country.

Moriyama: I would like to think that's true, but it may be a fantasy. The world no longer hangs on to a picture of that nature. It's not the reality.

Nash: Are you saying that we were born in a duality, but we've now grown up into a multicultural country?

Moriyama: That's right. You have to look at the whole multicultural aspect.

Nash: Some people have suggested that officially sponsored multiculturalism damages a sense of national unity because it tends to enhance people's sense of being Poles or Ukrainians or Vietnamese at the expense of a sense of being Canadian..

Moriyama: I think you have to ask yourself, what is being Canadian? Are we following the concept of the melting-pot of the United States? It may be a wrong path. I try to understand this when I look at my personal ethnic background and wartime experience.

Nash: What was your wartime experience?

Moriyama: For me, it's the most negative part of my experience with my own country. When your own country turns its back on you, there is very little that you can rely on. In my case, my solace was nature.

Nash: You were born in Vancouver and you had to go into the interior of B.C. to labour camps?

Moriyama: We were all incarcerated, whether one was born in Canada or in Japan.

Nash: What did that do to your sense of the country? How did that affect you, and is the residue of that experience still there?

Moriyama: Sometimes one has a tendency to kind of sweep it under the rug somewhere. Psychologically, you protect yourself from your own sense because it hurts so much. It's really like getting raped and not being able to expose that rape – the traumatic experience of a rape and the shame. As much as the mind says, "I am not the guilty party," you are perceived as the guilty party.

Nash: It's interesting that you use the word "shame" because I would have thought the shame would be on the other side, the side of the government, the side of the rest of us, not on your side.

Moriyama: That's what I am talking about. As much as I am aware that I am not the guilty one, that I am the victim, somehow one starts to think, well, maybe I am guilty.

Nash: Even with that thought, you have done so much for your country since then. You have made such a contribution to it.

Moriyama: I learned in the experience that democracy is really fragile. It also became very clear to me that by insensitivity, not by malice but just by sheer insensitivity, an institution, whether it is government or big business or a school, could diminish the need of each individual to grow spiritually, and thereby cause a loss to the family, to the neighbourhood, to the city, to the country, to the world. So one has to be very sensitive about the individual's need, and that's really affected the way I think about architecture. I felt that having gone through a negative situation doesn't mean that I should be bitter about it and carry a big sledgehammer all my life. If anything, I should use the experience to benefit others. This is part of the positiveness that I feel about Canada.

Nash: How long were you incarcerated during the war?

Moriyama: It started in 1942. I was eleven. My father pulled me aside one day and said, "Look, I think this is the first time I am speaking to you as a man, but I have to go to a road camp. First of all, in two days I cannot conclude the business of the store. Secondly, your mother is pregnant. And thirdly, the most important thing is that I came to Canada for democracy and the democratic principle of protecting human rights and this is happening to me. I must fight the contra-diction." I always admired my father for taking a stand. It took a lot of guts to do that. I was incarcerated from 1942 to 1944.

Nash: It was obviously a very searing experience, and it affects how you think of this country, but, despite that, your thoughts are positive. How so?

Moriyama: I have often wondered why. The Japanese Cana-dian community tended to come out of it basically with, I wouldn't say a positive attitude, but maybe less harmed than one would expect. Maybe this was a characteristic of the Japanese.

Nash: What's your sense of what is going to be happening to Canada over the next few years?

Moriyama: My sense of it is that if we don't get off our butts, we are slowly going to go down the drain. If we don't start thinking in terms of the quality of our country as a whole, the quality of production, quality of thinking, and that includes equality, then we are really, to exaggerate, down the drain.

Nash: Down the drain in an economic sense?

Moriyama: In the sense of being non-competitive, but that's going to affect the quality of life. We are so spoiled here. Cynicism and negative thoughts are going to create a faster downhill slide.

Nash: If we go downhill, what's at the bottom of the hill? Is the bottom of the hill being integrated with the United States, or is the bottom of the hill becoming Albania?

Moriyama: We are starting to become a Third World country now. It's just that Canadians don't recognize it. If you look at the world picture, I think we tend to fool ourselves in think-ing we have a great life-style. But look at the shift that's happening.

Nash: What can we do to change? Is the country better off if we split, or is a whole new reshaping of our attitudes and our country needed?

Moriyama: I hope Canada doesn't split apart. But really,

would it matter if we split, insofar as the international situation is concerned?

Nash: You travel all over the world, but do you travel in Quebec at all?

Moriyama: I lived in Montreal for a long time. I can understand what the French are saying. They want to be recognized. Canada is a country that is shaped as a duality, but the French feel it treats them like a small brother. If I compare it to a much smaller situation, like a company or an organization, it's clear you cannot work with a duality.

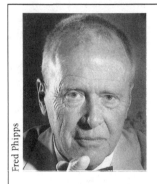

Fred Phipps

ALEX COLVILLE

*An eminent Canadian artist, Alex Colville came to promi-
nence as a war artist in Europe during the Second World War.
After the war, he taught at Mount Allison University in Nova
Scotia until 1963, when he resigned to devote himself entire-
ly to painting. His hyper "realistic" painting style has won
him acclaim both in Canada and around the world. Colville
designed the Centennial coins, minted in 1967, and the Governor General's Medal, in 1978. He was made a Companion of
the Order of Canada in 1982.*

"The Maritimes would become part of the U.S."

Nash: The Maritimes has always seemed to feel short-
changed by Confederation. Why is that?

Colville: In the 1850s and 1860s, Nova Scotia had more ships
at sea than any other nation. It's just mind-boggling to think
of it. This was a great Maritime nation, which traded all over
the world and had close connections with Boston and New
York. A city like Halifax would have been at that time far
more civilized than Toronto. I have often compared the Maritimes to the American South – there are a lot of similarities.
Both were, in effect, defeated in the 1860s.

Nash: Do you think there is much movement towards a unified Maritimes?

Colville: I think not. I don't think Maritimers would go for
that, really.

Nash: What about some economic association?

Colville: The premiers are now talking together. Personally, I think Wells is something of a nut. Certainly Ghiz is a very bright guy. McKenna, I think, is a pretty bright guy, and so is Cameron. They are talking together, but I don't think it is likely that there will actually be political union.

Nash: What about the broader sense? What's your sense of Canada?

Colville: As a person, I think I am a Canadian, I always vote in elections, I follow politics very closely. I am serious about it all. As an artist, I don't feel that I am a nationalist. I think in principle I disapprove of the idea of nationalism in culture. In the Middle Ages, artists weren't Italian or French or anything, there were simply sculptors or painters.

Nash: Yet many, if not most, in Canada's cultural community are nationalists.

Colville: And in this, I think they are wrong. To me it's just the most appalling stupidity that the artists banded together and opposed free trade. I couldn't believe it when I saw the names listed. For one thing, it seems to be so obvious that culture requires economic prosperity. If you don't have money, you don't have culture. Culture is expensive. I am on the board of the National Gallery, and I think the program of the gallery isn't to promote Canadian nationalism or unity. This is essentially nonsense. The artist has a role in making people have a deep and significant experience, but it is not some kind of nationalist bonding or something.

Nash: What about the question of a Canadian identity? We are always looking for it. Is there one, and if so, what is it?

Colville: I think there is. There's the climate. There is the fact that we are, as someone has said, all people who have been defeated: the Scots beaten by the English; the French beaten by the English; the conservative people who left the U.S.A. for being against the revolution.

Nash: You have seen Quebec's proposals in the Allaire report and other reports. What's your sense of whether we will be able to make a deal?

Colville: I have the feeling that we will get along. I guess I think that economic success is enormously important. All culture is expensive, universities are expensive. In order to keep these things running and to make them better, we have to be more prosperous. It would be economic stupidity to split the country. I think, in the end, most people know this.

Nash: What's your reaction to those people who say, "Well, let them go"?

Colville: In some parts of the country there is some kind of actual hatred of the French. I tend to like the French Canadian people. When I was in the army I became friends with quite a few French Canadians. Montreal is a city I like a lot. I think it would be a terrible loss if Quebec separated. For the Maritimes, ultimately, I think we would become part of the United States.

Nash: Part of New England?

Colville: Yes.

Nash: Why would that be the ultimate outcome?

Colville: With Quebec a sovereign state, I think we would be too isolated. For one thing, Ontario then becomes half of Canada, and this is one really unfortunate consequence of Quebec's splitting. I am not a born Maritimer, so I am not a real Maritimer. But I have been here since I was nine years old. When we are in Boston, we feel very much at home. Of course that whole part of the U.S.A. is not doing well economically, so maybe they wouldn't want to take on another.

Nash: You're saying a Maritimer often feels more at home in Boston, more, say, than in Edmonton?

Colville: Yes.

Nash: You have a greater sense of identity with the New Englanders than with the westerners?

Colville: I quite like the West, but I don't feel at home there. I don't like B.C. For one thing, I think there are a lot of people there who sort of ran away. It's a kind of lotus land. Also I don't like mountains.

Nash: To meet some of the requests from Quebec, how far do you think English-speaking Canadians should go in terms of the transfer of power from Ottawa to Quebec?

Colville: I don't see why a loose federation wouldn't work. I would be inclined to give Quebec virtually everything they want. Then you say, in effect, to the other provinces, if you want this, you can have it, too. What's wrong with that?

Nash: Some people would argue how do you thereby maintain national standards in things like medicare and labour practices, or how do you make effective economic treaties with other countries?

Colville: To split the country up economically would be a disaster. The other more bizarre thing that I wonder about is, is it possible that the U.S.A. will split? One wonders. California is soon going to be the fifth biggest economy in the world.

Nash: What do you think the outcome is going to be for Canada? Will we get through this crisis?

Colville: Yes, I think we will. I think we will make it, and five years from now the country will be significantly different. I am so glad that Joe Clark is getting the respect that he deserves.

Nash: You think that Clark's community of communities idea is a good one?

Colville: I am opposed to multiculturalism, but community of communities is not the same thing.

Nash: Why are you opposed to multiculturalism?

Colville: I think it is perfectly foolish for a government to be giving money to Ukrainian dancers. My father was an immigrant from Scotland, and I would never think of speaking Gaelic or learning Scottish dances. If people want to get together and do something, that is fine, but this is not something that the government agencies should be involved in.

Nash: There is, though, a whole new wave of immigrants coming in now who are changing the face and nature of the country.

Colville: The country is changing so much with the immigration, which I am all for. All this business about the oath to the Queen being dropped, I would agree with the NDP. It means something to me, it doesn't mean much to someone from Southeast Asia.

Nash: Something like 40 per cent of the country is now non-British, non-French.

Colville: Here in the Annapolis Valley, my wife's family has been here since way back. After the war, the people who came in and ran the successful farms were Dutch and German people, who just ran circles around the local people, who were third- or fourth-generation farmers. People came over with nothing, worked like hell, and now they are almost dominant figures around here. With all the immigration I think something new is stewing away in this country, and I don't think anyone really knows what Canada in the future will be like.

LISE BISSONNETTE

Lise Bissonnette is publisher of the influential Montreal daily Le Devoir. *Educated in Montreal, Paris, and Strasbourg, she started at* Le Devoir *as a reporter in 1974, became parliamentary correspondent both in Quebec and Ottawa, and later served as an editorial writer. Ms. Bissonnette became editor in 1982. From 1986–90 she wrote a column on Quebec affairs for* The Globe and Mail, *wrote magazine articles, and appeared on Canadian radio and television networks as a commentator. She was named publisher of* Le Devoir *in 1990. She also is co-chair of* The Canadian Journalism Foundation, *which is dedicated to the promotion of excellence in the media.*

"I don't feel any sense of belonging."

Nash: What does Canada mean to you, and what does Quebec mean to you?

Bissonnette: Quebec is my country, there is no doubt about that. I feel a sort of a relationship with Canada, but I don't belong. I do feel that I know Canada better than any other country on earth, and I can talk about Canada much more than any other country. So I wouldn't say that I like France or the United States better. I have a special relationship with Canada, but if you ask me, "Are you a Canadian?" I might be on paper, but I don't feel any sense of belonging. I don't want to say that I feel rejected. I am always upset when I read something saying we feel rejected. I am sick and tired of people in Quebec saying, "Because of Canada we are so unhappy." I don't feel rejected, because I don't think it should be put on that emotional basis. People in Canada have their own interests and we have ours. They happen to conflict, but they are both perfectly legitimate. My sense of not belonging to Canada is one that is shared by many, many people, not only of my generation, but the generation after, and the previous one. My parents probably felt a bit better about Canada, but I am not sure that's true today. They are about eighty, and I should ask them how they would vote in the next referendum.

Nash: How would you vote?

Bissonnette: It's very difficult to say until you see the question, but I voted yes in 1980. I would still probably be looking at what's in it for Quebec. Is it going to settle the question? I don't expect anything much from Canada right now.

Nash: So you have a feeling that we are on a collision course.

Bissonnette: Yes. It's something that you almost can't prevent. That's why I don't believe in the Spicer Commission and all that soul-searching because, in the end, if your interests are not the same, what can you find as a common ground? You can find some functional arrangements, and I would be very interested in getting some kind of functional arrangement because we've lived with Canada for so long, and its history is closer to me than the history of any other country. I think we could find some arrangement, but I really don't feel that I belong. It is difficult to understand why. It's difficult to say why. It's just not there.

Nash: Is it a fair assumption that, for the most part, the élites of Quebec are essentially sovereigntists today.

Bissonnette: You still have within the intellectual community quite a strong consensus geared towards some kind of sovereignty. It's quite soft in some cases because people in that group are a bit tired. I've had a feeling for the past while that the intellectuals now just are going through the motions. Yes, we have to have sovereignty and all of this, but they would like to turn their minds to something else.

Nash: What do you mean by something else?

Bissonnette: Discussing social issues, discussing other issues. They still take it for granted that Quebec should be sovereign, but at the same time they are asking all sorts of questions: "What will that be?" "Is it going to be business people who are going to define what is going to be an independent Quebec?" And they worry very much about it. "Is it going to be a capitalist independent Quebec?" You can feel these questions. The business élite is quite different. There you've got a divided group. The large businesses are very angry at English Canada for all sorts of reasons, business reasons very often. But if you look at small and middle-size business, that is quite different.

Nash: One thing that puzzles me is, what does the word sovereignty mean? It seems to mean different things to different people.

Bissonnette: Absolutely. And at this point, I don't think you can ask for much more than that. If you look at Quebec opinion right now, you get polls saying that two-thirds of the people want separation or some kind of sovereignty. If you poll deeper and ask real questions about what they really want, you will soon find that it is more like sovereignty association, or a European parliament, or a sort of very loose confederation. We had a poll where the conclusion was that what people want in Quebec is really many more powers, but not really separation. They call that sovereignty. The Parti Québécois knows what sovereignty is. It's making all your laws. You can have some links, but you don't keep a common parliament. So most of the people in the Parti Québécois have a clear idea that sovereignty means independence. Sovereignty has become a password in Quebec that everybody is using. It has come to take on a Quebec meaning, in a way.

Nash: But it can range widely in meaning.

Bissonnette: I use it almost every day in my writing. I almost never use the word independence, but I use sovereignty all the time.

Nash: What would be an acceptable transfer of power in your judgement?

Bissonnette: It's always been this division of powers. As far back as the sixties Quebec was asking for a new division of powers. I travel a lot in this country and I hear people saying, "Well, we have given everything to Quebec and they're never satisfied." And that's a great misunderstanding.

Nash: That's something I heard in Alberta, for instance, this past weekend.

Bissonnette: They keep saying that, and I understand quite well why. Trudeau came in and said, "We will give them official bilingualism and they will be happy with it, don't worry about the division of powers." It didn't work. Never did Quebec ask for federal official bilingualism. But the federal government has always tried to appease Quebec through a federal solution, which would be sort of, "Give them more." Well, Quebec has been saying since the sixties that what we want is a new division of powers. If you could touch the division of powers today, maybe there would be a solution. I am not so sure, but at the same time, it is the first time ever that I've had a feeling that in some parts of the country, some very serious people, both in the business and in the political circles, are beginning to look at devolution as a real solution for Canada.

Nash: I think it really now depends on what kind of devolution of power you are talking about. The Allaire report spelled out basically what Quebec wants. Do you think that is a bottom line or a negotiating position?

Bissonnette: Oh, it is a negotiating position, there is no doubt in my mind. Even more than that, it is a strategy to wake up the rest of Canada. I am convinced that it was a kind of shock treatment.

Nash: What do you think would be a Quebec bottom line in terms of the devolution of powers?

Bissonnette: Social affairs, education, culture, immigration, regional development. About ten areas.

Nash: Not the twenty-two areas of Allaire.

Bissonnette: No, not the twenty-two. Some of that was very unrealistic. Communications is a big thing, it's part of culture. Energy. You would have to go to a list of ten or twelve, and then you can begin to talk. The problem as I see it right now is that a lot of the people who are speaking about devolution or decentralization, as they put it, are not talking about real decentralization. The Quebec National Assembly will never accept national standards in terms of education, for example.

Nash: What about medicare?

Bissonnette: Or even medicare if it's a provincial jurisdiction. There is no way. What you are doing is making the kind of proposal Bob Rae has made, saying the provinces are subordinate to some norm, some national standards that are put in the Constitution. I can't believe that someone as intelligent as Bob Rae and as knowledgeable about Quebec can make that kind of proposal.

Nash: Maybe he's bargaining, too.

Bissonnette: Well, it's not bargaining. I think it is all part of the big misunderstanding.

Nash: Which is what?

Bissonnette: If someone like Bob Rae doesn't understand that this is absolutely contrary to the whole philosophy in Quebec and the principles that the province has been fighting for for the last thirty years, I mean, we are out of the picture. We are not in the same house, the same river. Why should we talk?

Nash: You know a lot about the mood, the feel of Quebeckers. You also do a fair bit of travelling in English-speaking Canada. At this point, what is your educated guess as to the outcome?

Bissonnette: Oh, God, confusion. I really think until the referendum we might end up in total confusion both in Quebec and in English Canada.

Nash: You think there will be a referendum in October 1992?

Bissonnette: I am not sure. Bourassa is always playing for time. I am sure that in the end that if there is any sign of interesting offers to Quebeckers Bourassa may say, "Okay, we promised a referendum but it doesn't make sense any more. We should really be serious and look at what is happening in Canada and maybe this will lead somewhere." He might call an election instead of a referendum and say, "Do you give me the mandate to postpone the referendum?"

Nash: Because things would look good now?

Bissonnette: Things look good, so he might say, "Let me work this out, and in six months or a year from now, I promise that there will be a referendum. We are so close to a kind of agreement in all of this."

Nash: You sound a bit of a sceptic.

Bissonnette: After my studies in Europe, I came back in 1970, and thought I would vote yes anytime. I voted for the Parti Québécois. You would vote for the Parti Québécois, but you knew in your right mind that you were just pushing this thing ahead a little bit. You never thought that at some point it would become very serious in that it would come to the point it is today. What is so frustrating about it is that we are not talking about the issue any more. We are just talking about how is this going to come about, and the plumbing of all of this. We've got mechanical solutions to everything, such as whether we should have a Senate. But we are not talking about what's really at stake here. Pepin-Robarts was really quite close to getting at duality and what it means. They came to the conclusion that this country is founded on duality. No one is discussing these views of Canada any more. It is just all the plumbing. I guess we are getting very close to some kind of separation, but how is this going to be done? I don't think it is going to be as clear as a couple of parliamentary commissions and then a referendum, or any-thing like that. It's going to be much more confused than that. It is going to be much more angry than that.

Nash: Angry on whose part?

Bissonnette: On both sides.

Nash: Why would there be the anger?

Bissonnette: Because it's normal and human. It's going to be angry, though I feel less of a threatening mood in Quebec than I find in the rest of Canada. But I am not surprised about that, because threatening is normal. You are angry and you threaten. In the end, they will have to do like Bob Rae when he said Canada is not negotiable, and I am not in any hurry, and the Bélanger-Campeau Commission is not going to push me. Once people have vented their impatience with Quebec, I think there will be some kind of, not offer, but some kind of movement at the table.

Nash: Do you think there might be enough movement to create the pause you spoke of earlier, and that Bourassa might delay a referendum?

Bissonnette: My own reading is that this is a country that, even without Quebec, would have trouble putting its act together, because I sense that there are two deeply colliding visions of the country. People in business want to reduce government because they think that if they cut programs they are going to reduce the debt, and it is going to be better for their business. So how do you cut programs? Well, you shove them onto the provinces, and that would be one way out. At the same time that you have this trend in the business community in Canada, you've got people in the intelligentsia who don't want devolution on that scale.

Nash: Was Canada emotionally and economically an impossible dream?

Bissonnette: I think that Canada went on the wrong track in the sixties. Bill Thorsell said in *The Globe and Mail* that, in order to accommodate Quebec, we changed the whole of Canada. We had official bilingualism and all these institutions, and we had a strong central Canada where French Canadians were represented. There has been a real effort, and I think that people of good faith and people in the élite in Canada believed really that that's the way to win Quebec. It was Trudeau and the French outside Quebec. For what bilingualism did for small communities outside Quebec, I am still willing to support it, but it didn't do much for Quebec. The French CBC, Radio Canada, was a superb achievement. But bilingualism was not really an answer. What Thorsell was saying is that we should have given Quebec more elbow room in the province. And that is what Trudeau didn't want, because his view was if you are sufficiently represented by good people, the French power thing, then you can run the whole country, or at least co-chair it, and then you have real influence and real power. That is intellectually something you can agree with, but we are a minority, and you are never really able to co-chair equally at the federal level. There's a resentment I feel about that. The elbow room was never really there.

Michael Bedford Photography

TOM AXWORTHY

Winnipeg-born Tom Axworthy was principal secretary and primary speech writer for Prime Minister Trudeau from 1981 to 1984. Previously, he had been senior policy adviser to the prime minister. He is now executive director of the CRB *Foundation in Montreal, established by the Bronfman family. He also is a lecturer at the John F. Kennedy School of Government at Harvard University. He is the author of several books and many articles on public policy.*

"Sovereignty. A code word for pride."

Nash: Did Pierre Trudeau make a fundamental mistake with his bilingualism and biculturalism policies, and with the idea of French power in Ottawa, when Quebec, according to some people, wanted power within the province, not power on the national scene. Was his approach a mistake, do you think?

Axworthy: There is, to me, a tremendous divergence between the people who make up the nationalist élite of this province, who have their own value systems, their own set of interests, and their own sense of psychic deprivation relating to the rest of Canada, and what the average working man and woman of Quebec wants, which is no different than what other Canadians want. If a country means anything, it is that people should feel at ease to live and move into any part of it. Therefore, on official languages, surely federal institutions have to be bilingual, so that both language groups could be served in their own language? That's a basic right. How could you have a country that would deprive its citizens from being served in their own language? And then, for example, the famous Corn Flakes box debate. Isn't it important that French Canadians be able to read labels that tell them what is in their products? And on education rights, for a French Canadian to take a job in Alberta, what choice is there if he or she knows that it means the children must be educated in English. They instantly almost lose their French. The whole concept of nationhood begins to diminish if you can't think of the territorial entity as your home. Because we have two large language groups in our country, without language rights, Canada can't survive. So those people who say it was a mistake, in my view, just have no appreciation of what it means to be a citizen in Canada.

Nash: You think most of the Quebeckers who want to ignore French in the rest of Canada and concentrate on the province, are sovereigntists?

Axworthy: If you are in the Quebec élite which has no interest in Canada, very little interest in partnership, and only wants to have the fun of running its own place, and is interested only in powers for itself, what do you care about the French Canadian who may want to take a job in Newfoundland or Alberta, and what do you care about the French-speaking minority in Alberta? My focus is Canada, my desire is to make Canada a society with equal life chances for all Canadians. That means, unlike many countries, that Canada has to define language as an equal right. I have no interest in creating a state of Quebec, because I believe that the welfare and the future prosperity of Quebeckers is best achieved in cooperation with other Canadians.

Nash: On the question of the difference between the élites of Quebec and the people of Quebec, the polls still suggest that most Quebeckers do want sovereignty, whatever that word sovereignty may mean.

Axworthy: Public opinion is very volatile. One can't put an enormous amount of credence into polls because they are a snapshot of opinion. The choice where it really counts, in referendums or elections, is a much more important choice because it is a considered one. Sovereignty doesn't mean now what it means in the dictionary. It has become a code word for a greater sense of pride and legitimacy. Sovereignty means, in the dictionary, an independent state with full legal powers. When you look at Quebeckers who really want that, suddenly those numbers drop radically.

Nash: You really are talking then about pride rather than power for Quebec.

Axworthy: Yes, I am. The bureaucrats, the politicians, the power-mongers, they want power. But for Quebeckers, sovereignty has become a symbol for the fact that people want to be treated as an equal partner in Confederation.

Nash: How should English-speaking Canada respond to what they are hearing that Quebec wants?

Axworthy: Start by making a distinction between the Quebec élite and what's good for Quebeckers. We have a body of people here who have no interest in Canada. They are strategically placed through a whole series of institutions. They are not bad people, they just have a different vision of the future. They want the fun of running their own country. Those people can never be appeased. They won't be appeased until they have a state.

So what do you do about division of powers? You start off, not with what these politicians and bureaucrats want, but by asking what is an intelligent division of powers according to functions. I believe in change. What's the change for? It's to deliver services and goods and life-chances more equitably, more fairly, more efficiently across the country. Does that need some rejigging of powers? Probably a little. Does it need the twenty-two of the Allaire report? Nonsense.

Nash: How do you characterize the Quebec government, and Premier Bourassa specifically?

Axworthy: You can't find an intense commitment to Canada in anything that Mr. Bourassa has ever said. On the other hand, he also knows that there will be a terrific price to be paid for the psychic satisfaction of becoming a rather tiny nation state in the latter part of the twentieth century. It's just so hard to delve into where this man is really coming from, and if he knows himself. He may not. I have a feeling that Mr. Bourassa is as ambivalent about Canada as many of his fellow Quebeckers. He knows how good a country this is, but he also feels the desire to be supreme in his own. I think that he is very spooked by the nationalist élite and their ability to turn the hard core out on the streets. I think he sees himself in the tradition of Quebec premiers who have sought more powers for Quebec, but I think he is worried about the ability of Quebec to go on its own. So he would like to have a much looser Confederation with more powers for Quebec, but all the economic advantages accruing.

If you look at Quebec opinion, it varies from about 18 to 30 per cent who are pretty hard-core separatists. Separatists, not sovereigntists; they want an independent country. Similarly, on the other far extreme, is my group which is the hard-core federalist. They are heavily among the anglophone community, but there is a band of 10 to 15 per cent of French Canadians as well, who believe strongly in Canada. Then we have this vast group in between of about 45, 50 per cent, who want to get on with their lives. They don't travel across Canada all that much, but they like the idea of being Canadian. But they are also very proud of being French Canadian. They are worried about their ability to maintain the language and culture in this part of North America. They feel very favourable towards Canada, but they feel stronger about Quebec. So we have got a group of Quebeckers who reject Canada. There are equally strong Canadians who are among the minorities, and then there is a broad mass of French Canadians who are now saying they are for sovereignty, but they are not for independence.

Nash: What do you think the odds are for a form of sovereignty for Quebec?

Axworthy: There either will be independence or there will be renewed federalism. What will not fly is sovereignty association. It makes no sense for English-speaking Canadians to agree to it, and it makes no sense for French Canadians to follow this will o' the wisp that they can have their cake and eat it, too. That is the crucial choice that the Quebec nationalist is going to have to face.

Nash: Is there time enough to formulate a renewed federalism by the October 1992 deadline?

Axworthy: That was always a foolish deadline. As soon as I saw that I said, he is not serious about really wanting a renewed deal. You could begin to have the framework of one, but you could never have a signed, sealed, and delivered deal at that point.

When you look at the kind of revised federalism that we need, it strikes me that you have to look at movement on four or five basic fronts, all of which can be do-able. The first is the free mobility of capital, labour, and goods. It is so infantile and stupid that the European Community has a freer common market than Canada has. The provinces prevent Ontario bricks from coming into Quebec. That really is nonsensical. We need a strong Canada clause for trade and commerce and mobility. Again, my point is that Canadians should feel free to move and earn a living and settle right across the country. The second point is that I have always been against the notwithstanding clause in the Charter of Rights. My whole argument is that we have rights, they are inalienable, and they should be right across the country. No province should have the power to take away the right of free expression as Quebec, or Alberta, and Saskatchewan have done. At a minimum, as a federal government, I would say that I will not use the notwithstanding and I would try to have a constitutional amendment which other provinces could opt into.

Do we need some shifting in the division of powers? Yes. We could look at powers such as manpower training, where the provinces are closer to the local needs. The manpower area can be delegated intelligently to the provinces. The provision of immigration is another area. Canada has to set the levels, but the government of Quebec could decide on the kinds of immigrants that it wants. That, too, is a power that I could see devolving to provinces, because that's one where they could allocate it more efficiently.

West Germany is a very interesting, functioning federal system, where the national government keeps its powers, but they are administered by the provinces, i.e., they have one civil service; the Länders, or the states, are delegated by the federal government to administer a whole series of federal laws, but you lessen the bureaucracy by having one bureaucracy doing this function. That could be a very interesting way of reducing the duplication in Canada by having provincial bodies administer these sets of laws and be paid a certain amount, but the federal ability to change the law, jurisdiction, would hold.

Communications worries me. I could see why Quebec would want the ability to license their own cable people, but I would be very careful because we need national communication, Canadian content, against the beam of the United States. I would look at a functional division of powers on who can best do what. Federal power should probably be strengthened, for example, in the environment, because the environment knows no provincial boundaries. So I would look at who best can deliver what kind of powers in this latter part of the twentieth century, and I would be prepared to switch quite a bit. No question about it, we have to move on the representation issue. The West demands an elected Senate. I believe in that. Ontario and Quebec are going to have to give up dominating not only the House of Commons because of population, but dominating the Senate, as well.

Nash: You would be in favour of a Triple-E Senate – elected, equal, and effective.

Axworthy: In theory, yes. The problem would be how many senators and how many districts. In theory it makes very good sense for a federal system to have that kind of power. Let's bring the regions into the centre. Ontario and Quebec are going to have to understand that the West demands it, and the Maritimes demands it, as well. That representation at the centre is as important for the psychic pride of western

Canadians as a greater devolution of powers is for francophones. We also now need some major moves on aboriginals.
Most of the country knows that they need a fair deal. If we
put together that kind of basket of a renewed federalism – a
changed division of powers; stronger Canada clauses; new
representation; and an aboriginal deal – then that is a deal
that would fly in every part of the country. What won't fly is
some system which says all these powers for Quebec and
nothing for the rest of the country, or twenty powers to the
provinces, leaving the federal government nothing more than
a postman.

TED BYFIELD

A Toronto-born westerner, Ted Byfield is president of United Western Communications Ltd, which publishes Alberta Report, Western Report, *and* B.C. Report, *weekly public affairs magazines. His first job was as a copy boy for* The Washington Post, *and later he worked with the Ottawa* Journal, *the Sudbury* Star, *and the* Winnipeg Free Press. *He left journalism for teaching in 1962 but returned to it when he started* Alberta Report. *A popular commentator on western politics and attitudes, Byfield writes a weekly column "Westview" which appears in all three of his magazines.*

"Quebec never was part of Canada."

Nash: People in the East don't realize there are many differences among westerners and so many western points of view.
Byfield: There isn't any such place as western Canada. Some of the people in the Prairies speak of the Prairies as being the West. The people on the coast don't really call themselves westerners so much as British Columbians. Even within the Prairies, Manitoba is a very different sort of place than Alberta. There are real differences within British Columbia. A Vancouverite has very little in common with people from Abbotsford, or from Prince George.
Nash: With all those separate identities, how do we get a national identity as Canadians?
Byfield: Our history is really the problem. Prior to the

Second World War, people in English-speaking Canada including, I think, even people of Eastern European origins, tended to identify with the British element. I can always remember in Ontario the red boxes that said Royal Mail, and highways that were named the King's Highway. There was a very powerful national identity, and it was British. There was a very conscious effort made, beginning with the Pearson government and accelerating under the Trudeau government, to destroy that national identity. I think it was murdered. Perhaps it had to die anyway, but its death was certainly hastened, and we have never been able to replace it with anything else.

Nash: What we were trying to replace it with, I suppose, was a bilingual, bicultural country.

Byfield: That was the idea, and a country that was caring and sharing and all those things. But it was totally divorced from our history. I don't think nations are concoctable. What we are now doing is suffering the consequences of that failed experiment. We don't really have anything to hold us together, and we know it.

Nash: What about the role of Quebec in all this?

Byfield: Quebec has always been a nation. Go back to 1760 with the surrender of the armies at Montreal. The town of Quebec had fallen the previous year. Quebec was left destitute. Quebec didn't come to Canada and say, "I want to belong to you." We went in there with muskets and took them over, and it didn't work. We were continually warned, of course, by Lord Durham, in particular in 1840, that if you don't destroy the nationalism that's resident in Quebec, eventually it is going to separate. That's what he was telling us, and he was certainly right. So it is not as though Quebec is leaving Canada. Quebec never was part of Canada. It was always a country unto itself. It has everything. It has a continguous geography, it has a language, it has a culture, it has a common religion. It has all the attributes of nationhood. I think it is a country, but the question is, what are the rest of us?

Nash: Do you think that we shouldn't be spending time now trying to find ways to keep Quebec within Canada?

Byfield: I think that's a lost cause. If they don't separate this time, they will the next time, because they have been working on this for more than 200 years, and they know exactly what they want. What we should be working on is a workable nationalism in the rest of the country.

Nash: What kind of a Canada do you envision?

Byfield: Countries don't come about because people envision them. We live in an era of social engineering in which we think we are going to have a country and put together a recipe for it. You can't do that. I think the first thing we have to do is to solve our economic problems, and there are cultural consequences of doing that. We have a $400-billion debt, and we don't know what to do with it. When we go through the unquestioned agony that is going to be necessary to solve that, we might come out of it with something of a national identity. What we should do is face our economic responsibilities and begin solving problems. As we solve them, we will begin to become a nation. Nations are born as the consequence of history, not as the consequence of social engineering.

Nash: You think Canada historically was inevitably going to have the break we now seem to be facing?

Byfield: We were never able, or at least willing, to terminate the French fact. Begin with the proclamation of 1763, the policy then was to terminate the French fact in Canada. That's what the Brits saw right away that they had to do, and everything was calculated to do this. For Quebec as such, its boundaries were restricted down to the St. Lawrence Valley. The government at the time simply said we've got to end the French fact in Canada. Immediately they were threatened with the American Revolution, so they had to purchase the loyalty of the French. So they passed the Quebec Act in 1774, which went in the opposite direction. It guaranteed their religion and language and schools and everything else, thereby assuring the French people of a continuity. The next milestone you come to is Lord Durham, who said this has gone too far. He wanted to unite the country into one and stop the French fact from spreading. Today we've got to terminate it again. We didn't resolve it in 1763, we didn't resolve it in 1774, nor in 1867, and we still haven't.

Nash: We now seem to be heading in the direction of some resolution.

Byfield: Well, yes. It is going to resolve itself in the sense that exactly what had been foreseen all along is now going to happen.

Nash: You think that might be a catalyst then for the rest of the country to find itself?

Byfield: The rest of the country will either find a common ground or disappear into the United States. We can go either one way or the other.

Nash: What's your best estimate?

Byfield: If we resolve to solve our economic problems, we will become a country, and if we continue kidding ourselves with one sort of ineffectual government after another, we won't. We will simply go bankrupt and be bought. We should quit playing around with Quebec and say, "Look, if you want to be part of the country, you are one province of ten. You can have your language, and all the provinces can decide language policy. If you don't want that, go ahead on your own and set the thing up independently, but the rest of us must decide how we are going to live, because we can't continue with this uncertainty. All it is doing is tearing us apart. If you are in, you are in like every other province, with one distinction and that's on language." If they say they are out, and that is the probability, then the rest of us should get together and say, "Okay, how are we going to solve this financial problem?"

Nash: Constitutionally what do we do then, devolve powers from Ottawa to the provinces, make stronger regions? What do we do?

Byfield: You have to retain strong central authority in the federal government, but it should be mitigated the way the Americans mitigate it by the Senate. Whether you call it the House of the Provinces or whatever, as long as the Triple-E principles are maintained. The federal government must retain all the powers it has now and possibly more, but it must be subject to the veto of a Triple-E Senate.

The thing that destroyed much western allegiance to Canada as such was the national energy program. It just hit Albertans, as though to demonstrate that Canada is essentially a fraud. They changed the rules. They simply said we are going to impose taxes and drain the money down east. A hundred billion dollars was transferred from Alberta to the central authority in fifteen years, of which ninety billion went to Quebec. The people at that point in Alberta, and I don't mean a few kooks, I mean the rank and file in Alberta, began to suspect the Canadian connection. And then they elect a Tory Government, and it takes the Tory Government a year and a half to repeal the national energy program. They wait, and then there is this CF-18 contract, and stuff like this. This is supposed to be our government, but it's still working on behalf of the centre.

Nash: You're distressed with the way all recent governments have handled the economy.

Byfield: It started with Diefenbaker. We adopted Keynesian economics. It says that in adverse times you run at a deficit and in prosperous times you run at a surplus. Well, we took half the advice. We simply spent more than we could afford. We have made medicare into a national icon, and yet everybody knows of stories of just unbelievable waste. To suggest some sort of user fee on medicare is almost blasphemous. The consequence is that we are destroying medicare.

If the country decides we are going to solve our fiscal problem, then out of this will emerge a very much stronger country. The politicians don't seem to want to do that, but I think of the people who are now being laid off in one place after another in Ontario. These things are coming home to us, and whether we want to face them or not, we are going to have to.

Nash: They are coming home because of what? Because our taxes are higher, because we're less competitive?

Byfield: Because we live beyond our means. We have to

discipline ourselves or we will be disciplined. There is a tremendous unwillingness to face these realities. But we've got to cut back, we've got to spend less, especially through government. It's not a glorious thing to do, to save money, but it has the effect of saving the country.

Nash: Look forward to the year 2000 and tell me, what do you think Canada may look like?

Byfield: I don't want to hazard a guess, because the most dangerous thing that is going to happen is going to be what I think of as the Save Canada Movement. I think that Quebec will ask a ferocious price to remain even nominally associated with the rest of the country – a price that on the face of it is ludicrous. The Ottawa establishment, particularly the bureaucracy, will say that unless we sustain Quebec's participation on any basis at all, we are finished. Therefore, they will say, the Canadian thing to do is pay the Quebec price and save Canada. We are going to be assailed with the most unbelievable propaganda emanating from Toronto and Ottawa to save Canada. The consequence of this is that we are going to make a deal with Quebec in some sort of last effort to save them that will be absolutely disastrous to the rest of the country. Quebec will prosper through this deal and the rest of us will be destroyed. There will be voices in the wilderness saying what we are doing is not saving Canada, what we are doing is destroying it, because we are refusing to face the reality that Quebec is another country. But these voices will be dismissed as bigots and rednecks. The consequence will be a country in the year 2000 that is really two countries, with practically no federal presence in one of the provinces – that province controlling its own destiny to a degree that's really so close to autonomous that the difference is almost impossible to define – and the rest of the country still striving to retain this thread and, in consequence, left destitute. The question is, can we resist the force of the Save Canada Movement and use our heads instead of our emotions?

Nash: That's a pretty gloomy outlook.

Byfield: Now if we can say, look this is phoney, Quebec wants to be an independent country. We are virtually making it an independent country, so bite the bullet and make the best deal with them we can and stop this nonsense. If we are clever enough to do that, then I think we might have a country in the year 2000 with a promising future.

ROBERT STANFIELD

Leader of the national Progressive Conservative Party from 1967 to 1976, Robert Stanfield came close, but never won the prime ministership of Canada. Born in Truro, Nova Scotia, he became premier of the province in 1956 and was re-elected in three subsequent elections before taking over the national party leadership from John Diefenbaker. After three defeats at the hands of Pierre Trudeau, he resigned. Between 1979 and 1980 he served as special representative for Canada to the Middle East and North Africa. Stanfield was chairman of the Institute for Research on Public Policy from 1983 to 1987, and he was appointed the first Canadian chairman of the Commonwealth Foundation in 1986.

"We make a fetish of every province having exactly the same power."

Nash: If you were prime minister, how would you respond to the conditions that Quebec has set for continuing on in the federation of Canada?

Stanfield: I would find them very difficult to accept, of course. I guess I would proceed in the hope that if we can get talking again, we could work in something considerably more moderate. It's essential that the people of English-speaking Canada recognize that things just won't be hunky-dory for Canada if Quebec left, as some English-speaking Canadians seem to think. On the other hand, it is important that Quebeckers realize that there's serious risk in separation for the people of Quebec. It is really not an easy thing to be a small country in the contemporary world. If both realize the problems, then I think it becomes possible to negotiate more moderate changes.

Nash: What kind of moderate changes are you thinking of?

Stanfield: There may be some powers, some roles that could be transferred from Ottawa to the provinces without loss of efficiency or effectiveness. I don't know what they are. I think more in terms of reassuring Quebec about its culture. Begin with the notion that all provinces are equal under the Constitution, which is a recent myth that some people have tried to develop.

Nash: You think there could be a special status for Quebec?

Stanfield: There have always been special differences. For example, in the area of education, Nova Scotia since Confederation has had powers that Quebec or Ontario have not had. In Ontario and Quebec, the legislators had to respect the religious school boards. There was no such restriction put on Nova Scotia. It caused some problems in Nova Scotia, but it didn't weaken Confederation.

Nash: So, we have been different from the start in a number of areas?

Stanfield: From the start there have been some significant differences in the powers that the provinces have, and therefore I think it is unfortunate that we make a fetish of every province having exactly the same power. There are obvious reasons why one could object to Quebec having powers in foreign affairs, because it would make it very difficult for Ottawa to conduct a coherent foreign policy. If one is careful to make certain that any power considered for the province of Quebec does not impair the ability of the federal government to do its job, then I don't think we should necessarily get all steamed up about this, although I agree that we should be careful.

Nash: Should those powers, such as culture and communications and immigration, if they are given to Quebec, be given to all the provinces?

Stanfield: Not necessarily. In a very real sense, the Parliament of Canada represents the culture that prevails in the other provinces and is very able to protect the people in the other provinces.

Nash: There is a certain feeling among some provincial premiers that they would like those kinds of powers.

Stanfield: That may be. But, as I said, provinces are not necessarily equal, and the provinces are not always the best judges as to what is in the best interest of the country.

Nash: Do you think this might be an opportunity to look at some kind of overall renewed federalism, not only *vis à vis* Quebec? Things like dealing with the Senate, or dealing with representation in national institutions.

Stanfield: There has to be a re-examination of Confederation as a whole if what is proposed is going to be supported by the country as a whole and by Canadians in all parts of the country.

Nash: There has been an almost universal downgrading of respect for politicians in recent years, and it particularly accelerated following the Meech Lake processs – a feeling that there wasn't enough public participation. Do you think that there has to be more of a public presence in trying to find some kind of new federalism?

Stanfield: Apparently there has to be more consultation than took place in the Meech Lake process. We have not made it a practice in Canada to take constitutional considerations to the people. They have always been dealt with by governments and members of Parliament and members of legislatures. There is a desire on the part of Canadians for more involvement in these questions, and I think we should start satisfying that desire. Surely we are smart enough to work out some method of greater consultation.

Nash: Many Québécois seem to have a sense that English-speaking Canada has failed Quebec. Has it?

Stanfield: I don't think English-speaking Canada, or parts of it, were very smart in connection with Meech Lake. I think it was a very inexpensive way of bringing Quebec fully into the Constitution, having Quebec formally accept the Constitution which it formally rejected in 1982. It was asking an amazingly small price.

Nash: Now we are hearing some fairly tough words out of Quebec about the conditions for continuing in Confederation. What's your educated guess about the odds on the outcome? Will Quebec separate, do you think?

Stanfield: The people of Quebec are a cautious lot on the whole. Perhaps they are beginning to wonder and worry a bit about what life would be like for them off on their own. I hope they are beginning to worry. The odds will depend to some extent on what the reaction is in English-speaking Canada. Are English-speaking Canadians prepared to make any concessions? Some are clearly not prepared. As long as any significant number of English-speaking Canadians are saying, "Well, Quebec can accept Confederation as it is or leave," then Quebec will probably leave. In my judgement, it's not just attitudes in Quebec that are important.

Nash: You are saying that English-speaking Canada has to come back to Quebec with some kind of package that would indicate a willingness to recognize the distinctiveness of Quebec and those areas in which Quebec could have some new authority?

Stanfield: They have to recognize the duality of Canada in some sense and the important role that Quebeckers played in the birth of Canada. After all, Confederation could not have taken place without the cooperation of the French-speaking people of Lower Canada.

Nash: Can you really have a successful duality within the multicultural society we are increasingly becoming?

Stanfield: It doesn't become any easier, but it would be helpful if more Canadians knew something about their history. I get the impression that Canadians today don't know very much about the history of Canada. There is room for discussion as to how far you take the duality question. Certainly the people of Quebec have to feel they can communicate with and be served by the federal government and its agencies in their own language if Canada is going to mean very much to them. Surely we have to be prepared to go that far.

Nash: Do you think negotiations for a separation, if it came to that, would get pretty tough or even nasty?

Stanfield: I do expect a good deal of bitterness to develop. There would be fierce disputes about how much of the national debt was attributable to Quebec, what assets Quebec should get for nothing, what it should pay for others. Then the discussions and arguments would go on for some time, and a tremendous bitterness might develop.

Nash: That might endanger any ability to have close economic relations and cooperation.

Stanfield: This is something that Quebeckers should consider. They will be on their own.

Nash: How do you describe what a Canadian is? We are forever searching for our identity, do we have one?

Stanfield: One of the things I like about Canada, as contrasted to the United States, is that we do not have in Canada a strict, orthodox definition of patriotism, a strict code as to what you have to do or believe to be a Canadian. Whereas I have the impression that in the States there is an orthodox view of what you should think and how you should behave. I have always admired the approach we have taken. Being patriotic is nothing more than being a good citizen.

Nash: Do Canadians really understand each other? Do we really know and hear each other or is it a dialogue of the deaf?

Stanfield: It is easier to describe what the problem is than to find the solution. We have to persuade people in English-speaking Canada and people in Quebec that it's important we understand each other. I am not sure what the solution is, but I think we have to make a much bigger and more sustained effort than we have made in the past to try to undertand each other. The problems that the West have complained about have been dealt with. The tariff problem is pretty well historic, the energy policy they objected to has been done away with. They say their voice is not heard in the East, but they have the deputy prime minister and the minister of Finance and there's Joe Clark. They think some kind of an elected Senate would help them. I don't think it would.

But let's talk it out, let's have a real discussion on how institutional reform could create more confidence among westerners, without tying up and making it virtually impossible to conduct the public business in the country.

Nash: Again, we are talking about the reshaping of the Constitution. What about the institution of the monarchy?

Stanfield: The monarchy is important in a Commonwealth sense. I feel that the Commonwealth is a very important institution in the modern world. It is extraordinary that these countries, most of which were former colonies and frequently oppressed to some extent, should have some sense of cohesion, some sense of commonality. They represent about one-fifth of the world's population, all different colours. We would be very stupid to let it go down the drain. The Queen is the head of the Commonwealth and the Queen is a very real symbol as far as the Commonwealth is concerned. What do we substitute for the Queen, anyway?

Nash: Much of what we are talking about and many of the reshaping proposals tend to push us away from the British style of parliamentary democracy and closer to the American style.

Stanfield: That's quite right. It's rather paradoxical that many Canadians who are maybe not pro-American have advocated the adoption in Canada of American institutions. The Bill of Rights was there for nearly 200 years in the States before we were attracted to the idea, and I doubt if we have done anything since 1867 that is going to change the country and some of our institutions as much as we did when we adopted the Canadian Charter of Rights. If we adopt an elected Senate, that again will be a move towards the American system.

Nash: Do we expect too much from our government?

Stanfield: There are times when I have felt that most Canadians do feel that governments can solve any problem. We expect far too much from our politicians. Politicians are not any more evil in my opinion than they ever were.

Nash: Could you tell me what you would like to see Canada look like at the dawn of the twenty-first century?

Stanfield: I would like to see it geographically intact, running from sea to sea, proud of its political institutions, to be prosperous as a nation and among ourselves. It is hard for me to bring myself to believe that the country will separate.

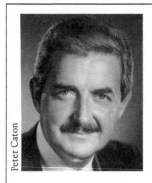

Peter Caton

MATTHEW BARRETT

In his twenty-seven years at the Bank of Montreal, Matthew Barrett has risen from trainee to chairman and chief executive officer. He was born in County Meath, Ireland, and, at age eighteen, joined the bank at its old Waterloo Place branch in London, England. He transferred to Canada in 1967. He has served as vice president of the British Columbia Division of the bank, and as deputy general manager of the bank's international Banking Group. He became president in 1987 and was elected chairman in 1990. At age forty-seven, he is one of the youngest senior banking executives in the world.

"It's tragic if this country breaks up."

Nash: Could I ask, as an immigrant, what does Canada mean to you?
Barrett: I have a tremendous love affair with the country, and one of the things I would like to see expunged is that you have to make apologies for giving I Love Canada speeches. What are we doing to ourselves when you feel ashamed to say you love the country? I came here as a young kid from the Bank of Montreal in London, England, and you can't travel this country without falling in love with it. It is the greatest country in the world. And it has wonderful values. But there is a gap now between our self-image and reality. We see ourselves as a tolerant, caring, compassionate society, and yet we make jokes about each other, about the East and West,

French-English. We need to reexamine that.

I grew up in a small country (Ireland) that was broke, and I saw what that does to people. Then I moved to the U.K. and worked for the bank for five years in England and saw that system fall down around its ears. When I came to Canada in 1967 I was breathless because it was such a fabulous country. I remember when I got off the plane they were singing "Canada We Love You ... "

Nash: Bobby Gimby and his band of kids.

Barrett: And this was in Montreal. It was a wonderful party. How things have changed in twenty years. So the country has everything in the world going for it.

Nash: What happened to that spirit of 1967, the spirit of our hundredth birthday? Where did it go? We were on such a high at that point.

Barrett: I think the country became fiscally irresponsible, and you pay the price. Every country in the world that has gone down that route has paid the price. Every one. We came out of the sixties with great optimism, tremendous promise, a decent fiscal situation, and it has deteriorated. We have an imbalance between our appetite for government services and safety and security – to be protected. I think we lost sight of the best elements of democratic capitalism and got the balance wrong. When the economics go wrong, it tends to bring up an awful lot of stresses and strains.

But, you know, this country is a miracle. It has no right physically to exist. You wouldn't design a country that's three thousand miles long, with the north-south pull. It has required some extraordinary vision and devices and engineering to keep it going, and I think what happened in the last twenty years is that we just got it wrong. We put the wrong set of incentives and disincentives into the system generally, and it has eroded our competitiveness. As well we seem to have been very inwardly focussed for a couple of decades while the rest of the world has had a tremendous external orientation, and therefore we are caught in a time-warp in our thinking.

I would also argue that the political leadership in the

country has not been burdened with much preoccupation with economics. We have had a lot of lawyers, who enjoyed government. I mean, it's sexy. But I don't think you've had an awful lot of pragmatic common-sense people focussed on the economy.

Nash: What do you think in your heart that Canada will be like in the year 2000?

Barrett: In my optimistic scenario, it would be a country that strikes the right balance between social policy, social justice, and economic development. It would be a country that gets its act together in competitiveness and realizes that it is part of a global world, that it can't withdraw into itself without entropy. I hope it will be a country that will put greater emphasis on individual freedom than it now does, and will be a lot less corporatist or statist; a country that doesn't look to government to solve its problems. I would like to see the country move back to its traditional values of individual responsibility, individual freedom, less government.

Nash: What do you see as the biggest obstacle to our constitutional confrontation? One obstacle that really stands out.

Barrett: We are debating pieces of the problem and not integrating the pieces. Constitutional issues are about values and about organizational arrangements. There is an economic crisis, and there are ten thousand voices debating bits and pieces of that, and then there are all the social policy issues. These things seem to me to be debated as if they were independent variables when, in fact, they are interdependent variables, and you can't tackle one without understanding the impact it has on the other areas, and vice versa. My concern is that the debate so far has been purely on cultural and political lines, as if they could be resolved independent of the economic backdrop and the social policy backdrop of the country. You need to come up with a holistic solution, because if you don't, you will merely have deferred the problem, you won't have solved it.

Nash: Is there time to do all of that? Looking at deadlines, looking at, say, October 1992, is there time to do that?

Barrett: We have to make time. There is a great old cliché that if you haven't got the time to do it right, when are you going to have the time to do it over? My concern is that it get done right once and for all, and end this disruptive and divisive overhang on the country. You now hear referendum or referenda being talked about for the fall of 1992. That's a short period of time to do the kind of ambitious integration that I'm talking about. But I would argue that you can't afford to have the agenda for the country set by one province's agenda. I think that if you get the process going, and if there seems to be good progress being made, and the issues are surfacing, then you would find that perhaps Quebec will defer or delay the referendum date.

Nash: Of all the various options that have been talked about, what's your choice for Canada?

Barrett: I think it's unnecessary and tragic if the country breaks up, and I would consider sovereignty association or independence as a breakup. So, the question is, can you reconfigure arrangements – political, fiscal, everything else – so that you can renew the Canadian miracle? I think you can. The vision I have is that there would be a significant decentralization of powers. Whether you are talking of a country or a business, I think the forces at play everywhere in the world these days are the need for people to feel responsiveness. They want local authority, local decision-making. Local empowerment has sensitivity to local issues and needs.

The other reason I am in favour of decentralization is to push accountability, political accountability, down to where the public has the best chance of holding politicians to account. The problem we have today is that, somewhat unfairly, the entire country blames the forces of darkness in Ottawa. And the provinces, of course, are not unskilled at blaming Ottawa, as well. There is this distant abstraction, this straw man, that the public gets to bang away at. What I would like to see is that you push some of these things down, and then if provincial governments don't strike the right balance between social policy and economic development, they will be held to account. So, I am in favour of, to the maximum extent possible, pushing appropriate authority down into the places where, one, the service can be best delivered, and, two, where the public can hold political leadership accountable for results.

Nash: Would that then mean a lot of shared responsibilities in the economy, for instance, so that some would be federal and some would be provincial?

Barrett: Yes. We have a relatively small domestic market, and the problem is that we have a tremendous amount of government overhead proportionate to the population, proportionate to the gross domestic product. It's like having too much overhead in business. We want to eliminate as much duplication in governance as possible.

Nash: What are the areas you think might be best served as exclusive federal jurisdiction? Areas like foreign policy or defence?

Barrett: That's obvious. I think foreign policy, defence, the national infrastructure.

Nash: Breaking down provincial trade barriers, perhaps?

Barrett: Absolutely. I mean there are some nonsensical things going on in the country. Certainly economic policy, monetary policy, has to be maintained by the government. I think environmental issues, also. Acid rain doesn't know which border it's supposed to stop at, and rivers have this unfortunate habit of flowing from one province into the other. There is no point in trying to deal with environmental issues locally because, as I say, acid rain, pollution, all these things, are not local issues, they are global issues, national issues.

Nash: Do you think Quebec would find that kind of federal authority comfortable, acceptable?

Barrett: I don't know yet, Knowlton. I can only guess like everybody else. I think the Allaire report is an aggressive opening chess move. It is exactly what I would do. I don't know why people are getting all upset. The good news is that the Allaire report is saying, "I want things very decentralized; maximum power short of separation." So they have put a stake in the ground, and no doubt somewhere in the psyche of the people in Quebec there is a bottom line below which they won't negotiate. We don't know what that is.

Nash: But you don't think Allaire is the bottom line.

Barrett: No I don't. I think the Allaire report was an extreme opening gambit and that they will settle for considerably less than that.

Nash: Is there not a danger that once having stated an extreme position, it becomes entrenched in the minds of people, and they will have political problems in settling for anything less than that?

Barrett: There is a danger of that, but I don't think we are there yet. I have great faith in the common sense of the public, and I think the public recognizes that Allaire was an opening move. It's a wish list of every possible thing you might like to run yourself. But I suspect the bottom line revolves around culture, language, communications, immigration – the things that they deem to be critical for the protection of their language and culture. I would say those are probably not negotiable. The rest that deal with economic powers and trade and other things are probably negotiable.

Nash: Do you think there is more than a fifty-fifty chance of getting a consensus on the Constitution in the rest of Canada?

Barrett: Yes I think there is. But Knowlton, you can't separate the debates on the Constitution from the debate on the economy. In the end, the real social activist is an economic realist, and it is a fact of life that you can't protect social policy, cultural policy, or any policy, if you are broke.

Nash: Let me be a pessimist for the moment. Supposing it doesn't work. Supposing Quebec doesn't find acceptable the proposals that will be coming forth, what happens then? What are the implications?

Barrett: We have a big Canada today that has problems. I am hard pressed to think how several small Canadas would solve the problems because within each province, the problems are ingrained. In a world in which everyone is snuggling up into larger and large relationships, I can't see how Canada imploding and fragmenting could be good for the country. I would see it as a significant negative effect on the economic development of whatever the number of regions is that emerge. They would be weaker. The standard of living would fall. Foreign investment would be weak. Continuing funding of our debt abroad would mean paying a higher risk premium. What I am saying is not economic terrorism, but this is a fact of life that's going to happen. I think people who dismiss the economic consequences of the breakup of the country on the standard of living and jobs in this country are doing a tremendous disservice. It's manipulative and deceptive of them to pretend to the public that everything is going to be fine. It's just not going to be fine. And that's why you find people saying things like sovereignty association. But if you break up into independent, fragmented, small countries, the economics are terrible.

The ordinary Canadian, the ordinary citizen, the factory worker in Quebec or the logger in B.C. or the fishermen in Newfoundland, he is the one who will suffer. It's not the urbane, sophisticated cosmopolitan, fluently bilingual, Harvard-trained Ph.D. He is going to be fine under any scenario. He is mobile, his skills are portable, he can go anywhere in the world. But what happens to the poor average Joe who has got to go to his job every day, if the people who say everything will be okay are wrong?

DAVID BERCUSON

Born in Montreal, David Bercuson is Dean of the Faculty of Graduate Studies at the University of Calgary. He is a graduate of Sir George William University in Montreal and the University of Toronto, and is one of Canada's top historians. He has written and edited numerous books and articles with particular emphasis in recent years on the Canadian constitutional dilemma. He joined the University of Calgary as a visiting assistant professor in 1970 and has been associated with the university ever since.

"The duality doesn't work."

Nash: With so many competing visions of Canada, are we a nation at cross purposes today?

Bercuson: I am not even sure I could use the word nation any more. I think that historically that was always a rather problematic definition of what we are as a group of people in a country. Today it just doesn't apply any longer. We have two competing visions of Canada. I think they are very separate visions of Canada and I don't see them being accommodated within the bosom of a single state.

Nash: You must agree then with Lord Durham, who felt French Canadians would need to be assimilated into the country. We didn't do that. We went the other way, and we went for duality.

Bercuson: We went for duality, and I think it was a good try, but duality doesn't work. And it has been especially brought out that it isn't working in the last half of the twentieth century. Anglicization certainly isn't going to work either, so what are you left with? You are left with some kind of mutual accommodation within one state, and I don't think that works. Then there's nothing left but the dissolution of the state as we have known it and something else emerging on the other side. As much as I am not particularly happy about that prospect, I think that at the moment it is probably the least lousy solution.

Nash: Are you saying that it is a waste of effort and energy now to try to find a solution to our constitutional crisis in the context of a single state and that we should concentrate on the divorce?

Bercuson: It is a waste in the sense that it will not produce a solution. All it can do is to put the inevitable off for who knows how long and continue us in this constant dance with the devil. I think that the country as a whole is rendered poorer by it. We're poorer both physically and spiritually as a result of this constant wrangling, constant going around in circles. So in that sense, it is a waste. It's not a waste in the sense that maybe the country does really need one more try in order to recognize that there really is an irreconcilable difference between these competing views of the country.

Nash: Are you suggesting that we might be richer if we did split in two? How would we be richer?

Bercuson: What I would see on the other side of the crisis is two states that I think will have a relatively friendly relationship and certainly will probably have a working relationship in a variety of ways, as Canada and the United States do. I don't see anything like sovereignty association or anything like that.

Nash: Just total independence.

Bercuson: Total independence. And after independence you negotiate as independent states do, as we have done with the U.S., all kinds of agreements and treaties. What we will be left with is a country that has a more standard vision of itself. Canada outside of Quebec has really emerged full-blown as a liberal democracy. I think that Canada without Quebec will become a country which will be based on constitutionalism, on the Charter of Rights, on individual liberty, and so on, and will probably accommodate many disparate groups, much like the United States does now.

Nash: Is it then simple romanticism to think that we would lose part of our Canadian soul if Quebec left?

Bercuson: No, it's not romanticism, it's a reality. It's a truism. I teach Canadian history, where you'll start with aboriginal people and go on to New France, and then all of a sudden you will be saying, "Yes, that was part of us at one time, but it is no longer part of it." It's not an easy thing to adjust to. What I've been forced to face in my own thinking in the last twelve months is we have all that history, but there are costs that we now have to pay. Demands are being made upon our political system. We are basically being asked to accommodate a sovereign state within one country. We are being asked to accommodate a political philosophy within this country that is no longer viable for most of the people. It is a constant attempt to fit a square peg into a round hole – continuing constitutional crisis; a thirty-year constitutional crisis and no end in sight. The government becomes paralyzed, unable to deal with economic and industrial problems. We are going into the twenty-first century totally unprepared for the kind of globalization and competitiveness that we need to bring to bear. We have to focus on saving what we can of the country.

Nash: What happens to the rest of the country after separation? Do we fashion a new kind of federalism or do we carry on with the status quo?

Bercuson: I think we will fashion a new kind of federalism, but it will probably be very much like the one we have now. Canadians are basically a conservative people. When you ask people to specify those powers which need to be decentralized, they come up with almost nothing. The issue which is of the greatest concern to people today outside of the economic issues is, of course, the environment, and there is no question whatsoever that the central government has to be predominant in the area of environmental protection. You may have a rationalization of powers – some that are now exercised by one level of government will go to the other – but it won't necessarily be a one-way street. There will be some greater feeling for centralization as a result of Quebec's departure, rather than the other way. I think there will be a backlash against decentralization.

Nash: That's not what the premiers of British Columbia and Alberta have been saying.

Bercuson: The current premiers are playing the same game they have played for years, and that is, "Give us more. We want more because we want more." I am not sure how sympathetic people are going to be to that, especially in the light of the trauma that will be caused by Quebec's departure. There will also be the other question, and it is one that will be raised increasingly, and that is, who says Quebec will have the boundaries that it has now? There isn't anything sacred about those boundaries. You may even see an attempt on the part of people in northwestern Ontario to disassociate themselves provincially from people in southern Ontario.

Nash: Have a separate province?

Bercuson: Absolutely. There has been a lot of talk up there for many years about how their needs are not met

Nash: You hear a lot about western alienation from central Canada. How real is that?

Bercuson: Realistically, a lot of western alienation has been not simply from central Canada, but from Quebec, rightly or wrongly. There is a lot of jealousy of Quebec, much of it totally misplaced, but it is there anyway.

Nash: Jealousy in terms of economic favours?

Bercuson: Economic favours and the perception of Quebec as having greater political muscle in Confederation than they do, because they have been better organized. They got their act together. Western alienation goes back one hundred years, so it's not all Quebec-related. But there has been a tremendous amount of alienation over the issue of bilingualism and biculturalism. I think with Quebec gone, that issue is going to die.

Nash: Bilingualism will die?

Bercuson: Oh sure. Of course it will die, because in a country with twenty million people, of whom nineteen million are English-speaking, you may get people who will stand up on a sentimental basis and say we should continue this, but there will be no logical reason for it. And if the country is going to be based on individual rights and a charter of rights, very much like the one we have now, no one is going to be able to make a case for special language rights.

Nash: Much of the West strongly favours Senate reform – a Triple-E Senate – what in effect would be a House of the Provinces. Wouldn't that take away a good deal of authority and power from the provincial premiers?

Bercuson: I hope so. Because we don't have an effective Senate, and haven't had one for a long time, somebody had to assume the responsibility of voicing the regional concerns. The provincial governments took that responsibility on their shoulders. The problem is that they are imperfect defenders of regional interests. I want my regional rights and interests to be protected, and I know an elected senator in Ottawa is going to do a damn sight better job of doing that than Don Getty can.

Nash: What is your greatest fear about how these negotiations will go leading up to the next referendum in Quebec?

Bercuson: My greatest fear is that we have Meech, cubed; that in their unwillingness and inability to face reality, as I see it, people will go to such lengths to accommodate Quebec's requirements that they will endanger the very fabric of this country. They are going to try to go back and resell Meech, but a worse Meech than we had before. I don't know if this country is really going to break up. I am not happy at the prospect that it will. But, in my opinion, the only chance that Canada has not to have Quebec leave is to be absolutely steely nerved and steely eyed, drive this thing right to the wall, and say to Quebec, "You are welcome to leave if you need to. We will do without you rather than accede to these demands." Then just maybe some common sense will arise in Quebec and they will say, "Really, we haven't had it so bad." There is probably a one in fifty chance of that happening.

Nash: You see the option as being between an eviscerated Canada and a truncated Canada?

Bercuson: I would rather see a Canada without Quebec than a Canada that really doesn't exist as a nation any longer. Don't get me wrong. I love Alberta, I am glad I live in Calgary, but I am a Canadian. I was born in Quebec, and I'd love to include Quebec in Canada, but Quebec obviously wants to exclude itself, or at least it is asking me to pay a price that endangers all the rest of it.

Nash: Some have suggested that for Quebec it is a matter of pride rather than power.

Bercuson: It has become that now. It started as a question of power, but it has become an issue of pride in the last three years, and that is why I despair of their finding any solution to it. If Quebec didn't have as much pride invested in this whole process as it now has, it would probably not be doing some of the things it is doing. You wouldn't have the referendum threats. You wouldn't have the folding of arms and waiting for the telephone to ring. If they really want to make it work they'd stop, but they don't realize how badly that is going down out here. They are saying, "You rebuffed us, so we are not going to pursue you any more. You are now going to have to court us." People here are saying, "Forget it!"

Nash: But there is a real feeling in Quebec that English-speaking Canada rejected Quebec with the rejection of Meech.

Bercuson: That feeling is based on (a) an almost total ignorance of what English-speaking Canada is all about today, (b) an almost complete lack of desire to find out what English-speaking Canada is all about, and (c) a fairly high level of disdain for English-speaking Canada. We are to them pale imitations of Americans. I realized this during a conference I was at in Ottawa about a year ago which brought English- and French-speaking Canadians together. All I heard was, "If it wasn't for us, you would be part of the United States. You have no culture. You have no identity." And I thought to myself, I am living in an environment where the culture and the identity are so strong. Every day you can see it in the literature, poetry, films that are made here, hear it in the music. If you think we have no culture out here, it's because you are either ignorant or you deliberately choose to pay no attention. They simply don't understand what we are all about.

ED BROADBENT

Former NDP leader Ed Broadbent is now president of the International Centre for Human Rights and Democratic Development, headquartered in Montreal. Born in Oshawa, Ontario, he graduated from the University of Toronto and the London School of Economics. He became a professor of political science at York University in Toronto in 1965. Three years later he was elected to the House of Commons for the NDP and became leader in 1975. He retired from politics at the end of 1989.

"I would bet marginally against the survival of Canada."

Nash: If you were a betting man, what odds would you put on Canada remaining united as a country?

Broadbent: If I were a betting man, and if I were sitting comfortably in Washington or Venice or some place other than Canada, for the first time in my life I would bet marginally against the survival of Canada. That's a very significant turnaround in my judgement, but not a big turnaround from what it was at the time of Meech. I was apprehensive then that this might happen, and my judgement hasn't changed. If anything, it's become somewhat more pessimistic.

Nash: You were strongly supportive of the Meech Lake deal.

Broadbent: I was a strong defender of Meech Lake because I thought it was absolutely essential for the survival of Canada. The defeat of Meech Lake will be seen, I think, as a turning point in our history. Certainly it will be if my moments of pessimism turn out to be true and we disintegrate as a nation. What has happened since has accelerated the feeling in Quebec that English-speaking Canada was rejecting a special place for Quebec in our federation. It is now taking on mythological proportions in that province.

Nash: Quebec is now asking for Meech-plus – a lot more than Meech. Do you think the rest of Canada will respond positively to Quebec's demands?

Broadbent: I hope they will to some of the demands, but it is my impression from talking to Canadians in other provinces that there has been, if not an acceleration, at least an entrenchment of feeling that Quebec ought not to have certain special powers or its distinctiveness accepted and recognized in a way that clearly distinguishes this province from the rest of Canada. The intensity of that feeling has grown in a minority. I still think it is a minority of English-speaking Canadians that are intensely opposed, but it is a strong and significant minority with the potential of having majority support in English Canada. I am more pessimistic about this than I have ever been as a Canadian. I don't see the strong desire by a sufficient number of Canadians in either English-speaking Canada or Quebec to resolve the crisis.

Nash: What brought us to this crisis?

Broadbent: Pierre Trudeau had unquestionably a number of virtues both as a person and as a political leader. I think perhaps he was a saviour of Canada in 1968, but he was the creator of the problems of Canada for my generation right now. His particular vision was an updated, more cerebral version of John Diefenbaker's vision of pan-Canadianism that has had many more dangers than solutions in it from the point of view of the unity of Canada.

Nash: What's your vision of Canada? What would you do if we could start over and reshape a new Canada?

Broadbent: We would have to be much more positive about Québécois nationalism and link it with an English Canadian nationalism. Mr. Trudeau's generation of intellectuals, both in English- and French-speaking Canada, by and large, were opposed to nationalism because they came of age in the thirties and forties and they associated it with a kind of right-wing, fascist view of society, which they correctly rejected. But they were blinded, in my judgement, to the creative possibilities of a positive form of nationalism, of a creative nationalism that would see two cultures living side by side with a fair degree of independence one from the other, working together with a zest for life. I've always been somewhat reluctant to describe myself as a Canadian nationalist because very often Canadian nationalists have an irrational antipathy towards the United States unequivocally across the board, and I've never felt that.

My form of nationalism has never been negative. I feel very positive about English Canada's accomplishments, especially since the Second World War, in almost every field of interest to me in my personal life. Canadians, whether it's Glenn Gould or Margaret Laurence, or architects and painters, have been terrific, and I know they also exist in Quebec. My view of Canada is that we should be celebrating this. We should be, in our political institutions, much more open to a higher degree of sovereign activity within a federal union, and see it as a terrific opportunity to work together. We don't have to view the emergence of a Quebec nationalism as a threat to English Canadian nationalism.

Nash: What do you think of the idea of provinces taking on what are now national powers, and then delegating them back, as they wish, to the federal authority?

Broadbent: Asymmetrical federalism is the current term for that, and all it is, is a new term for special status or distinct role. Everyone wants to come up with a politically safer description of what has been the age-old dilemma of Canadian federalism. The birth of Canada saw Quebec as a distinct society, as a unique province, and we've had the task of playing with words in every generation since. I haven't the slightest doubt in my mind that there has to be some form of asymmetrical federalism or distinct society recognition. That's a continuation of the Canadian tradition, this is not something new.

Nash: How far would you go in delegating authority for foreign policy, economic policy, social policy, the environment?
Broadbent: I think you have to make a deal which is exactly right. A deal that sorts out in a practical way, going into the twenty-first century, all those areas in terms of global markets, in terms of the interpenetration of all cultures.
Nash: Would something like a whole series of sovereignty-association relationships work, such as B.C. and Alberta, as well as Quebec, having a sovereignty-association relationship with the centre?
Broadbent: I don't think so. I don't think that would work because English-speaking Canadians in western Canada and in Ontario and Atlantic Canada, by and large, wouldn't want that. They want something more than that. They want the central government to have more powers than the people of Quebec want the central government to have. We have to find a way of changing our federal institutions to give greater representation to western Canadians in the central decision-making authority in Ottawa, as opposed to giving more powers to western provinces. The West wants a greater sense in determining decisions in Ottawa, unlike the people of Quebec, who want a greater say in being able to make their own decisions in the province of Quebec.
Nash: Is there a constitutional umbrella that would encompass both the western desire for a stronger presence in the federal system as well as Quebec's desire for less federalism and more provincial power?
Broadbent: I think the answer is yes, we could work out a package of proposals. The key to doing that is for the federal leaders to come together. If the federal leaders don't come together in an acceptable way, the chance of unity is greatly diminished. If this becomes a partisan issue it will be disastrous because of the nature of Canada. But I don't think the same degree of unanimity is required by the provinces. I deeply believe that we could get a majority of the premiers, six of the ten, and the federal leaders to do something that would give a greater degree of autonomy to the province of Quebec and a new sense of real participation in our federal

institutions, particularly to western Canada. An aboriginal package of proposals also has to come in. We can accept a certain framework of aboriginal law, under which they control decisions over their life in their territories. Then I think we would have to go to the population as a whole; the people of Canada have to be brought in on this through a national referendum.

Nash: In a national referendum would you require a majority vote in each province?

Broadbent: If we have the three federal leaders and six or seven provinces, including at least the majority of provinces in the West and Ontario, Quebec, and a majority in the Atlantic, that should be sufficient to put immense pressure on those who vote, even with the existing amending formula, to carry that through. Such a majority would have a great moral force on legislators, including the Parliament of Canada, to match that disposition in their legislative decision.

Nash: Is there time enough to get that package of proposals if you look at a deadline of a referendum in Quebec, possibly in the fall of 1992?

Broadbent: Absolutely. I think there is. We could have a vote as early as next summer. Maybe have it in September of 1992, and have the whole summer to have the debate of our lives from coast to coast.

Nash: That assumes a lot of speed and effort being made to build a consensus to respond to some of the needs Quebec has articulated. We haven't demonstrated that speed of decision-making in the past. How do you generate that sense of urgency?

Broadbent: Obviously, our political leaders have that task. Other Canadians, trade unionists, farmers, business leaders, have to start seeing what's at stake and start making their proposals, too.

Nash: As an individual, should I really care what happens?

Broadbent: Absolutely. We have tremendous prospects for a civilized, decent, just, and exciting life in this part of North America. We have a diversity of people unmatched in most other countries. We have a richness and beauty and resource in our geography. We have language. We have a cultural political tradition that embodies not only individual rights, but a certain notion of community equality that's far advanced over the United States'. We have all the elements needed, not to create perfection, but to create one of the best places to live on the planet. I strongly believe it's worth doing if enough of us in this country can get the creative energy to make it possible.

SYLVIA OSTRY

Sylvia Ostry chairs the centre for International Studies at the University of Toronto, is chancellor of the University of Waterloo and chairwoman of the National Council of the Canadian Institute of International Affairs. As one of Canada's most distinguished economists, she has been the country's Chief Statistician, deputy minister of Consumer and Corporate Affairs, chairwoman of the Economic Council of Canada, deputy minister of International Trade, and ambassador for Multilateral Trade Negotiations. She also served as head of the Economics and Statistics Department of the Organization for Economic Co-operation and Development in Paris. She is a Companion of the Order of Canada and has received numerous national and international honours.

"The nation state is a nineteenth-century illusion."

Nash: What do you think is at risk in the constitutional debate insofar as our economy is concerned?
Ostry: The preoccupying debate on the Constitution and earlier on the Free Trade Agreement, which was construed rightly as an issue that affected sovereignty, has removed from the public's understanding, and from the agenda of the politicians, what is clearly a crisis in this country's competitive position. That is, the erosion of Canada's capacity to compete internationally and to sustain a high standard of living. The underlying situation is really very serious. It has

not been understood, the public doesn't understand it, it's been neglected and crowded off everybody's agenda. If you add on to that the uncertainty that the present constitutional crisis creates and the possibility of serious fragmentation, you are giving another enormous shock to an already serious economic situation. The real issue that we should now be looking very hard at is what our productive capacity is going to be like in the future.

Nash: But then, we don't know what that future is going to be.

Ostry: We have to come to grips with fundamental factors like our lack of research and development, the extraordinary decline in our productivity over the eighties, the deep troubles with our educational system, our training capacity, and a whole array of issues. There are portions of the so-called Third World that have a much greater capacity for growth, much more emphasis on innovation, and the capacity to penetrate markets than anything we have been able to pull together. The constitutional debate is layered on top of existing problems, and one of the most serious issues is that if we are to grapple with these issues, we need cooperation between the federal government and the provincial governments and among some of the actors – the unions, the employers, and linkages between the unversities and industry.

Nash: This need is clearly being overlooked, you feel, with our preoccupation with what kind of a country we're going to have?

Ostry: We have ignored the competitiveness issue. The preoccupation with the constitutional debate is with issues of the nineteenth century – sovereignty. The nation state is a nineteenth-century illusion. We are having a ferocious debate about the past. We have never injected into the debate what I think would bring us together – like facing the prospect of being hanged in the morning – that everything we have come to regard as unique and desirable about our country is at risk because the only engine that will supply it is the capacity to generate high producivity.

Nash: In your travels around the world you meet economists and other officials both in the public and private sectors. What's their sense of what's going on in Canada today?

Ostry: Canadians have to understand that beyond our borders there is a massive ignorance of and indifference to Canada, but that the image others have of us is by and large favourable. We are a boring, worthy country. We do a lot of good things in international places, we are known as strong defenders and participants in the post-war international system, but there is not really a great deal of understanding or knowledge of Canada.

Nash: Is there awareness of the current constitutional debate?

Ostry: It's gradually coming. My own view is that we are very lucky that there is not a greater awareness.

Nash: Why?

Ostry: Because I think it would begin to affect the views about foreign long-term investment in this country, and this would be very serious.

Nash: One of the things Premier Bourassa is talking about is the possibility that Canada should be more like the European Community. How valid is that concept?

Ostry: My reading of the European Community is the exact opposite of what Bourassa seems to be implying. Its common market is a very good example of the opposite of what is happening here. Europe has been attempting since the Treaty of Rome in the fifties to try and really create a common market: the free flow of goods, of people, of services, and of capital. The thing that has galvanized them in the most astonishing way is exactly what I am saying, which is the fear of loss of competitiveness. They knew if they did not get their act together they would never be able to compete against the Japanese as the decade wore on. Therefore, they would really have to move to create with great speed a genuine common market, followed by monetary union, followed by political union. What this has meant is a continuing erosion of the sovereignty of the nation state and a continuing expansion of the scope at the supranational level, which is

the exact opposite of what Bourassa is saying. You can only
get away with saying that if you can rely on the enormous
lack of information or knowledge in the Canadian public
about the lessons from Brussels. Again, the lessons from
Brussels are the exact opposite. In the evolution of the European Community since 1985, there has been more and more
erosion of individual national sovereignty, and it's been put
into the supranational. They mobilized, they acted when
they understood that if they didn't do so they would not be
able to maintain their position in the world. We have not,
and yet we are under greater threat than they were. We have
not mobilized and pulled together the political will and the
public understanding which would say this is a terrific
opportunity to rethink a constitution. We are talking about
emotion, we are talking about the nation state, we are talking about language, we are talking about emotional things,
which I find are nineteenth-century phenomena, not twenty-
first-century phenomena. The world is changing, it's transformed. The Fathers of Confederation did a great job, but the
world is different. It is now the world of the twenty-first
century. We have an opportunity now to rethink the kind of
federation we need in the light of the need to maintain and
improve our position in the world. We are all in the same
boat. If we don't hang together, we will hang separately. There
is just no question about that. So let's use this occasion to
have a real discussion.

Nash: The whole debate, then, you feel, is focussed on the
wrong object.

Ostry: It has ignored the catalyst that would pull us
together.

Nash: What would you do to improve our national competitiveness?

Ostry: There are issues, for example, the fiscal deficit, which
are both federal and provincial responsibilities. We have no
coordinating mechanism. Monetary policy has to be guaranteed independence in order to entrench its credibility. Education is a provincial jurisdiction, and we are the only country

in the world that doesn't have a national debate on this most basic of all issues. But we can't do anything unless we come to grips with the dimensions of the problem

Nash: How do we come to grips with it since we are focussed on the question of national unity, and our motivating force is not competitiveness?

Ostry: There are only two avenues. One is at the level of the political leadership, both federal and provincial, where the debate has got to be couched in these terms, and the other is at the level of the private actors. The business community catalyzed it in Europe. I am not saying we could do that, but our business community has not played that kind of role, although our academics are participating, our unions, our consumer groups.

Nash: Is time limited not so much by the deadline of the Quebec referendum as it is by the competitiveness deadline?

Ostry: By both. I don't dismiss the referendum deadline. We have a lot of work to do, we have to get the debate focussed, and we want to think about these issues.

Nash: What do you think will happen as we go into the twenty-first century?

Ostry: Our history on this has been that, in the end, we muddle through. It strikes me that there are lower probabilities of that happening this time than at any time in the past. Countries that have been devastated, like the Latin American countries, have now mobilized the political will after decay and unbelievable misery. In the end, they came to the conclusion that, if they were to get out of the incredible pain that they had suffered, they were going to have to focus on one or two things, and that is what they are doing. The same thing is happening in central Europe. Fear of the devastating effects of not taking the opportunities sometimes produces the necessary response.

Nash: On this question of competitiveness, how do you bring it down to the level of the individual so he or she can understand it?

Ostry: Yesterday I was in a cab, and I always ask the same questions, "How is business?" and what not, and you get this incredible outpouring. The cab driver gave me details on how this recession is much worse than the one in 1982, and then he said he is sick and tired of governments not being able to come to grips with the economy. And he gave me a dozen examples of how various things were affecting him. There is a great understanding that jobs and livelihoods are at stake.

MICHAEL WALKER

Economist, journalist, lecturer, and public speaker, Michael Walker is executive director of the Fraser Institute of Vancouver, a research body concerned with public policy. He has authored or edited twenty-two books on economic affairs and has spoken at universities and conferences around the world. He is a member of the International Trade Advisory Committee to the Government of Canada. Prior to joining the Fraser Institute, Walker taught at the University of Western Ontario in London, Ontario, and at Carleton University in Ottawa, and worked with the Bank of Canada and the federal Department of Finance.

"The nation state is under transformation."

Nash: How do you assess the constitutional changes that Quebec is seeking?
Walker: I am quite sympathetic to the idea of decentralization, and I am quite sympathetic to the notion that decentralization does not necessarily mean the breakup of Canada. From the very beginning I have insisted that people be very careful in their vocabulary, because people have a tendency to use the term balkanization to describe the decentralization of Canada when, in fact, they might mean canonization. Balkanization is a negative term. It's a notion of fragmenting, in the sense of falling apart. Canonization, or regionalization,

conveys a sense of getting together in a particular way, rather than falling apart. The aspect of the sentiments that are being expressed in Quebec that I want to focus on for an optimistic viewpoint is to say, look they want to respect some sort of tribal boundary. They want to have a greater measure of independence in certain things than they have had. They want to have a confederation which is more autonomous, more autonomous from the point of view of the provinces without, in fact, competely giving up the notion of Canada as some sort of larger whole. Autonomy or sovereignty doesn't mean separate existence. It means separate existence from some points of view and integrated existence from other points of view.

Nash: So do you see a model in something like European Community, which Premier Bourassa talks about?

Walker: Exactly. I think that more and more, not just in the U.S.A. and Western Europe, we are going to find people trying to respect their tribal boundaries, on the one hand, without giving up the benefits of economic integration, on the other.

Nash: I guess it basically boils down to how much devolution of power there is, and of what powers. At what point does a nation become just a shell because it has allowed too many powers to go to the provincial level?

Walker: I don't know that I have an answer for you, and I don't know if anybody has an answer. I think probably the notion of the nation state itself is under transformation. The time has gone now where governments could exert themselves over people in the way they did when we conceived the nation state. I think that devolution or decentralization by itself is not a bad thing, but one has to draw a sharp line of distinction between, say, regulatory decentralization and decentralization over expenditures on matters like unemployment insurance, or training, or medicare. For example, we do not want to have ten demagogues regulating the securities industry across Canada, which is what we have now. We want to make uniform and harmonize our standards and our regulations. The vision that I have is of decentralization where that is sensible and centralization, like in Europe, where that is sensible or where it reduces costs.

Nash: For instance, getting rid of trade barriers between the provinces?

Walker: Well, exactly. We don't have a common market at the moment. We have more trade barriers between the provinces of Canada than there are between the countries of the European Community. The guiding principle ought to be towards cost minimization, so that you are going to minimize costs by decentralizing in some areas and by centralizing in others. It just so happens that a lot of those things are coincident with the desires of the people of Quebec for completely other reasons, for the reason that they want to respect their tribal urges or cultural affinities, or whatever you want to call them. There is a nice overlap of interests for the most part, but in the end, it is going to be a matter of the soul, not a matter of the pocket-book.

Nash: You mean the heart will win out over the mind at the end of this debate?

Walker: In terms of the choices that people will make on this issue, yes. It is going to be a question, from Quebec's point of view, of emotion. The challenge from the point of view of the rest of us is to find out what kind of system permits people to reflect their tribal urges, while doing the minimum amount of damage to the whole. It's a devolved system; it's a system that respects the local autonomies in a wide range of areas, but still has centralized treaty-making power, standards, and so on. It's a country that looks very much like the European Community as it is emerging.

Nash: Do you think of Canada as a bilingual duality, or a community of communities, or something else?

Walker: What I see in Canada is very many cultures. We have a number of souls. In Newfoundland, there is no question that there is a Newfoundland soul. There is no question that there is a Cape Breton soul, as distinct from the rest of Nova Scotia. There are probably two cultures in New Brunswick, the Acadian culture and the old English Maritime culture. There is obviously the province of Quebec. I must confess having some problems with Ontario. I don't see any kind of culture in Ontario. Somebody said that Ontarians are people who define themselves by a common distaste for Americans. Clearly there is a culture in the West. There is a Prairie and western culture that is not as well defined as the Maritime culture, but it is close.

Nash: Do we define ourselves essentially then as Nova Scotian or British Columbian before we think of ourselves as Canadian?

Walker: That has been my experience.

Nash: The exception may be Ontario.

Walker: Yes, that's right. Ontarians are like failed Americans.

Nash: The ancestors of a lot of them fled from the United States.

Walker: We have a major project on right now on North American economic integration. What North America will look like in 2020, I think, will be very much like Europe is starting to look now. If you look at the innards of American society as it is evolving now, you can see so many of the characteristics of the Canadian debate. By the turn of this century, it will be inconceivable for anybody to be elected governor of California unless he is bilingual, because almost the majority of the population will be Hispanic. There is a very significant chunk there now, in Florida, and Louisiana, too.

Nash: There are some worries that, if Canada breaks up, our economy will become much more integrated with the United States, and that we would further lose a sense of identity.

Walker: People are concerned that we are going to fracture, that we are going to break into little pieces and will be sucked up by some sort of economic manifest destiny. If that is going to happen, it is going to be the result of people choosing it. It's going to be the result of British Columbians surmising that, everything considered, they have more in common with people in Oregon or Washington State than they have with people in Manitoba. Nobody is going to merge with the United States unless there is some overarching economic push for us to do that, because you simply wouldn't get the sort of political support that you need. Quite apart from trying to convince the lumber manufacturers in Oregon, for instance, that this would be a good idea. These are the chaps who have the 15 per cent import duty levied on us because they didn't want to have to compete with our products. Eventually it will be meaningless to talk about markets other than the world markets. We are going to be integrated into world markets.

Nash: Do you think that deadline of the proposed referendum in Quebec in October 1992 is realistic in terms of deciding these issues?

Walker: I have spent some time in Quebec recently and have talked to a lot of very sensible people who, ten years ago, would not have felt that way and who are now talking sensibly about having a much more sovereign relationship than they have now. Now, whether that means a unilateral declaration of independence is another matter.

Nash: Sovereignty means so many different things to so many different people.

Walker: Exactly. There is a whole range of opinions. There is no question in my mind that the average opinion in the province of Quebec today is more oriented towards sovereignty than it was ten years ago.

Nash: Is the whole idea of the nation state crumbling?

Walker: Think of it as a demand and supply problem. The nation state was really responding to a perceived need. Well, if those perceived needs are no longer there, if you don't need to maintain a big army, or perceive that it is a very expensive thing to have, then maybe the demand for the nation state is declining, and so we will have fewer of them.

Nash: Is Europe already beginning to re-form as distinct tribal areas with an overall regulatory structure?

Walker: Europe is recognizing that in order to have cultural affinity you don't have to bear the cost of the nation state. It is easier for them in some sense because of language. The cultural definitions are much more evident than they are here. We must take enormous optimism out of the fact that these people, who have been trying systematically to eliminate each other for hundreds of years, are now getting together. In doing so, they are willing to surrender the kinds of things that are surrendered within a city, where you have the agglomeration of different cultural affinities. They are creating in Europe one big metropolitan area, which happens to have a bunch of different people, who happen to have different affinities, but who are not going to allow demagogues to put up walls to collect tariffs. If they can do it, then we, with so many overlapping interests and contacts with the province of Quebec, we should be able to do it.

Nash: How is all this going to play out politically?

Walker: The next federal election is going to be critical, because I think we are likely to see in the Parliament of Canada the kind of regional representation that some people are trying to achieve in the Senate.

Nash: Five parties vying for power.

Walker: We will see members from the Reform Party and the Bloc Québécois. I don't perceive how Ontario will be represented, but I do know that they will have Ontario's interests at heart when it comes down to some sort of negotiation. In Atlantic Canada the premiers are now getting together and recognizing their interests as a group. Now impose upon that there having been a referendum in Quebec. I don't think the question is going to be complete separation. I don't think that the question is going to be as strong as that, but whatever it is, it will be put to that new Parliament, which is now going to be kind of a regional representational body. Let's suppose we get a strong representation of the Reform Party from the West, a good slug of NDP, and then the odds-and-sods grouping from Ontario. From Quebec, the majority will certainly be Bloc Québécois. Can you imagine any other constellation of events but that the Reform Party will represent western interests and the Bloc Québécois will represent Quebec? Whatever parties came from Ontario will represent central interests. It will be more like the Italian parliament.

Nash: Do you have hope that there will be a relatively united Canada in the end?

Walker: Absolutely. At a human level, and because there are significant costs involved, I certainly would like to see Canada as a country maintained, but I think that, if it is going to be maintained, it has to be a more flexible kind of Canada than the Canada we have had in the past. I think that the attempt to rigidly adhere to some historic notion of Canada in the face of the enormous changes around the world will not be successful because of the way things are changing around the world. A transformed view of Canada, which is flexible enough to accommodate the appetite of people for tribal affinity, will be successful, and indeed more successful than the Canada we have now.

BOB WHITE

Bob White, Canada's most visible labour leader, was born in Northern Ireland and came to Canada at the age of thirteen. He started work in a factory as a teenager and rose through the union ranks to become president of the United Auto Workers' local union in Woodstock, Ontario. In 1972 he was appointed assistant to the UAW Canadian director and replaced Dennis McDermott as Canadian director and international vice-president in 1978. In 1985 he led the 12,000-member Canadian wing of the union out of the U.S. labour body and formed the independent Canadian Auto Workers. Today White is also general vice-president of the Canadian Labour Congress.

"We have to pay a price for being Canadian."

Nash: Could you tell me why your Quebec labour colleagues are as strongly sovereigntist as they are?
White: In the labour movement we have held the right of Quebec to self-determination for a long time, and we have made accommodations in the Quebec labour movement over the years. For example, the Quebec Federation of Labour takes on a lot of responsibilities inside Quebec that the Canadian Labour Congress does in the rest of the country. Most unions in Canada have made accommodations to the distinctiveness and uniqueness of Quebec. All we have said

is that we will fight strongly for Quebec's right to make its own decision.

Nash: What's your own sense about Quebec's demands for transference of power, particularly the twenty-two items in the Allaire report?

White: The problem we are having in Canada is that some people can't come to grips with the fact that Quebec is different. If these people maintain their position, Quebec is going to have to be separate to be different. Then the question in English Canada will be, can they be different within some form of Canada? The danger is that there are some people, including those in the Business Council on National Issues, and some others, who have a different agenda for Canada and who see Quebec's proposals as an opportunity to significantly decentralize the country. In other words, to say to other provinces, "Well, you should demand some of this yourself and push a lot of this decision-making down to the provincial level." I am not going to argue that there isn't some duplication or that there shouldn't be some changes, but I think at the point we give more powers to all the provinces, we really start to break up the country, especially now we have free trade with the United States. The twenty-two points will be difficult for English Canada to deal with. When you look at them in totality, they are not very revolutionary. But the problem will be to get people to agree to them without demanding some of them for the rest of the country.

Nash: Should there be an asymmetrical relationship, should Quebec have special status?

White: In my union I say to Quebeckers, "I am prepared to give you much more than you want today. If this thing goes through, you really have to talk about a separate union in Quebec." Today, they would want to remain a part of our organization. But I didn't leave one international union to set up another.

The next constitutional discussions can't just be about Quebec. There are other issues. If we talk about these other issues and, at the same time, clearly recognize that Quebec is different, and do a number of things within the constitutional framework that will recognize that distinctiveness, then I think you can maintain a relationship with Quebec.

Nash: You think the best approach would be special status for Quebec rather than devolving power to everybody?

White: Definitely. I just don't think devolution to all provinces is the way to maintain a country. One of the problems is that Quebec has a sense of what it is about, but the rest of the country doesn't have a sense of what it is about. Maybe it is because we are bigger and more diverse. What we don't want is a massive decentralization. What we do want is to maintain a nation, with Quebec having a somewhat different relationship. We need to recognize the distinctiveness of Quebec, but also have a nation in which, outside of Quebec, we make major decisions centrally.

Nash: What about other suggestions, such as changes to the Senate?

White: I really can't get very excited about the Senate. I am not sure that having an elected senator gives you much more input into the system than you have today.

Nash: What kind of a role do you see for the monarchy, if we are really looking at changing the nature of the country?

White: I came from Ireland when I was a kid, and my parents used to take me to see the Queen when she came. It was a big issue back then, but I think the role for the monarchy is diminishing today. We have a lot of people from other countries now who don't have that attachment. I think the monarchy is still going to be part of the Canadian system, but a diminishing part in the future.

Nash: How would you treat the desires of the aboriginal people?

White: They have to be totally involved in the discussions. I don't think the Constitution can just be a legal document about the sharing of powers. Constitutional discussion has to talk about what kind of a society we want socially, economically, politically, and culturally. It has to take into consideration one of the other founding peoples, the Native peoples. They certainly have to be at the table in a much different fashion than they have been in the past. The discussions about the Constitiution can't just be about Quebec's demands. They have to include the Native people. You have to talk about their right to self-determination, self-government. You also have to talk about collective rights, economic rights, what kind of a system we are going to have in this country, what kind of a relationship we are going to have economically.

Nash: Looking at that much broader sense of what this country is, what's your own particular vision of Canda?

White: My vision of Canada is a country that recognizes the distinctiveness of Quebec, that has a strong central government, that has clear lines on issues of health care and child care, that recognizes that the country is also multicultural, that recognizes the rights of women, the rights of minorities in society, that recognizes the rights of Native people. But I also envision it starting to have a much more independent voice. The free trade thing scared me in that we seem now to be so closely associated with the United States and, on international issues, we are not seen as having a voice. We have got to get back to where we were, when Canada was a voice of reason around the world, when Canada had something different to say from the Americans on a number of issues. That is not to say we are enemies, but it is to say you have to fight hard to maintain an identity.

I am really concerned about the vision that says the only thing that counts today is that you have to be the most competitive, you have to do whatever it takes, even if it means closing up factories or moving jobs out of the country. If that happens, at the end of the day you will have a much less kind nation. You will have a nation that doesn't work properly.

Nash: Are you saying there is a fundamental conflict between the desire to be internationally competitive and Canadian nationalism ?

White: If you make international competitiveness the only yardstick, whether it's labour costs, regulations, health and safety, Sunday shopping laws, if you have to get rid of those to be internationally competitive, then I say we are trying to run the country like a corporation, and you can't do that. We are a people who are supposed to be concerned about each other, a nation that needs good health care, quality education, child care, human rights, needs a whole range of services, and you can't run that on the corporate bottom line. If you are going to have a nation you have to have balances; you have to have social planning as well as economic planning. And you have to pay a price. We will always have to pay a price for being Canadian. The thing that worries me today is that there are a lot of people who are saying they are not prepared to pay that price any more.

Nash: Are most Canadians prepared to pay that price today?

White: They are if it is explained to them properly. If we put the balance sheet up and say, as a nation, we have something going for us here that is different from the U.S.; it is going to mean a different tax structure in some ways, but it is also going to mean a different health care system, different cities, different attitudes towards life. The difficulty is that people from the business community are saying competitiveness, free trade, internationalism is the goal, but when you talk that way to people, they say, "Well if that's internationalism, why don't I shop in the United States? Why don't I move to the United States?" And once we start losing our tax base, our social agenda becomes much more difficult.

Nash: One of the things that we are looking at is whether we do have a Canadian identity. Is there such a thing?

White: I am having more difficulty with it today than I used to, but I think there is. Quebec gives us a Canadian identity as well, and if Quebec separates competely, it will be very difficult to maintain a Canadian identity. There is already an enormous north-south pull. Our forefathers knew that from day one, and so they deliberately structured the country east-west.

Nash: Aside from the identity question, if Quebec did separate, what are the implications for both Quebec and the rest of Canada?

White: It would overstate the case to say it would destroy the country. It won't. But there would be enormous social impacts, because if you thought you could just sit around the table and just do this nice and quietly, and nobody would get upset about it, well, you can't. Not many countries have done that. I think the backlash between the francophones and the rest of Canada would be heightened by a major break. There would also be some economic dislocation in the meantime, and a lot of it will be felt by Quebec and Ontario.

Nash: Would there be an increase in the north-south pull?

White: I don't think there is any question about that. Look at the Maritimes, for example. It would be easier for them to travel down to Boston than to Toronto. It would make for an enormous north-south pull.

Nash: What do you think is going to happen from what you see at this point?

White: Unless we get together and decide what kind of nation we want, I see us becoming much more integrated with the United States. I see us having a lower standard of living in terms of social standards, if we follow the competition argument. The country has great potential, but in many ways I don't think we are living up to that potential. I am more troubled about Canada than I have ever been, and there is no simple answer. Canada is going to go through some very difficult times in the next ten years. Unless we start having a much stronger national voice on behalf of the whole country, I see it becoming very regionalized.

Nash: How do you maintain national standards in medicare or labour law or welfare if you don't have a strong central force?

White: That's the issue. You can't do it just by saying you must have national standards. You have to do it by attaching funding to those national standards. The medicare debate was very crucial when doctors were opting out and the national government said, "If you are going to do that, you are not going to get the funding." I just don't buy the argument that you can put in a program and allow each province to determine its own standard, as long as it meets some sort of minimum national standard. Poor provinces are not going to have as good a health care system. We should understand those values are very important to this country, and along with that goes a number of other issues. The tax system may be different, but again, our quality of life can be much better if we are prepared to pay a little for it.

I don't think what we have today is the only system that works, but you have to be very careful in talking about decentralization and increasing provincial powers. I would be very nervous about a massive decentralization of Canada. I don't think we want to dismantle the nation as we have known it; to be a collection of economic sectors, some weak and some strong. I don't think that is what this nation is about.

Nash: In the early days of the Spicer Commission, Keith Spicer talked about the need for more poets to articulate what Canada is about.

White: There is need for more people who believe in this country as a nation to speak out. You have to have a belief that this is not just a piece of land in North America, but this is, in fact, a nation with great potential, and that we will always have to fight to have an identity.

Nash: Can we do all those things by 1992?

White: No. But by 1992 there has to be some kind of consensus around what the relationship is going to be within the constitutional framework, and that has to deal with collective rights, Native people, economic issues, and Quebec. I think that can be done, but it will take a lot of discussion and understanding across the country. I don't underestimate the difficuty of getting a consensus, but it has to be tried. I think it can be done.

JEFF MCCONAGHY

Jeff McConaghy was the winner of the Junior Achievement Junior Executive Award for 1989-90. He attended high school in Fredericton, New Brunswick, and plans to do undergraduate and graduate work in business before establishing his own consulting firm specializing in budgeting and finance. He was a 1991 Deloitte & Touche Scholarship winner and between 1990-91 was president of Clownin' Around, a Junior Achievement company producing and selling decorative models of clowns.

"We don't promote our national heroes."

Nash: Jeff, you are a teenager. What do people your age think about Canada? Do they talk about it much at all? Do they have any sense, any vision, of the Canada of the future?

McConaghy: It all depends on when you are talking to them and in what area. I was at the Encounters with Canada program recently. There people from all across Canada, including Quebec, interacted with one another, getting to know each other and becoming friends. There you get a stronger national feeling, and you don't get the regional rivalry.

Nash: You think as a Canadian rather than as a New Brunswicker.

McConaghy: Exactly. You are looking at the entire country instead of just your particular region.

Nash: What is the Encounters with Canada program?

McConaghy: It is a program set up by the government to promote Canadian unity. Each week 150 kids from across Canada get together for a conference in Ottawa. You visit the Parliament Buildings, the Senate, different political places in Ottawa, and this is done each week throughout the school year.

Nash: Tell me a bit about your attitude going into the first meeting and coming out of the last one, in terms of what you thought of the Prairies, Ontario, other parts of the country.

McConaghy: I have had a lot of involvement with people across the country because I have been to two national Junior Achievement meetings and I was in Winnipeg for another program, too. So I realized very early that there is not a big difference between the East and West. I like to think that I am pretty open-minded about this already, but I noticed a difference in other people. For instance, the guys from Alberta would walk into a room, and they'd hear French, and they would walk right back out. But they weren't doing that at the end of the week. The eight people from our school who've been there have just been in awe; they talk about how great the program is. They come back and say, "I met the greatest person from B.C., and the French really aren't that bad." That's the type of attitude they get.

Nash: I guess our future depends on getting the younger generation involved.

McConaghy: Yes, exactly. I don't want to say that the older generation is hopeless, but soon enough the younger generation will be the older, and as you continue these programs, you won't have the uneducated, narrow-minded opinions that we've had before.

Nash: What does Canada mean to you?

McConaghy: I would like to think that Canada is one of the greatest places in the world to live because we've got a high standard of living, we have a lot of programs that help us in our social services. But I also see a lot of confusion and a lot of problems that have to be corrected. I think the only way we can do that is by having the people across Canada communicate with each other, because you don't solve a problem by just fuming about it, not getting your opinion out, because it just builds up and eventually explodes. If you get to voice your concerns to the person you have the concerns about, at least you've got communication there and can help solve the problem.

Nash: What do you think might happen in New Brunswick if Quebec did separate? Would that tend to encourage people to think about getting closer to the United States?

McConaghy: I don't think you would see us joining the United States. I think there would be more of a union among the Atlantic provinces. They are already talking about an economic union between the Maritime provinces.

Nash: Would that be a good thing for Atlantic Canada?

McConaghy: Yes, as far as the economy is concerned. I am not sure about political union. If the four provinces join together, you've got a bigger market. You've got more people working together. And if you bring down those trade barriers, then it can't do anything but improve our business.

Nash: You'd probably have more political clout in discussions with the rest of Canada, too. Do you have a sense of identity with those people in the rest of Canada? We're so spread out, so far apart. Do you share anything with them other than just a continent, things like values?

McConaghy: Yes, of course. We do share the history, and I do feel that they are part of the country. They have been part of the country almost as long as we have. I don't want to see Canada separate or divide up into groups because we've survived since 1867.

Nash: You want to go into business in a few years. Will you stay in New Brunswick, or move to another part of the country, or to the States or Britain?

McConaghy: I have always planned on staying in New Brunswick. I'm proud of where I have come from. We are considered to be an economically depressed region, but I think we do very well for ourselves. I definitely plan to help build on what we have and improve our area of the country.

Nash: You were speaking a moment ago of being at a meeting with people from all across Canada, and you mentioned that a lot of them had a sense of national feeling when they were together. How strong a feeling did you sense that was?

McConaghy: Pretty strong. You could actually tell the difference between the first of the week and the end of the week just by how people sung the national anthem.

Nash: What happened to intensify their sense of national pride?

McConaghy: When everybody gets together like that they realize that, whether you live in Nova Scotia or Alberta, you are not really that much different. You are still Canadian. That is also the case with the people from Quebec meeting people from the West and from the Atlantic provinces. A lot of the people from Quebec didn't speak a lot of English and the majority didn't speak French, but everybody made an effort, and it worked out fine. There wasn't any tension at all. The problem is to get people together to educate them, make them more aware of what other areas are like, so that they don't feel this isolation and build up that wall.

Nash: Do you think there is enough being taught about our history and our traditions and values in schools?

McConaghy: There is not much at the high-school level, in New Brunswick anyway. They probably could do more.

Nash: What kind of future do most of your friends see for themselves? Are they full of optimism about their own future within Canada, or do they have some hesitancies, some doubts, some worries?

McConaghy: There are definitely hesitancies and worries. A lot of that is just the uncertainty of what's for you personally in the future. Then again there are a lot of people who are very confident. They have a strong feeling of what is going to happen, that Canada will survive.

Nash: Canada's adult population is beginning to get involved in the national unity debate. What I am hearing from you is that it isn't that big a deal for youngsters, at least not yet.

McConaghy: High-school students seem to be very unaware. They are more concerned about what's going to happen on the weekend than about national unity. But they are not completely unaware of what is going on around them. When people turn eighteen and are old enough to vote, then I think you will see their interest grow.

Nash: Should there be a deliberate effort by schools and teachers and parents to stimulate more interest in history and more interest in the country itself?

McConaghy: If more history was taught, and there was more understanding of exactly what went on in our past, so that we can understand where we are going in our future, then that would probably help ease many of the tensions people are feeling.

Nash: What's wrong with Canadian history? Is it a boring subject?

McConaghy: It tends to be less exciting than the Americans'. We never had a civil war. There just doesn't seem to be much interest in history. Another thing is that we don't promote our national heroes. In the States, if they have a national hero, whether it is in sports or anything else, they become celebrities. Here we don't even celebrate Sir John A. Macdonald's birthday, the Father of Confederation. It makes you wonder. We have to try to boost Canadian morale.

Nash: In many ways, the Maritimes have traditionally felt somewhat deprived by Conferederation, in the sense they haven't got out of it what they thought they would. Is that still a feeling?

McConaghy: Yes, there is a lot of that. My economics teacher said that we have been called the parasites of the East and that sort of thing, but really, we've paid a price for the success of the rest of Canada. It would be more sensible for us to trade with the United States, the New England states, since it's a larger market and it's closer. Within Canada, we've worked with the old Canadian railway linking one country east to west, and we have paid increased prices to have your goods shipped to our area. We don't have as much clout as you do, but we have also helped southern Ontario to be what it is.

Nash: You are going into business as a young entrepreneur. Would you be willing to pay a price to remain Canadian?

Suppose you made 5 or 10 per cent less profit by trading in Canada instead of trading with the United States.

McConaghy: Definitely, because there are so many more benefits to being a Canadian as opposed to being an American. The Canadian passport has a much better track record. Then there are social benefits, medicare, that type of thing. It makes Canada worth being in. That's what's so frustrating. There is a lot of cross-border shopping in New Brunswick right now. It's frustrating because we decided that, as Canadians, we would like to see central health and welfare services, but we are not willing to pay the price. People are just not thinking.

Nash: In much of Canada people are turned off the political process. Is that true for young people as well? Is there an anti-government, anti-politician feeling, and a sense that they are all out to lunch?

McConaghy: To me, people who just complain about government are not helping the situation any. If you don't like how something is being done, or how something is being treated, get involved yourself and try to make it better.

Jewel Randolph

PETER RUSSELL

Professor Peter Russell is director of graduate studies in Political Science at the University of Toronto and is widely recognized as an authority on Canadian constitutional affairs. A former Rhodes scholar, he is president of the Canadian Political Science Association, and has been a visiting professor at Harvard University, the Australian National University, and Makere University in Uganda. He has served on numerous royal commissions and task forces.

"We have shown the genius of diversity."

Nash: If we were starting over again to build Canada, as we may well be doing, in broad terms how do you think it should be changed?

Russell: Number one in terms of the justice of our political community we should treat aboriginal people as full peoples. They were here first. They have the right to negotiate the terms on which they want to join with the rest of us who came later. We have been in an imperial relationship with them for the last 150 to 200 years. First they were our partners militarily and economically, and then when we got the upper hand, we just dominated them and treated them in a way that's unjust.

Nash: How would you do that?

Russell: The first step would be to discuss with them what their prime condititons are for membership in a common

Canadian community. If it is to have special positions reserved for them, according to their population, in our national institutions, in Parliament, fine. That is what the Maori worked out with the New Zealanders over a hundred years ago. If that's what our aboriginal people want, I would certainly support it. If, in addition, or instead of that, they also wanted a much larger degree of self-government in those areas where they still occupy ancestral lands and have a good economic base from which to have more control over their future development, that, too, I would support. But my main point would be in terms of the covenant that creates a country, the social contract on which a constitutional democracy ought to be based. They should be part of it, as they have never been before.

Nash: How would you treat the other question facing us, of Quebec?

Russell: We have now a population which is 40 per cent neither British nor French. There is a three-way situation in terms of the non-aboriginal population. You have British, French, and the multicultural community. That means you can't build the Canadian social contract on just a dualistic French-English basis, but nor can you build it on a basis that ignores the historic role of the Québécois as a people who have been on the banks of the St. Lawrence for hundreds of years. So I think you have to accommodate both the multicultural and the bicultural aspects.

Nash: When you say "accommodate" them, that implies that Quebeckers have to have some powers that they don't now have. What do you envision as a transference of power?

Russell: They have to have some constitutional recognition of their status and some security within the powers they are given under the Constitution, so they won't be forced to comply with national standards that threaten their distinctive way of life. I think one of our big problems will be our desire to have common social objectives in the areas like medicare. Quebec may well be interested in cooperating in achieving national objectives, but according to its own programming and its own way of realizing those objectives. If we are designing a new Canada, we must have some trust in the different elements of the country, including Quebec, to realize national standards. We should look much more to the European way, which is to have a social charter that doesn't have the threat that some people in Brussels will go to Paris and tell Mitterand what kind of social policy he must have. And yet, it is a meaningful charter since it establishes objectives. It's that kind of balance we need; to have national objectives, which Canadians share, but not to force them constitutionally down the throat of Quebec.

Nash: So you differentiate between national objectives and national standards?

Russell: Yes I do. We don't need national standards that are forced on a province on the grounds that we just can't trust the majority in Quebec to elect a government that will provide decent medicare and other decent programs for the people of Quebec.

Nash: Does that lead inevitably to some kind of patchwork quilt of standards?

Russell: Patchwork quilts are the essence of federalism. But we shouldn't use terms like patchwork. Why not say diversity? Throughout our history, we are a people who have shown the genius of diversity. Where did medicare come from? Did it come from a uniform national policy? No, it came from the laboratory of Saskatchewan.

Nash: In general terms, what kind of minimum federal powers should there be? What should be exclusively controlled by Ottawa? Defence, foreign policy, the economy?

Russell: Certainly defence and external affairs, although we already have a shared set of activities, in that the provinces historically have been active in different forms of external relations. I think the major commitments of the country diplomatically and in defence and certainly in economic policy, international economic policy, have to be federal. Domestically, I think the major things that most Canadians want leadership on in Ottawa, I call the three "Es." First is an effective, thriving economic union. The second is that this country, unlike the United States, is quite committed to equalization of public services and facilities across the country, regardless of the revenue base of the less prosperous areas. In the United States, the policy is to let people go to where the opportunities are, so instead of taking money and transferring it from California to New England, you let the New Englanders drift down to the sun belt. That's their method. We've chosen a different way. We've chosen within some limits to not force the people out of Saskatchewan, Manitoba, and the four Atlantic provinces, but to maintain a decent level of public sevices there without forcing them to resort to exceptional taxation. I think the program of equalization is one that ties Canadians together. The third E is environmental protection, which is a recognition that environmental problems don't recognize borders. If you have strictly provincial approaches to major environmental problems, you won't deal with them effectively.

Nash: You sound like a bit of an optimist in terms of the possibility of making that kind of arrangement with Quebec.

Russell: I think there is a fighting chance. It isn't easy, but I think there is a potential package.

Nash: If you allow a major transfer of powers to the provinces, wouldn't you wind up with a federal boneless wonder?

Russell: I would be very worried about massive devolution. But I don't think for a moment there is a chance of selling the majority of Canadians on massive devolution. That's just not on.

Nash: How then do you achieve the objectives you are seeking and satisfy Quebec?

Russell: You work at it both ways. There are some things that we must do more effectively at the national level. The economic union is a good example. After 124 years, and even though we are in an international free trade arrangement, we still don't have really an economic union internally. That is a national purpose that requires national action.

Nash: It also requires the ending of provincial restrictions.

Russell: Yes, but it may very well be one of those distinctive roles of a new revitalized upper house that, in a systematic way, identifies the barriers that are causing most disruptions within our economy.

Nash: Speaking of the upper house, how would you change that?

Russell: I am very partial to a regionalized upper house. I think it should be elected, although I can imagine an effective house also being developed in the West German way, where there would be representatives of either provinces or regional governments. I also think that the upper house should have the distinct purpose of looking after elements of the federation that are neglected by the House of Commons and have particular regional dimensions, and I speak of equalization. It's a waste of time to have the upper house redebate every bloody bill that goes through the House of Commons. I'd rather see the House of Commons strengthened and party discipline relaxed and really give members of the House of Commons something to do.

Nash: But party discipline is such an element of parliamentary democracy, how would the government be able to operate without it?

Russell: Authoritarian control of members of Parliament has had more to do with the cynicism among the public about politicians than any other single factor, because they see the whole life of the House of Commons as a mock, a façade. If a party has a majority, as the current government does, and the prime minister says the party position is this, and you must hew it or you are out, then what's the point in the whole debate?

Nash: What you are seeking is more political responsiveness on a continuing basis to the public.

Russell: Yes, absolutely, and we don't have that with the strict party discipline. It's far too strict. I happen to think we also should relax the rules about what is a confidence vote.

Nash: What role would you see in a future Canada for the monarchy? Same as now or different?

Russell: Same as now. I think the monarchy is an extraordinarily cunning device, and that the republicans who think they can create a ceremonial head of state that works better, that is more unifying, and who think they can do better with some elected or appointed person, are naïve.

Nash: We were talking earlier about greater regional and provincial influence on national affairs. Should there be much greater provincial involvement, say, in appointments to the Supreme Court of Canada, or to the regulatory agencies, or to the Bank of Canada governors?

Russell: For sure on the Supreme Court. There should be for the first time a check and balance on the federal politicians of the government party who control judicial appointments. It's very unhealthy to have that much power over the judiciary in so few political hands. Whether that check and balance comes from provincial premiers or from a committee of a revitalized Senate is another question. I prefer the latter, if we had an elected Senate that really meant something and had real legitimacy with the Canadian people.

Nash: Is there enough time left, assuming a deadline of a referendum in Quebec in October 1992? That's not far away. Is there time for Canadians to develop a consensus on what they want?

Russell: There's time to get close enough to seeing whether that is a pretty good possibility. There's time to see if there is a ghost of a chance of pulling together a set of constitutional changes that can command respect and support in all parts of Canada. We may not have all the *i*'s dotted and *t*'s crossed and all the arrangements finally made in some sort of binding way, but I think we can be close enough to know, yes, we are getting it together and it's worth forging ahead for a few more months, or, no, we are not getting it together.

Nash: One wonders if there is a difference between what the élites of Quebec are saying and feeling and what the people there say and feel.

Russell: I think they speak for most Quebeckers in the sense of feeling insulted and abused as a result of Meech Lake. Their ego has been insulted and that is a broad-based, deep feeling. Whether it's justified or not is irrelevant. It's there, it's a political fact. But I think the sovereigntists have been doing a con job on the Quebec people. Quebec people may wake up and realize that what they are really talking about is not sovereignty but independence, and that any economic relationship with Canada, including the currency and all of that, is very dicey, and that there is enormous economic risk. The sovereigntists have been glossing over this and saying that it will be a piece of cake: "We'll be independent and there will be no problems." But I think there's some common sense in the ordinary person, and they might see through that as a bit of false advertising.

Nash: What about the consequences outside Quebec for the rest of Canada were there to be a split?

Russell: Economic consequences all around will, in the short term, take the form of a much higher price for borrowing money from the outside. People abroad will have less confidence in us for a while, because we'll look very confused and mixed up, and if you can put your foreign currency in a more stable environment, you will. So we will all pay.

Nash: How would the individual be affected? Would it mean each of us would have to pay more money for mortgages, car loans, and so on because of higher interest rates?

Russell: Sure, you will pay more money for mortgages and car loans, absolutely. Not only that, you will be taxed more heavily. They certainly will be taxed more heavily in Quebec. They already are taxed more heavily there than anywhere else, practically, in North America, and that will get a heck of a lot worse.

Nash: If it came to a split, would it be acrimonious, or would we still be relatively friendly?

Russell: It depends on how it's done. If we move into it in a systematic way, having first looked carefully together at the possibility of staying together and found we couldn't, and then saying, "Let's draw up arrangements for a divorce," then I could see it being done quite smoothly. On the other hand, if it's done abruptly and abrasively through some unilateral move by Quebec that plunges us into a chaos of illegal action by a provincial government, which simply claims that it's now an international state, well, then you are certainly plunged into possibilities of civil disorder.

Nash: How much does Canada mean to you and your family?

Russell: We go back to the eighteenth century in Canada, and we came here because we did not like some of the elements of the new democracy that the Americans were building. We built a different kind of country that's offered the world a great deal. People may think that's a little corny, but I don't think it is. I think we have had a lot to do with the protection of the democratic world. We have done things that we ought to take great pride in, and to break up means we will have much less of a role in the world. I think humankind would be considerably worse off with a broken Canada.

Nash: We seem to look down on patriotic corniness.

Russell: That's the American thing; the flag-waving and so on. I wouldn't want to see us as a bunch of horn-blowers. I like our low-key approach, and I think it is part of our effectiveness internationally. We don't push ourselves in quite such a chauvinistic way as the Americans.

Nash: What do you want Canada to look like by the turn of the century?

Russell: A united country in which the aboriginal people have for the first time a place that recognizes them as a founding people. A place in which the Québécois can feel secure in preserving their distinct culture. And a Canada in which those who are neither British or French can take pride and feel at home in a federal system that operates more smoothly with less cost and tensison. And I think in the future Canada, we must overcome and get rid of this colonial treatment of the North. It's just plain wrong.

WILLARD "BUD" ESTEY

In his renowned legal career, Willard "Bud" Estey has been Chief Justice of Ontario and a Justice of the Supreme Court of Canada. Following his retirement from the court, Estey became Chancellor of Wilfred Laurier University and counsel to the law firm McCarthy-Tétrault. He is also chairman of the Canadian Law Scholarship Foundation, chairman of the Ontario Press Council, and special adviser to the chairman of the Bank of Nova Scotia. Estey has been a member of several royal commissions. He is a graduate of the University of Saskatchewan and Harvard University and began his career as a professor at the College of Law at the University of Saskatchewan. He also lectured at the Osgoode Hall law school in Toronto. He is a Companion of the Order of Canada.

"We've got the powers to solve the problem."

Nash: How serious do you think this constitutional crisis is for Canada?

Estey: It could be the end of the road. I have watched this come now for half a century, and I have taught constitutional law for most of that half-century. It's a shake-down. We are either going to make it or we are not. I don't think we are going to go broke, or go down to two meals a day, but we may lose our national structure and go down to a Hanseatic League of a sort.

Nash: Do you see any consensus at all in English-speaking

Canada on the substance of a new Canada, of what changes there might be?

Estey: Yes. I think there is an awareness building, and I think that English Canada, if there is such a thing, will coalesce around a few fundamentals that are compatible with what they think their way of life is. Sure, I think it's possible.

Nash: What are some of the fundamentals you think might be possible?

Estey: One of them is language. The anglophone has to get it through his skull that Quebec wants the right to say that there will only be one language in Quebec. They don't care what language is spoken in St. Boniface, Manitoba, or anywhere else, just in Quebec, and we have to grant that right. It's true that we are selling down the river a little bit the one million anglophones in Quebec, but that's evolution. Once they have the right to insist on French, what they will exercise is something else. The big bogeyman is language. I think we've got to acknowledge that Quebec is the master absolute of language – commercial and political language.

Nash: Would you apply the same principle to other provinces? Could Alberta, for instance, use the same rationale and say no to French?

Estey: Same thing. Stamp it right out.

Nash: That would basically be the end of official bilingualism.

Estey: Absolutely. That was a non-starter to begin with. It's expensive beyond belief. It's a retardant in trade, it scares foreign investment off, it accomplishes nothing, because if people want to speak French, they will acquire it as a second language. But commercial use and compulsory public use is something else. That was one of Trudeau's very few mistakes.

Nash: Do you think that the government would be prepared to end official bilingualism?

Estey: Absolutely. I think the people are going to force it on them.

Nash: What other things that Quebec is seeking do you think English-speaking Canadians are prepared to give?

Estey: Quite a few. One of them is control of social services, social-spending programs. They should be able to get the federal money, without strings, and administer their own health plan. If they don't have the same standards, so be it.

Nash: If Quebec and other provinces run many programs that are now federal, how can you get national standards in things like education?

Estey: You can't. I was going to come to that. That should be the number one problem, education, because we are going to die if we can't compete globally, and that means education. In education, I think we have to swallow a few hard things, Quebec among us. We have to make some concessions to nationalism and have national standards in education, maybe a national exam. We also must face the Native problem head on. It is a horrendous problem.

Nash: How should we face it?

Estey: First of all, we must recognize that they have an absolute right to certain parts of the surface of the country. It was dedicated to them in the Treaty of Paris. We haven't bought it from them since, they haven't waived it, and therefore you start with that recognition. We can't run roughshod over them, we've got to work it out.

Nash: Should there be Native provinces in the country?

Estey: I think so, yes. They may not be provinces, because they haven't attained that level of economic productivity, but they have to have a big element of self-government, not just municipal government. I'd also abolish the Department of Indian Affairs and put the money into Indian schools.

Nash: It sounds like you feel there should be a fairly large transfer of power from the centre to the provinces.

Estey: No. I would push a lot down, but we are caught up in our buzz-words on that. People have a battle flag: strong central government. Another battle flag: strong provincial government. Well, neither one is a reality. What is a reality is the practical locale of the immediate power in which you are interested. For example, trade marks. There's got to be national power in trade marks. Taxation has to be national, because of the differential of income. Trade has to be national, because you have to have a strong international voice. You can't bargain with the United States if you are going to have ten voices. There has got to be a powerful, national, tough voice. It's a pragmatic exercise. You go through a whole zylophone of powers and needs and you say, "National or provincial? National or provincial?" If the total comes out in favour of national, then I guess you've got a strong national government.

Nash: So you think Quebec will be practical about the constitutional arrangements, and that practicality would lead you to think that there can be some form of federation, and yet you are pessimistic about our united future.

Estey: I'm pessimistic because I think the Anglo response is too slow. We are jeopardizing our good relations with Quebec by appearing to straight-arm them. We are not, but we appear to be.

It is not sound to say the federal government is going to speak for the other nine provinces. That's the last thing they are going to accept. I have always pushed a citizens' assembly because I've come up the old-fashioned jury side of the law, and I'm greatly impressed with the ability of the common man to make sensible decisions.

Nash: That common Canadian man or woman doesn't seem to have much nationalistic patriotic emotion, or at least, doesn't express it.

Estey: No, we don't. It is one of our voids. We've never had a George M. Cohan in our make-up who could write patriotic music. We don't want to be seen singing patriotic music. Most of us can't mutter "O Canada" unless the Maple Leaf Gardens has that line going by. We like to attack the memory of Billy Bishop for no reason other than the fact we must not have a hero. Even during the Gulf War, everyone was critical. They would interview some flight lieutenant saying, "I don't know what I am doing over here," while the Americans, on the other hand, were marching back and forth on the desert.

Nash: We are both inhabitants of the North American continent, though, so why would one stream to the south of us grow up with that patriotic fervour when we have not?

Estey: I don't know. The Anglos blame it on the French, the

French blame it on the Anglos. I don't know why that is, but it is certainly true. We didn't have a war to start with. It's too bad we didn't kick the British out instead of letting them withdraw as dignified as they did. We should have thrown them out.

Nash: We don't have a violent history. We didn't have a civil war. We didn't have the violence in the West the Americans had. Maybe it all comes back to the original idea of "Peace, Order, and Good Government," which carries a significant psychological message of quiet conformity, compared with "Life, Liberty, and the Pursuit of Happiness," which is more individualistic and enthusiastic. But, looking to the future, what do you think might happen if Quebec did seek to separate?

Estey: If we came to that, it would be a peaceful separation. We would have an independent Quebec, and we would have the rest of Canada carrying on the federal system. Eventually, the bonds would get more complex and more daily, and we would be back into some kind of federal union.

Nash: How long a period of time would that take?

Estey: Not very long because the world is moving so fast. At the absolute outside, twenty years.

Nash: It's an enormous exercise to go through to separate and then eventually pull back together again.

Estey: A convulsion. Just like a young kid who's eaten too much at a picnic and then everything has got to come back up.

Nash: Our immigration has changed the nature of Canada. If Canada has been a duality in the past, we are less so now.

Estey: Much less so. Did you ever think that maybe our whole concept in the British North America Act is contrary to the United Nations Charter? We are racist. We say we are two founding races. That means there is no room for a third. You can't do that. The 1960 United Nations treaty said that people are all entitled to be treated equally. So we have been bringing in all kinds of people, and thank God for it, to build a new society here. And it's loosened all our fabric of bonds. We don't have any institutional bonds now.

Nash: What happens to the monarchy in that situation?

Estey: It might survive, because we can't figure out what to put in its place. It's a silly kind of thing. There is no bond there at all.

Nash: What role is there for the Supreme Court in all this discussion about restructuring Canada?

Estey: Not much.

Nash: There are suggestions that the provinces should have a greater say in appointing members to the Supreme Court.

Estey: That's more of our divisionalism. The United States has a nine-person court, same as we do, and lo and behold, they have two from Minnesota. They've got fifty states, and one of them has got two. There was no rhubarb about that. The court is not an instrument of regionalism, nor is it representational. And furthermore, in the problems you and I are talking about, if Quebec has the power of self-determination, the court can't reverse it.

Nash: Does Quebec have that power of self-determination?

Estey: Undoubtedly. In my opinion, indubitably.

Nash: Where do they get it?

Estey: They get it from a combination of things. One of them is the 1960 treaty, to which Canada is a signatory in the United Nations, that says people have the free and unlimited right to self-determination, and Quebec is a people. They have a language. They have a locale. They have a history. They are a people. Unfortunately for Quebec, the Indian in its midst is more of a people and has more of a right. They have a 1763 Declaration of Paris, which clearly describes on a map Indian country right across all of those hydro dams.

We fought the Second World War on the North Atlantic Charter theorum, which gave you the right of self determination. It was aimed at Europe, not aimed at us, but it's in broad terms and that's what Roosevelt and Churchill signed out there on that battleship in Conception Bay, Newfoundland, and so Quebec's got the right to separate. But it's also a practical matter of who is going to stop them? We are not going to go to war over that.

Nash: In the English-speaking part of Canada, can we

develop a consensus on proposals to Quebec within the time frame we've got?

Estey: Sure, easy. I think we are getting frightened. We are seeing our jobs go south. They will never come back, and we are losing them in the hundreds. We are frightened, and we are going to get a lot more frightened. We are non-competitive, which is a nice word for saying we are going to go broke; from three meals a day we will go down to two. We cannot compete with the Japanese, with the Americans, with the Europeans.

Nash: So, in a way, the setting of a deadline is a good thing in focussing our attention on our economic as well as our constitutional problems?

Estey: It did us a favour, absolutely did us a favour. The timetable is simple. If we decide we have something to talk about, we can easily call a meeting. We have the meeting. We don't agree, then we get frightened. We wonder what happens if we walk out of here in disagreement. So we come back again, like an accordion, and eventually we agree. We don't get everything we want. We don't settle everything. Maybe we only settle four things and that will leave forty-four left to be settled. Then we will build a new contract, and we will all sign that, and we will go back to work on the next struggle. That will all happen in twelve months. It's easily done. I think we've got the powers to solve the problem.

MARJORIE BOWKER

Born on Prince Edward Island, Marjorie Bowker moved to Wetaskiwin, Alberta, at an early age and has been a westerner ever since. She has a law degree from the University of Alberta and was admitted to the Alberta bar in 1940. Always active in community organizations, she has been outspoken on the role of women and the future of the family. She was named a judge of the Family and Juvenile Court of Alberta in 1966. Her national fame came with the publication of her best-selling books on the Canada-U.S. Free Trade Agreement and on the Meech Lake accord. Ms. Bowker was named Woman of the Year by the Business and Professional Women's Club in Edmonton in 1989 and received the Distinguished Canadian Award from the Council of Canadians that same year.

"Will they ever be satisfied?"

Nash: How would you describe a Canadian?
Bowker: I don't know if we can define ourselves. Too often the answer is what we like to say and what we think you want to hear. But one important facet is the caring attitude of our country, which is reflected in the kinds of programs we have had for the last twenty years.
Nash: The social safety net?
Bowker: That's right. The concern about economic disparity. We have the regional development programs, we have univer-

sal health care, and we have transfers to the provinces in order to equalize opportunities across Canada. That symbolizes in my mind a caring society. But one negative thing is that multiculturalism has been very destructive.

Nash: Tell me how.

Bowker: Because it focusses on the differences between people, and it does not encourage a Canadian identity. I think that all of us, particularly immigrants, must identify with Canada before we focus on our ethnic heritage.

Nash: We have always tended to pride ourselves on our mosaic, as distinct from the American melting-pot. Are you suggesting we should do more melting and have less distinctive ethnic groupings?

Bowker: Well, yes. I think it is very destructive. There must be some way to encourage newcomers to keep their culture but not be funded by governments for it.

Nash: We are talking about multiculturalism, but what about biculturalism and bilingualism?

Bowker: Well, I think we should have bilingualism from coast to coast at the level of the federal agencies, but apart from that, it should be left to the provinces. The French came to the conclusion some time ago that French was not succeeding elsewhere in Canada, and therefore they must concentrate on their own borders. Here in the West, where we don't have much opportunity to speak French, people are sending their kids to French immersion schools, which I think is utter nonsense. I think they are depriving themselves of an English education. Our own kids learned French after they left high school by going to Quebec.

Nash: What do you think of what Quebec is seeking in terms of new powers?

Bowker: It's certainly excessive in the Allaire report and the Bélanger-Campeau report. They are excessive beyond reason. But I emphasize, it's not the provinces that want the power, it's the premiers. One of the real threats to our country is the fact that it is the premiers talking, not the people. The Meech Lake accord gave powers to the provincial governments, sometimes it was to the people, but in essence and practice it would be that this massive power would reside in the premiers.

Nash: And you think the Canadian people should seize back some influence and power from the political leaders?

Bowker: This is the issue right now. The Meech Lake accord is dead, but it will never really be dead because it marked the beginning of people's insistence on taking control. This to me is the great thing of the current debate. I call it a wave of populism. Never before has our country witnessed such a thing, and having exposed what they see as impropriety in the past, they are never going to give it up.

Nash: The public?

Bowker: The thing that absolutely amazes me is wherever you go, everybody wants a part in it. But I am afraid after all this fuss, it looks to me like all these commissions and task forces were just fronts, window-dressing to give the federal government time to decide what they are going to do. We can talk about the different options, but Mulroney and Clark will decide, and whatever they do will be in collaboration with Quebec. It will really be a Quebec-Ottawa deal. They will work out a deal, and it will look good, and Mulroney will quickly get the premiers together. I don't know what they will say, but in any case Mulroney will then go before the country as a saviour in the next election, which will follow shortly.

When we talk about saving the country, we've got to consider it's not just about making accommodation with Quebec. That seems to be the uppermost thing, and that is politically motivated, too, because Quebec is so important to Ottawa. But it will leave, just as Meech Lake left, a lot of resentment, animosity. Whatever solution is found to the constitutional crisis, it must be such that the cynicism that pervades the country has been overcome.

Nash: Tell me what you think would be the best kind of response to make to Quebec regarding the powers it wants to have?

Bowker: We should present a matching proposal to Quebec, which says this is the maximum extent of transfer of powers from the federal government to the provinces that we can give, this is the maximum degree. The powers that should be maintained are national standards of health care and education. We have to preserve national standards. We have to preserve regional development programs. We have to preserve the Charter of Rights, which Quebec has infringed upon in promoting its language, and the protection of minorities. Those are principles we have to maintain.

Nash: Using your ideas, supposing Quebec said, "We want more than that." Then what?

Bowker: I think we've got to say to Quebec that this is the Canada that we are going to have. Do you want to be part of it or not? No negotiations, this is it. Nobody has addressed the problem of Canada without Quebec and these studies should be two-pronged: a Canada with Quebec; a Canada without Quebec. Now we are only reacting to Quebec. There are other factors to be considered: What about the effect on other regions? What about the effect on Natives, minorities, on women?

Nash: Do we have enough time for Canada outside Quebec to develop the kind of country that we want to see?

Bowker: We should never be bound by a deadline set by one province. I think that the rhetoric in Quebec is softening and there's a mood of questioning right now. I don't particularly believe in polls, but I think that negotiation is going to be very popular.

Nash: You were speaking earlier about the differences between the political leaders in English-speaking Canada and the people. Is there also a gap between the political leaders, the élites of Quebec, and the people?

Bowker: I think very much so. The people have no comprehension about what they are being told. They have no way of testing the truth of what they are being told, and they are not being told anything good about the rest of Canada. But I think there is a lingering nostalgia and emotion, an attachment to Canada.

Nash: What's your educated guess? What do you think is going to happen?

Bowker: It's only a visceral feeling, but I think it is going to be resolved. My concern is that it is going to be resolved by compromise in such a way that we will be still faced with confrontation and more demands from Quebec. I think that we will avert a breakup in the fall of 1992, but my concern is, will it be lasting? Nobody wants another fifty years of wrangling, of a dissatisfied Quebec. I think that we in English Canada have to realize that Quebeckers, at least those who are very dedicated to the future, genuinely believe that they cannot have fulfilment of their dreams except through a separate country. We think that is ridiculous, but that's the way they see it. They genuinely do not feel any loyalty to Canada, any commitment to Canada. Their concern is at all costs, even at the risk of offending the rights of minorities, to promote their culture and their language.

Nash: There is also an economic facet in all this that has to be considered.

Bowker: As we proceed with this constitutional debate and our relationship with Quebec, in my mind the risk is that it will be determined on an economic basis. It seems to be focussing now only in economic terms. In other words, is it going to be advantageous to leave or remain? I think that that analysis will fail. There are already signs and studies indicating that it is going to be a terrible thing, a disastrous thing, economically. But it would be a shame if that became the basis of holding the country together. It should be one of those hard-to-describe feelings of attachment, commitment to the country. Quebec has been protected in our Constitution since 1867. It guaranteed their language, their civil law, and this has been preserved and added to, and yet they are not satisfied. And one has to ask, will they ever be satisfied? Maybe this independence movement began on the Plains of Abraham, and this is just the culmination of it. Maybe it's inevitable. But I think we have given so much to Quebec.

Nash: What should we do if there is a referendum and the vote is for soverneignty. What should the reaction of English-speaking Canadians be?

Bowker: I think that's the end of the line as far as English

Canada's intervention is concerned, but I don't think that the referendum will pass.

Nash: Why do you think we should be so concerned with trying to preserve the country?

Bowker: I had to ask myself that, because we've never had to question it ever before. I wonder what the value is if there is going to be continual squabbling. As to the alternative of a divided Canda, I don't know what the future of that is. It may be the trend in the world, the breaking up of countries. Eastern Europe has broken up. There's discord throughout the world. Maybe the human species can't live in harmony any more.

MAUREEN FORRESTER

A world acclaimed contralto, Maureen Forrester is one of Canada's most distinguished citizens. She was born in Montreal, where she made her debut at the Montreal YWCA and went on to become a favourite of many of the world's greatest conductors. In addition to her orchestral and recital appearances, Ms. Forrester is well-known on the operatic stage and in the recording world. She is an ardent advocate of twentieth-century music, especially that composed by her fellow Canadians. She chaired the Canada Council from 1983 to 88, and she was made a Companion of the Order of Canada in 1967, the year the order was created.

"I am passionate about my country."

Nash: What would your feeling be if Quebec separated?
Forrester: Inwardly, I would feel like I had lost a child.
Nash: What can we do to prevent it then? What can individuals do?
Forrester: We have to prove to Quebec that the rest of Canada loves Quebec, loves them exactly as they are, and that they shouldn't change. Nobody wants them to be anglophones.
Nash: They have a great sense of pride, and they feel that the rest of Canada rejected them on Meech.
Forrester: Yes, that's sad. They feel really let down.

Nash: What should be done to persuade Quebec to stay within Canada?

Forrester: The prime minister has to persuade Canada to persuade Quebec to stay. The government has to do a real PR job on the rest of Canada to say we can't let Quebec leave Canada. They were here at the beginning of our history, and it is very important that they stay.

Nash: How do you get that sense of urgency in the rest of Canada? How to you stimulate it?

Forrester: You have to invite people from all walks of life to Quebec and have them realize the joys of Quebec, what a wonderful province it is, and how lusty it is and passionate about itself. If only the rest of Canada were as passionate about itself as Quebec is, I think we wouldn't have any problems anywhere.

Nash: You are pretty passionate yourself.

Forrester: I am passionate about my country. I think I was fortunate to be born in paradise in Montreal. I travel so much, and I practically kiss the ground when I come home.

Nash: What do you think Canada will look like in the year 2000? Will we have survived the crisis?

Forrester: I really wish it with all my heart that we'll get over our petty grievances and look at a wider picture of how important this country is. People who come up here from the United States are always in awe of this country. It is so clean. I was in New York recently, and I was terrified to be there. It is so dirty, with people sleeping on the street. I always blow my own horn when I am away, urging people to visit Canada. It's got everything: mountains and water and plains and cold and warm weather and the best fall in the world. But we don't brag about it. We know we are a wonderful country, and we solve our problems without much hullabaloo. The Americans who come up here are always fascinated, especially when I bring an American pianist to play for me when we travel the country. He says people are nice. People in the United States are nice, too, but the cities are bigger, so everything is more impersonal in San Francisco or Los Angeles. It's just not the same.

Nash: How do you feel about all the arguments swirling around now about the Constitution? Are you sad, disinterested, disillusioned?

Forrester: I was brought up in Montreal in a French neighbourhood, and I remember when my francophone neighbours couldn't be bank tellers, couldn't be sales clerks at Eaton's, Morgan's, or Simpsons. The French always educated their children well because they wanted them to achieve something, but they would get to a certain position in a company and no further. They sent their children out of the country to France and different places, and when they came back they wanted their culture to survive. In those days, the church ran practically everything in Quebec. Now all these young bright lawyers and politicians, teachers and professors, they know what their past was like, and they want to see a better future for their offspring so that they will continue to have their language and their culture. But I just don't think Quebec should secede. I would hate them to separate. In Switzerland, they speak French in one part and German in another, but they all get along.

Nash: What differences do you see between English- and French-speaking Canadians?

Forrester: The French Candians are very outgoing, and they speak their mind. They don't hide their feelings. I still have a tendency from my Anglo-Saxon side to chew up my anger inside. I wish I could really be Latin and explode.

Nash: How much richness does all our multiculturalism give to the country?

Forrester: It makes it a wonderful patchwork quilt. Because they all bring their cultures with them. And the food! Look how we have changed in the way we eat in Canada. It used to be roast beef or chicken on Sunday, fish on Friday. Now we eat everything.

Nash: Do we need, in a sense, to try to overcome a feeling of being Maritimers or Quebeckers or Upper Candians, as the case may be? Do we need to have more national symbols?

Forrester: I think what makes people here interesting is that they are all Canadians, but they are a little different. They have their own character. We shouldn't put out people like cookies on a sheet.

Nash: You were obviously very much involved with the Canada Council as its chair for a long time. What's your sense of the role that culture can play in the future of the country?

Forrester: It's very important. People say that culture is something for the élitist. It isn't. Cooking is culture, too. Music and theatre make people express themselves. They express their anger and their happiness, and it gives you a thermometer of what's happening in the country. Sports and culture are an essential part of everybody's make-up.

Nash: Do we need more stories and visual arts about Canada?

Forrester: Yes, we do. We really have to encourage our writers and our playwrights. Their work reflects the time we live in, so that our children and our children's children can know. I also consider history a part of culture. I don't think people study enough about Canada. They don't travel around their own country enough.

Nash: Because of our relatively modest population base, encouraging more writers means government subsidies to an extent. How do you do that in this day and age when Canadians are worried about budgets and deficit spending?

Forrester: It's a drop in the bucket compared to how many people it services. It's a drop in the bucket compared to the whole budget of the government. Mind you, I feel the private sector always has to contribute, too.

Nash: Aside from the sense of how to improve the quality of our culture, what did you learn of Canada as chair of the Canada Council?

Forrester: That there is a tremendous amount of talent in this country, more than anybody ever thought. There is talent everywhere. Writers, painters, fabric-makers, all kinds of talent in this country.

Al Gilbert, Toronto

OSCAR PETERSON

Oscar Peterson began his profession as a jazz pianist in his home town of Montreal when he was fifteen, and launched his international career at Carnegie Hall in New York in 1949 at the age of twenty-four. Peterson's highly skilled and joyous piano technique has brought him world acclaim, as has his composing. In addition to extensive critical acclaim, Peterson has won awards around the globe, including Grammys and Junos. He is a member of the Juno Awards Hall of Fame and a Companion of the Order of Canada. He was appointed chancellor of York University in the summer of 1991.

"We don't know our own country."

Nash: What has the constitutional debate and all the turmoil meant to you emotionally?

Peterson: It has ripped me apart emotionally. I was speaking to my neighbour the other day, and he asked me about this problem, and suddenly I realized I had tears coming out of my eyes. I've never felt this helpless in my life, and I realize it is because of my true love for this country, which most people, I hope, have. To think of the stupid mistakes we have made as Canadians!

Nash: You work all over the world, outside of Canada more than inside, and you could live anywhere you wanted to, but you live here. Why do you choose to stay here rather than being in Los Angeles or Paris or London?

Peterson: For a very simple reason. This is my home. I have grown up here. I have family and friends here. As well, I love seasons, I am not a one-season person. I think that is boring. But I also had a vision, my own personal vision of this country, and I thought at one point that we perhaps would be able to overcome a lot of problems that other countries couldn't overcome. One of them was racial. I thought that perhaps because we had a more simplistic outlook, we'd be able to solve those things and say, "Let's all get together and do what we have to do." But I found out a very funny thing: human beings will be human beings, no matter where you go.

Nash: In all your travels around the world, does our debate about Canada's future come up, and if so, what are people's views?

Peterson: Yes, it comes up. It has been coming up more and more. Years ago almost everyone was in love with what they thought Canada was and represented, and now they look askance and say things like, "You guys are just as bad as the rest of us out here when it comes to bad politics and when it comes to racism."

Nash: Do you think Canada as a country is essentially a nation of two founding races, or is it a nation of ten provinces, or something else?

Peterson: The way I look at Canada now, unfortunately, is as a country primarily made up of two cultures in total disagreement. I believe that both French and English Canada have been caught in the middle of two opportunistic political systems that have caused this fracture.

Nash: You separate the politicians from the mass of the people, both English-speaking and French-speaking?

Peterson: That's right.

Nash: So do you feel that a referendum is a way in which you can tap the feelings of the people?

Peterson: Exactly, and go with whatever the answer is, whether you like it or not.

Nash: Do you think the breakup of Canada is inevitable? Say, by the year 2000, is it going to happen?

Peterson: It could, I think it quite possibly could. There are so many fragmented feelings right now, regionally.

Nash: Not just in Quebec.

Peterson: No, no. I am not even thinking about Quebec. I just think that there are so many needs that have been left unattended in this country, needs that we have glossed over and tried to put off.

Nash: What kind of needs are you thinking of?

Peterson: The most obvious one of all to me is the needs of Native people. Ironically, a lot of Canadians are embarrassed by this because they know the rest of the world has always perceived this country as being very fair and liberal. But underlying all of that, there is something that I have to be very frank about. I think this country has suffered for all these years with our own brand of racism. We look to the Indians and the Eskimos as window-dressing. We were pleased to have them because they didn't demand anything, they didn't bother us. Now they are speaking up for their rights.

Nash: Do you see other problems?

Peterson: I have to be very honest with you and say that we seem to be drifting towards being the underling of the United States. It seems that if the United States goes to war, we go to war. If the United States decides to have free trade all over the continent, we are going to have free trade.

Nash: You grew up in Montreal and have a real sense and feel for Quebec. You said the other day that, assuming Quebec goes, they should "go with love." What did you mean by that?

Peterson: I really don't think this issue is so big that the whole country should become so polarized that there is hatred between the rest of the country and Quebec. Look, they are not going to get a saw and saw off the province and sail it out into the Atlantic. They have to deal with us. They have no choice but to deal with the rest of Canada. Can we not try and understand part of what they want?

Nash: Do you worry that we may get into an acrimonious split?

Peterson: That is a possibility because of the economics that are involved. And it could be bad in subterfuged feelings. I know as a member of the black race, subterfuged feelings can hurt a lot more than displayed feelings. This stupidity of "I hate the French" and "I hate the English." First of all, that has to go. You can't sit down to a table with somebody that you really and truly hate to discuss something. You can't do it. And this thing about "Let them go. We are better off without them," that attitude doesn't work either.

Nash: What happens to the rest of Canada if Quebec does separate? Do we carry on as we are, do we break into small groups, do we get drawn to the United States?

Peterson: I will tell you one thing, if we are drawn to the United States, what happens to all of our history? If Canadians really want to give up their history, regardless of what region you are talking about that may go, then I am devastated, because I can't believe that people would give up something as important as their own history. We have within us the capacity to redevelop and restructure a new Canada.

Nash: Then the question is, do we have the will to do that?

Peterson: I hate to tell you, but I don't think some people do. Another thing that bothers me is that we are not really using the ethnic inflow that we have to its full capability. I think we could learn a lot from them. We could learn more about the world.

Nash: Doesn't there need to be more awareness of what is going on in the rest of Canada, let alone what is going on in the rest of the world?

Peterson: We don't know our own country. Does anyone really think that you could walk down the street in Vancouver and ask someone to describe Nova Scotia to you. Could they?

Nash: What can we do about that?

Peterson: We need a better educational system. That always is at the root of it. Our education system has slumped so badly in the last while that it's almost embarrassing. I know this from teaching music. Once you reinvigorate youngsters' minds, they start reaching out. As a teacher, you have to generate excitement.

Nash: And that is what we are missing, the excitement of what is Canada?

Peterson: That's right.

Nash: Will this debate help us do that, do you think?

Peterson: I hope so. The bad thing about this is that the problem at the moment is all being focussed on Quebec. It is not a Quebec problem. It is a Canadian problem. That is the thing we don't understand. If we gave Quebec whatever they wanted today, where would the rest of Canada be? We'd still be in trouble dealing with one another. There would still be trouble between people from Ontario and people from British Columbia. So, what we have to do is try to understand each other.

EDWARD MCWHINNEY

Edward McWhinney is professor of constitutional and international law at Simon Fraser University in Vancouver. He is a member of the Permanent Court of Arbitration and has been a visiting professor at the University in Tokyo. He has been a special adviser to the Canadian United Nations delegation, and is the author of twenty-two books.

"Break [Ontario] up into three provinces."

Nash: On the assumption that Quebec will separate, you've suggested the possibility of splitting up Ontario into two or three parts. Could you explain that a bit?

McWhinney: The reason for this, of course, is that a federal system with one unit that has 50 per cent of the population, 60 per cent of the wealth, and half the members of Parliament is just unacceptable. We in British Columbia would have to go ourselves, and others would have to consider separation, or we would have to consider rewriting the federal system. And the easiest way to do that is to break up a large province with disproportionate powers and population.

Nash: How many pieces would you break Ontario into?

McWhinney: Ontario couldn't be much more powerful than, say, British Columbia, so you probably would have to break it up into three provinces. You would probably add northwestern Ontario to Manitoba, and you would re-examine the area on the Quebec border. I am also an advocate for making large cities into provinces.

Nash: That would be Toronto, but what about Vancouver?

McWhinney: I think so. I think you can make a case. Vancouver probably is more marginal, because there wouldn't be much of the province left. There would be the minerals and the coal and the tourism, but you would miss the population base. But Toronto and Montreal are obvious examples of political units that should be separated from the hinterland.

Nash: Would that in a sense make Toronto, and perhaps Vancouver, something like a Singapore or a Hong Kong?

McWhinney: I think the better example would be Bremen, Hamburg, and Berlin. They are provinces, Länders they're called, within the German Federation. The really interesting government is in the cities, because that is where the problems are. The unemployed are there, the immigrants are there, the delinquent kids are there, the gangs are there, the drugs are there, and the exciting, interesting people are there. The media are there, the professions, too. So the city has a life-form and style of its own. You see this contrast somewhat unhappily in provinces like Ontario, where you have a conservative and traditional hinterland and an up-and-coming world city. The tensions are there, and they probably would be better off if they were separate.

Nash: Have you any sense of political support for that idea?

McWhinney: No. I am simply saying that, if I were advising, and if Quebec left, then one would have to tell the Ontario premier, "Look, we cannot tolerate a federal system in which Ontario remains as it is. There have got to be fundamental changes." We probably would have to consider geographic restructuring, and we have to take the lead. If Ontario won't accept, we simply lay down the law. The Constitution would be broken anyway, so we would have to have a constituent assembly and a new split.

Nash: Suppose Quebec does stay, and we fashion a new Canada, would your ideas about Toronto and possibly Vancouver still be valid?

McWhinney: They'd make a good deal of sense if what you

are emphasizing is modernizing the Constitution. But if what you are doing is simply solving the Quebec problem, they are not nearly as urgent. Our Constitution is out of date in many areas, and one of the areas is modernization, the restructuring of the provinces in their relation to the federal government, and restructuring provincial boundaries.

Nash: You would fundamentally redraw the map of Canada, whether Quebec is in or out?

McWhinney: The Constitution is overdue for modernization, even apart from the Quebec issue. If I were the prime minister, I would come out with a full program of modernization. I would give people some poetry. If it's just a matter of keeping Quebec in, it is very difficult to rally the troops, for example, of British Columbia, to the notion that they have to keep Quebec in because it is the number one problem. The number one problem in British Columbia is conquering the fear of economic insecurity and wondering about the future of Canada in this larger world.

Nash: You look on this constitutional crisis, not so much with a preoccupation with Quebec, but rather as an opportunity for a total rewriting.

McWhinney: I think every country should re-examine its fundamentals every now and again, and restructure its institutional processes accordingly. The failure of Meech was that the proposals were just presented by an élite in Ottawa and in the provincial capitals as a way of keeping Quebec happy. That's not a way to approach a people with constitutional change. You've got to get them involved.

Nash: You want people to get more involved in the process of governing.

McWhinney: I am a great believer in referenda, although plebiscite is the term I prefer, because I don't think they have to be legally binding. A plebiscite is an expression of opinion. Abortion, the mandatory retirement issue, the cruise missile issue, these are the sort of issues in my view that you should let people decide.

Nash: What's your sense about the outcome of all this? There is an effective deadline, if you will, of October 1992.

McWhinney: Under present conditions, I think there'll be a stalemate and then several things may happen that prevent catastrophe, assuming catastrophe is Quebec leaving. First, the separatist groups may find that economically the news from New York and elsewhere is bad. Second, Bourassa may finally assert his authority. He is a man who likes to react not to lead, he waits for a consensus, but he may have to assert his authority and make the decision himself that, on economic grounds, he wants Quebec to stay in, and he'll withdraw his ultimatum. He'll take more time.

Nash: What about the sovereignty association idea, which may overcome some of the economic implications?

McWhinney: If separation occurs, one hopes it will be civilized. If Quebec is to go, and we have the good sense to make sure that it is a peaceful and amicable separation, then sovereignty could work. You could probably have a Canada very similar to what we have now, except we don't now have two different sovereign entities.

Nash: Would that kind of thing be acceptable to the other provinces?

McWhinney: I think so. I think people have a remarkable capacity to adjust to reality when it's presented to them.

Nash: There seems to have always been a conflict between the federal centre in Ottawa and the provinces.

McWhinney: We are at the end of an era. We are at the end of half a century of strong centralization. All over the world, there's a feeling that government can get so big and so remote that you've got to bring it down to earth. The most exciting part of government in Canada is municipal government. It's where all the problems are.

Nash: How would you transfer power from Ottawa into the municipal areas?

McWhinney: I think you've got to make the municipalities a third element in Confederation. We've got this two-level approach, federal government and provinces, but when you look at the budget of Toronto, or Vancouver, you realize they have no independent financial autonomy, very minor taxing authority, no law-making power, only rule- and ordinance-making power, and no constitutions of their own. They are the creatures of the provincial government. The dynamic people are bypassing the provincial government and they are not going to Ottawa. You are getting a lot of interesting younger people in city government. So, give a new vision and power to local governmnent, where people can actively participate in legislation. But to achieve it you may have to go around the provinces.

Nash: In a way, you are advocating city states as against the nation state.

McWhinney: Nations are out of date, although nationalism isn't.

Nash: What do you think will happen in the next five years?

McWhinney: We are not going to get a repetition of Meech Lake, I am sure of that. I do not envision ten premiers signing an agreement with the prime minister and then going back to their legislatures and getting it ratified. First of all, the public is going to have to be involved. Provinces are going to have to go to their voters and say, "Here are the proposals," and they are going to have to take a position: "I recommend you adopt," "I recommend you reject," or "I am washing my hands of this." This is going to change the substance of the proposals. If a British Columbia premier comes to the people, and all he can say is that it will keep Quebec in, then he is dead and the proposals are dead.

Nash: Is there time?

McWhinney: Napoleon codified the French civil laws in three months. He insisted on presiding at the commission himself and he said, "Look gentlemen, this has got to be adopted in three months," and it was. It's beautiful. It's the leadership element. It's the confidence.

Nash: Do we have that confidence and that leadership?

McWhinney: The old political parties have all gone. They have been so lazy and, in a polite way, corrupt. I think people are getting really fed up and you will start seeing lots of new people in the political processes.

GUY LAFOREST

Professor Guy Laforest was born in Quebec City in 1955 and was educated at the universities of Ottawa, Laval, and McGill. He taught at the University of Calgary 1986–1988, and is now director of undergraduate studies in Political Science at Université Laval. He is the author of numerous articles on political issues within Quebec and has appeared as an expert witness at several commissions examining Canada's constitutional problems and Quebec's future. Professor Laforest is on the Advisory Council of the Institute of Intergovernmental Relations at Queens University, and is book review editor (French) for the Canadian Journal of Political Science.

"The man who really rolled the dice . . . was Trudeau."

Nash: What kind of response to Quebec would you want to see from English-speaking Canada?
Laforest: I don't think anybody in Quebec is expecting that all the powers required by Allaire will be offered, and I don't think they were meant for this. They were meant to make the rest of the country realize that the status quo will not be the option this time around.
Nash: If you don't have the status quo, what kind of change must there be?
Laforest: There must be devolution of a number of powers, including such things as language, culture, communications,

immigration, regional development, education, all the areas that are being invaded by the feds right now. This will be the easiest part to deal with – administrative arrangements and the division of power.

Nash: If that's easy, what's the hard part?

Laforest: The hard part is a mixture of two things. One is the symbols of nationhood. The failure of Meech is symbolically extraordinarily important. It was the first time that Quebec presented a self-formulation to the rest of the country and said, "If you accept this self-formulation, then we will feel reasonably comfortable within the federal system." But this self-formulation was rejected, and it was a devastating blow to the political-social contract in Canada. What will be required now is something similar but something more important than what distinct society means. On this level of symbols of nationhood and identity, Quebec can only come back with sharper, stronger demands, so it will be distinct society plus something like recognition and acceptance of Quebec as an autonomous national community.

The second thing is the Charter of Rights issue. We are often told that the fight between the Charter and the distinct society clause is a philosophical battle between defenders of the pre-eminence of liberal rights, individual rights, and defenders of the pre-eminence of collective or community rights. The scholars of the Charter tell us that it contains a mixture of rights, not only liberal, individual rights, but also community rights – Section 27 on multiculturalism, sections for aboriginal people, sections protecting endangered provincial communities' economic place. The Charter is a different bill of rights than the American one. It's more generous to particular ways of life than the American Bill of Rights.

The Charter is an attempt, and this was an intention on the part of its founders, Mr. Trudeau and the men around him, to make sure that there would be the creation of what Mr. Trudeau calls a new Canadian nationality that would be identical, homogeneous from sea to sea. At the heart of this there is a negation of Quebec's identity as a people, as an autonomous national community. Meech was English-speaking Canadians telling Quebec, not that they shouldn't have collective rights, but that they shouldn't have collective rights any different from the rest of Canadians. This is terrible. It is a rejection of distinct society. So, the federal government has to work on these three things: powers, symbols of nationhood, and the Charter. What Quebec is bound to demand is acceptance of the primacy of the Quebec Charter.

Nash: So the counter-offer from English-speaking Canada has to accept the duality, the distinct society, and then be specific about what that actually means in many areas.

Laforest: Quebec is bound to demand duality. You have to find a place for it somewhere in the political system. It is not going to be easy. It is going to be extraordinarily difficult. The failure of Meech raised the stakes with regard to this. And the man who really rolled the dice was not Mulroney. The man who rolled the dice was the man who undermined Meech in the first place, and that is the former prime minister himself – Trudeau. In his contribution to the Senate hearings on Meech Lake he said, "We have to be aware of the fact that there is a risk," and he said it is worth being taken. He rolled the dice then, and I think if the country ruptures, a fair share of the burden of blame should be on his shoulders. He wanted an absolute victory over his arch-enemies.

Nash: The gap seems to be so large at this point, what's your sense of what will happen and whether that gap can be bridged?

Laforest: Now, less than at any other moment in our political history in this century, do our politicians have full control of the situation. Nobody has control of the situation. My worst-case scenario is the federal government, out of despair, holding a Canadian referendum.

Nash: Why would a national referendum spring from such despair?

Laforest: Quebec nationalists like myself see Quebec as being autonomous, as having the right to self-determination. So the national referendum for us is a Quebec referendum. A referendum run by the federal government in Quebec is an illegitimate act, and I for one suggest it would bring massive civil disobedience.

Nash: Is there a gap within Quebec between the élites of academia, of business, of media, of labour, and the people themselves? The majority obviously are sovereigntists, but sovereignty covers a massive number of options.

Laforest: I think gaps like that exist in all liberal democratic societies. However, I think the thrust of Quebec nationalism has been changed by the referendum of 1980, and by 1981 and 1982. Quebec has had the momentum. There was that positive momentum building up from the Quiet Revolution. That momentum was stopped by 1980, 1982. At the level of the population, Quebec nationalism is now mostly a reactive phenomena. That does not mean it is a powerless phenomena. Actually, the power of reacting to events can be massive and extremely threatening for Canada. People at all levels of society understand in their bones what 1982 and the Charter of Rights was all about. It was like a second Conquest. The powers of the National Assembly in Quebec were reduced by the Charter, by the new Constitution, without the consent of either the government or the people.

Nash: What's your personal desire for the future of Canada?

Laforest: Associate states. The view that has been taken so far is that the European model is going the direction of political integration, and here in Quebec you have a movement that is going in the direction of past history. The real way to talk about these movements is to talk about the levels of integration desired by the people. Let's have a scale of integration, economic and political. Some people are saying that right now in Canada what we have is maximal federalism, with residuary powers in the hands of the federal government – a quasi-unitary regime. Let's call this a hundred on the scale, and let's say that Europe right now is at something between twenty and twenty-five and would like to go to fifty maybe in ten or twenty years. Quebec would be quite satisfied with what Europe could be like twenty years down the road. Quebec wants to reduce the degree of integration between our societies that we have right now. Right now, there is not enough distance between Quebec and the rest of Canada. Quebec wants to establish that distance, and I don't see how it can do that without first rupturing the federal arrangement, getting out of the federal arrangement. So I think it will be impossible for the feds to formulate an offer that will sell either in English-speaking Canada or in Quebec. The crisis will worsen, and there will be a referendum in Quebec, or the federal system will be paralyzed by an election, where Reform and Bloc Québécois will win. Quebec will go into a period of political sovereignty. So there will be some resentment. And fifteen or twenty years down the road you have a new form of association between Quebec and Canada, and that's what I call associate states.

Nash: So you see a total rupture at the beginning and then, in time, a coming together?

Laforest: The healing could be more rapid. I think a messy transition is in nobody's interst. Right now what you have is a compound crisis: a symbolic, economic, political, cultural crisis. English-speaking Canada is wondering what multiculturalism is doing to it. This crisis more or less has paralyzed the regime and, in a sense, it's Quebec breaking the impasse that could be the way towards a more lucid and functional restructuring, not only of the relationship between Quebec and the rest of Canada, but of Canada getting itself finally a national identity it can live with for a long time.

Nash: Don't you think the negotiations over debt and assets and boundaries could get pretty bitter and acrimonious, and that there could be some longevity to that distress?

Laforest: Undeniably so. There is that distinct possibility. Nobody thinks that this is going to be a cup of tea. Quebec is going towards this reluctantly. There is no ode to joy going on. We're aware of the perils, but measuring the alternatives.

Nash: Why do you think Quebec would be better off separately than as part of Canada? What are the benefits that the people of Quebec would gain?

Laforest: The prospect is for a relatively small, coherent, market-oriented society being efficient, finding niches out there in the world of competitive markets, with close relationships between the corporate world and the state. The market nationalists tell us this could be achieved in a much more efficient, rational, and cost-beneficial way if Quebec were alone They are saying there will be an economic cost for the transition but in twenty, twenty-five years, we'll have rearranged it to our advantage. You can make a reasonably plausible argument that, in the context of market globalization, the Quebec business class allied with the Quebec state would do a better job.

Nash: You are saying then that there would be obvious difficulties and problems for twenty, twenty-five years, but at the end of that time, Quebec would be better off?

Laforest: Yes. The argument still is that Quebec could be better off economically in twenty, twenty-five years than what it would be if we maintained the current situation. We in Quebec have a chance to formulate a new Quebec for the twenty-first century. It would be a predominantly French society, but not an exclusively French society. Some people, the old guard, are less enthusiastic about what the immigrants or what the anglophones can contribute to that new Quebec, but there are others, and they are gaining ground, who have a tolerant and generous vision of a new Quebec. They are saying that, in a sense, Quebec can be successful in accepting deep diversity, can be more successful than the Canada of 1867 to 1982 has been. That would mean, of course, guaranteeing minority rights, and being much more generous *vis à vis* public signs, control of institutions.

Nash: You are saying that a separate Quebec would be more generous to its anglophones than today's Quebec?

Laforest: Yes. Actually right now it's the weight of 1982 that, in a sense, prevents things from working much better between communities in Quebec.

Nash: There is the question of the Native people in Quebec and their desires. If Canada is divisible, is Quebec then divisible, thinking of the Cree in the north?

Laforest: No territory is indivisible. If there is a restructuring of one Canada from the Atlantic to the Pacific, there is strong likelihood that Ontario would have to be divided to keep the West content. The James Bay area is central to the economy and the development of Quebec, so it's in the immediate very best interests of Quebec to make the situation such that something like a matter of declaration of independence on the part of the Cree in the North will not take place. Quebec is not blind to the relationship between the federal government and some leaders of the Indian communities in Northern Quebec. We are in a power game and I think the Quebec leadership is aware of it, but it is not without means itself.

Nash: What's more important to you, power or pride?

Laforest: It's a combination of both. Pride alone is not enough. Symbolic powers will not be enough. Real power is necessary.

Nash: Reaffirmation of duality in a rhetorical sense won't be enough then. There will have to be specifics of how that applies?

Laforest: For instance, recognition of a distinct society in a preamble to either the Charter or the Constitution is not enough. That recognition has to be operative in what constitutes the essential functioning of the political regime. The distinctiveness of Quebec must have immediate, substantial, political consequences on how the system works.

Nash: The consequences that you want are so far away from what English-speaking Canada probably can manage to agree to that the gap seems to be almost unbridgeable. One wonders then is all of this a waste of time, and shouldn't we go straight to the divorce court?

Laforest: You have to recognize that if you want strong political integration with Quebec you have first to let Quebec assume its political autonomy as soon as possible. The longer we wait, the more difficult it will be.

Nash: Is a referendum the end of the road insofar as the united Canada is concerned?

Laforest: The road could be from federalism to sovereignty back to federalism. My sense is that, if an approriate offer containing a mixture of elements was offered, the majority of the Quebec population would take it. The discussion is about the threshhold of acceptability. When does an offer become acceptable? It would have to have ingredients under the three things that I mentioned: symbols of nationhood, relationship of the charters, and devolution of powers. You have to address concerns on these three to make an offer acceptable.

Nash: What devolution of powers?

Laforest: It's harder to give more powers to Quebec as long as it has the status of a province, than it would be if you said, "We are not a normal country. We must establish our own norm, and our norm is that we are a multinational state. We have nine provinces and one autonomous nation within the Canadian federal state." If you said that, people would probably accept more powers for Quebec more easily than if you said Quebec is a province. I think that would pass. The Canadian sickness is this obsession with normality, the thought that Canada must be a normal state. Canada has never been a normal state, and that drive towards normality will kill it.

AL JOHNSON

Saskatchewan-born Al Johnson has been in public service since 1945, serving as deputy treasurer in Saskatchewan for twelve years before joining the federal public service. Johnson was assistant deputy minister of Finance 1964–68, responsible for developing the equalization payments formula and medicare and post-secondary education financing arrangements. In 1966 he was appointed economic adviser to the prime minister on the Constitution. He was secretary of the Treasury Board, deputy minister of National Health and Welfare, and in 1975 became president of the CBC for a seven-year term. Most recently he has taught at Queen's University in Kingston, Ontario, and at the University of Toronto.

"An eviscerated Canada versus a truncated Canada."

Nash: You have very deep roots on the Prairies, but you've also had a great deal of national experience. Do you think Canadians really care about this question of the Constitution and the future of the nation?

Johnson: I think Canadians care very deeply about what they conceive to be their identity. They perceive their value system to be quite different from the one that we always compare ourselves with. Probably though, they don't usually think in terms of freedom and fairness and justice and so on. But I think this deepens the underlying, unifying bond. If you feel at home in B.C. or Toronto or Halifax, you have to ask yourself why. It isn't the trappings of Canadianism, it is talking to somebody and knowing that you are starting from the same base.

Nash: Do you sense that there is a will to preserve that identity?

Johnson: Yes. When I spent two weeks out west not long ago, I wanted to find out what people really were thinking, and I asked whether they thought if Quebec were to leave, Canada would fall apart, and they all just looked at me as if I were crazy. They said, "Absolutely not!" On Tom Courchene's argument that we would break into smaller sets of regions, I got two kinds of reaction. One was just complete puzzlement. "Why would we do that?" It just made no sense to people. When I asked one gentleman about regionalism, he said, "Do you mean the Prairies would form a region?" I said, " Yes, that is the argument," and he said, "Look, I just got one question now Johnson. Who is going to represent me at GATT? Is it going to be a giant, or is it going to be a minnow? I want a giant."

Nash: If he wants a giant, it's because he sees strength in a united Canada going to GATT. What would he be prepared to sacrifice to maintain that unity?

Johnson: I don't think the people I've talked to are prepared to talk about the devolution of powers. For them it's a Hobson's Choice. They are being told on the one hand that you might be able to keep Canada whole provided you eviscerate Canada. So it's an eviscerated Canada versus a truncated Canada, and they are not prepared to discuss that. Canadians to whom I have talked across the country have just said, "Look, we are past that stage. We are not prepared to discuss ripping up the national government, and then saying somehow or other we have retained Canada, because we haven't."

Nash: The powers that Quebec sees that it must have all involve the devolution of power from the centre to the provinces, and to Quebec specifically.

Johnson: Bourassa's agenda is to say, "Make me an offer." As you look at decentralizing, are you going to reduce the economic powers of Canada? The economic powers of Canada are not now sufficient to meet the challenges of the twenty-first century. We don't even now have the powers that Canada needs, that the national government needs, in the economic field, in the environmental field. You are not going to solve environmental problems by the devolution of powers to the provinces.

Nash: So, what has the Quebec premier done to the debate?

Johnson: What Mr. Bourassa has done in substance has been to say, "Because we want these powers, we are prepared to see the whole of Canada eviscerated in terms of its effective functioning in the future." I put it to you that Canadians aren't going to go along with that. Now in the process, Bourassa has done something else that makes it even more impossible, and that is, he has invited English Canada to make an offer. "Make me an offer I can accept." That turns the Canadian nation into a kind of auction. Who is the highest bidder? I think that repulses most Canadians. In substance and in form, Mr. Bourassa is wrong, and the problem for we who believe in a unified country, and who want very much for Quebec to stay, is that we have to find a way that is credible, that does not go the evisceration route and, hopefully, heads off the truncation route.

Nash: How would it hold off those routes if the only federalist thrust in Quebec is Mr. Bourassa, and he is federalist only in comparison with the Parti Québécois?

Johnson: This is a desperate situation in which we find ourselves, and it is the doing of Mr. Bourassa and of the nationalists in Quebec. If Mr. Bourassa had been a federalist, he would have stood up long, long ago for federalism, and he has not done that. If he listens to the swell of opinion among the élites in Quebec, and that's who he is listening to, then he has got to be a sovereigntist. If he is faithful to the Allaire report and to the nationalist colleagues with whom he is associated, how can he accept anything other than a massive devolution of powers to Quebec? He wants a Canada that would have the power to provide a safety net in the form of a monetary union, so that Quebec's balance of payments problems of the future would be Canada's and that Canada would still pay equalization payments to Quebec. There would be a constitutional safety net in that Quebec would have a veto over any constitutional change in Canada, and there would be a defence safety net in the sense that the Canadian army would defend Quebec.

Nash: Would those be acceptable terms to English Canadians?

Johnson: No. Everything I have read and everything I have heard is that the Allaire report is simply preposterous. It is simply out of the question.

Nash: You are very pessimistic, I take it, about the possibility of at the end of the day of there being a united Canada.

Johnson: I am very pessimistic indeed. I am fully convinced that the kind of devolution that is demanded will eviscerate the country. They would be saving the country in order to lose it. I think we have to say to Quebeckers one short thing and one long thing. The short thing is, "You must understand that if you vote for independence, it is independence, period. There is no assurance whatsoever that you are going to get the economic union that the Parti Québécois has been promising you since its very beginning." We will also have to settle the question of territory in the North, whether it really belongs to the Native peoples, because the territory was given to Quebec by a statute of Parliament, it's not in the Constitution. We will have to settle the question of a corridor to the Atlantic provinces. For any of us who have roots in the Atlantic provinces, and one side of my family came to Newfoundland around 1800, I feel we will insist on a corridor. Western Quebec may decide that it doesn't want to join an independent Quebec. There are terrible separation problems.

Nash: But those are the kinds of problems that can lead to acrimony.

Johnson: Lead to terrible acrimony. I would say to Quebeckers, "Look, understand that this is a vote for independence. Understand that the probability of there being an economic union is small, given the dynamics of the situation." Free trade, yes. I don't think anybody is against the free movement of persons and goods and services and capital, but an economic union, which involves a government apparatus, is very unlikely. The second, long thing I would say to Quebeckers is, "Look, we really believe in a complete overhaul of the constitution, an overhaul that would lead to some fundamental changes." That new constitution would have five pillars.

Nash: And what would they be?

Johnson: The first pillar would be ringing affirmation of Canadian nationhood and its values, identities, and the collectivities of Canada, starting with a distinct society of aboriginal peoples, a distinct society of Quebec, and all collectivities that have participated in founding this country and nourishing this country. The second pillar would be a charter of human rights and freedoms, and I would take the Charter pretty much as it is. The third pillar would be the overhaul of the institutions of federalism. The first part of this pillar would be that we had a free market, that nobody could erect official barriers.

Nash: Barriers between the provinces?

Johnson: Yes, between the provinces. Nobody could do that. Neither the provincial governments nor the federal government. This would have enormously beneficial economic results. The second part of the pillar is to reform the Senate so that we complement representation by population in the House of Commons with representation by province in the Senate. I would have an elected Senate. I would have an effective Senate, but not to the point of the Senate having a veto as the Senate has in Australia. Suspensive veto and no more than that. I would have a Senate more equal, but not completely equal. I would not go as far as the Americans, but I would greatly increase the representation of the smaller provinces, the Atlantic provinces and the Prairies. My fourth pillar would be a completely new approach to the distribution of powers. We should look at the distribution of powers in a functional sense: Which government is best able to do what.

Nash: So, zero-base constitution building.

Johnson: Zero-base constitution building. A principle you have to bear in mind is that the nation of watertight compartments is dead. There is a national dimension and there is a provincial dimension, not to all functions of government, but to a great many of them.

Nash: In other words, a good deal of shared jurisdiction.

Johnson: Yes. So I would have, in short, a complete review and overhaul of the distribution of powers. Then a fifth pillar with a new kind of right to complement the equality rights and the democratic rights and the mobility rights and the legal rights of the Charter. I would say we have to find a way of saying explicitly that some body, and manifestly it must be Parliament, must have the power to affirm certain social rights for Canadians. It's a kind of incarnation in national programs of the value system that Canadians share.

Nash: What kind of social rights?

Johnson: Let me give you two. One is we believe that all the citizens of Canada should be entitled to a decent level of provincial services, without paying exorbitant taxes, and that is the equalization formula. A second social right would be the responsibility of the national government to achieve a fair distribution of income and, at least for some people, to provide income support where they are unnaturally unemployed or employed at a very low income. And I would add to that medicare, and we would say that this is a social right of citizenship. Provincial governments will administer it, but there will be this affirmation by the national government. And over time, we will find other social rights we are prepared to affirm.

The people to whom I am talking when I talk this way are the people of Quebec, never the politicians. I spent so long around that federal-provincial conference table watching the battle over powers that was taking place to the almost total disregard of what happened to the people, that I am persuaded that the Quebec people may take a different view when faced with the stark realities of the situation in which their premier has got them.

Nash: What about bilingualism?

Johnson: Well, if Quebec departs, and if the people of Quebec say, "No, we would just as soon have our own nation," then I think the only realistic conclusion one can come to is that while you would have institutionalized bilingualism in New Brunswick, as more than three-fifths of the population is Acadian, you wouldn't have official bilingualism across the country.

Nash: You are directing your thoughts to people rather than to politicians and élites.

Johnson: Lying behind all of these discussions on the Constitution is your first question: Do Canadians share something? What do they feel they have in common? With almost all of us, we stumble. We are not good about beating our breast or talking about our flag and doing all the symbolic things that the Americans enjoy doing. But for our value system to survive, we have to see that it really exists in the rest of the country. We have to see one another and we have to understand one another.

REED SCOWEN

Reed Scowen is a senior adviser on investments to the Quebec Government and a former member of the Quebec National Assembly. He served as parliamentary assistant and economic adviser to Premier Bourassa and was executive director of the Pepin-Robarts Task Force on Canadian Unity. He has advised upon and written about the anglophone community in Quebec, and in June 1991 was named chairman of Alliance Quebec, the English rights lobby group.

"Most of what Quebec wants . . . is psychic satisfaction."

Nash: What does Quebec want, in your judgement?
Scowen: Most of what Quebec wants at the present time is psychic satisfaction. A little bit of what Quebec wants is freedom to do certain things without interference from Ottawa. Take the example of the environmental issue and James Bay. I think most Quebeckers would say they are as well equipped to make value judgements on their relationships with the Indians and their environment in the north of Quebec as Ottawa is.
Nash: How deeply is the demand for sovereignty felt?
Scowen: You can identify several things. Above all, you can identify the age-old linguistic, ethnic tensions between English and French. Secondly, from that flows a normal feeling that French-speaking Quebeckers should be allowed to do most things, unless there is a clearly stated reason why it's

against their interest to do things themselves. The other thing is a broad feeling, which has caught up the business élite of the province, that Canada isn't being run well, that the place is badly managed, and they are running up deficits in Ottawa that are unacceptable.

Nash: You have known Mr. Bourassa very well for a long time. What's your sense of what he's seeking in the end.

Scowen: His first objective is to stay prime minister of a strong Quebec. I think his basic inclinations are more for retaining a union with Canada than towards getting rid of it, but he's certainly not a strong Canadian federalist, and he certainly will be behind, not ahead, of the population in any decisions that are going to be made about constitutional changes.

Nash: Essentially then, he is more of a tactician than a strategist in all this?

Scowen: Yes. I think Mr. Bourassa's profound convictions are sound fiscal policies. You ask yourself, what do politicians think about when they get up in the morning and start shaving and there is nobody around to interview them and nobody to set the agenda for them? Mr. Bourassa doesn't think about the Constitution, and he doesn't think about economic development, either. He thinks about fiscal policy. The second thing he thinks about, or used to, is energy policy. The Constitution would come third. The part of the constitutional debate that he doesn't like is the emotional part, because he can't understand why people won't behave rationally. I think reason tells him it's best for Quebec to have a strong economic union with the rest of the country.

Nash: Would a strong economic union mean sovereignty association rather than being part of a united Canada?

Scowen: These words mean different things to different people. I think we've got sovereignty association right now. I think that's what the federation is all about. I don't think Mr. Bourassa would be upset if he found himself with an independent Quebec in a confederation rather than in a federation. That is to say, that the only central institution would look like the one in Brussels, with representatives essentially appointed by the sovereign states to make common decisions, majority decisions.

Nash: This is the European Community.

Scowen: Yes. I think an arrangement like that would effectively mean the end of Canada as we know it. Mr. Bourassa could live with that. It would provide him with the economic framework so that Quebec wouldn't be isolated, and it would provide Quebec with the psychic satisfaction of an independent country.

Nash: What's your sense of this country? What should it be?

Scowen: I'm almost ashamed to say that I am not a very strong Quebec patriot, and I am not a very strong Canadian patriot.

Nash: What are you?

Scowen: What interests me is the creation of a civil society in which people can first of all obtain a constitution and a charter that guarantees basic civil liberties. The second thing is I would like to find a place where we have an economic space that enables us to remain relevant in the world, and by that I mean competitive and prosperous. Unless you remain competitive and prosperous, your hospitals deteriorate, you can't take care of poor people, your roads don't function, and so on. The third thing I would like to see is a society in which those powers are placed at appropriate levels of government, so that the citizen is able to retain some contact with, and feeling for, and feel he has some control over, his elected representatives.

Nash: What role does emotion play in all this, the emotion you say worries Bourassa?

Scowen: Emotion makes analysis of these issues more difficult. Somewhere in each person's heart there is a small cell of Canadian patriotism, and there are places where the more dedicated patriots are grouped together. In some of the universities, in Toronto, for instance, the emotional fires are burning brighter in English Canada than I have seen in a long time. I guess what is fuelling them is essentially a reaction to Quebec.

Nash: Is it good for a resolution of the constitutional confrontation to have had those fires burning?

Scowen: In my ideal world they wouldn't exist, but they're a given, and a little bit of emotion is essential, because it provides a nice glue to hold something together once you have built it. It doesn't help you build it. I've always thought that one gesture that might be made, but I don't know whether we are ready for it yet, is to abandon our ties to Great Britain.

Nash: To the monarchy?

Scowen: Yes. I am not arguing about whether the Queen is a nice person. I think she is wonderful. But this is the New World, after all, and we came here, many of us, to get away from all that. Certainly we've got a supreme symbol in this country to which a very large number of one particular sect are hostile.

Nash: You are talking about Quebec.

Scowen: Yes. The English came here in 1759 and conquered the French, and so be it. But here we are 230 years later, and the Queen still stands there as the ultimate symbol of the unity of the country. To me, it's unnecessary, and we should be able to do better than that.

Nash: What's your sense of the implications if Quebec did separate or become sovereign?

Scowen: I can't see any way in which Quebec can, in fact, become very much more independent than it is today.

Nash: Mr. Parizeau certainly wouldn't agree with you.

Scowen: No, that's right, but there have always been people saying what Mr. Parizeau says. My guess is that a lot of the heat is going to go out of this debate over the next while, and as the heat goes down, the light will begin to shine, and we will begin to look at the real issues. Quebec cannot become separate. Quebec cannot be towed out into the middle of the Atlantic Ocean. It must have close economic ties with the people around it, unless it wants to become a sort of Albania. The strength of these ties and the skill with which they are created will be affected by the emotion generated in the debate between the English and the French. If we can cool it down to room temperature, we stand a chance of coming up with something sensible. If we have to do it in a climate where everybody is throwing verbal brickbats at each other, there is less chance that we will get it right.

Nash: What do you think the broad lines of a deal might be?

Scowen: In the Allaire report, there are twenty-two areas that they want to be exclusively under Quebec jurisdiction. As I recall, eleven of them are already exclusively Quebec jurisdiction anyway. So you are down to eleven, and I would have thought about half of those could be quite easily transferred exclusively to Quebec without any danger to society.

Nash: With all of the debate and discussion about transfers of power and relative strengths in the provinces or in Ottawa, does it really matter to the average Canadian or average Quebecker who is working in a bank or driving a cab or working as a clerk in an office? Does it really matter to that person's life?

Scowen: Of course it does. It doesn't matter in the sense that he cares every morning any more than he cares about the latest prejudice that has been articulated on a hot-line show, but it will come back to him some day in the form of taxes or unemployment, if it isn't done right. Believe me, the bottom line is the price the cab driver is going to pay for his car and his gas, and whether there are going to be any customers out there.

JOHN POLANYI

Born in Berlin and educated in England, John Polanyi is today one of Canada's most honoured scientists. In 1986 he won the Nobel Prize for Chemistry for his work on infrared chemiluminescence. He is internationally recognized for his research on the dynamics of chemical reactions and has lectured at universities and forums around the world. He is an outspoken participant in public issues and is a board member of the Canadian Centre for Arms Control and Disarmament.

"Make an asymmetrical Canada."

Nash: What is a Canadian in your judgement?

Polanyi: There is more than a single Canadian. There are the Native people. There are people who have a two-hundred-year investment in this country; their roots may be French or English. There is another group, to which I belong, who are the more recent immigrants. So in this sense there are many categories of Canadians. There are those who are Canadian first and those who are Canadian second. By Canadian first or Canadian second, I am saying that I acknowledge the fact that those who live in Quebec will regard themselves as Québécois first and Canadian second – if we don't throw that away. I would count them both as Canadian because we can build a nation out of both. Not only can, but should, and, I think, will.

Nash: Do we have the will, English- and French-speaking Canadians, to have a united Canada?

Polanyi: I think there is no doubt that we have the will. The real doubt, of course, is if we have sufficient will, because we have to be willing to pay a price. I think people are asking for a degree of uniformity as a requirement for the existence of a nation, which goes beyond what is needed. It doesn't daunt the Europeans that there will be some sort of asymmetry there, comprising at least an inner and an outer category of membership in the new European Community.

Nash: What degree of asymmetry should we have in Canada? How different from other provinces can Quebec be?

Polanyi: Some say that we seem to be going in the opposite direction from Europe – disintegrating while Europe is integrating – and claim that as a paradox. I would say that it isn't quite as much of a paradox as it seems. What you see in Europe is what you see in Canada, which is a feeling that world history has reached a turning point and we can now re-examine in a fundamental way the manner in which we conduct our affairs. We should have the imagination and courage to try to build something new. That something new is going to be asymmetric because we must deal with an asymmetric reality. At this juncture, to treat other regions of Canada in the same way as we do Quebec is to me just unimaginative. What I hope we can do is make an asymmetric Canada, which is so attractive at its core that, as time passes, all the elements are drawn inward.

Nash: The worry that a lot of people have about extensive asymmetry is that you may weaken the centre, so that you have ten rather different little entities rather than a single strong nation.

Polanyi: I would argue that, on the contrary, this will happen if we insist on symmetry. Why should we take it for granted that the degree of devolution that Quebec today demands is advantageous for every region? Of course every region is entitled to claim it, but they'd be foolish to do so. We have a central government because it benefits us to have one. I might add that I don't think Quebec needs the degree of independence which it presently says it needs to have, by the way. Its distinct culture is guaranteed except for certain forces which have nothing to do with the rest of Canada. Nonetheless, we should not begrudge it the special status which flows from the Meech accord to which, in a fit of sanity and largesse of spirit, all the premiers of Canada at one time put their names.

Nash: Do we have enough time to come to an agreement?

Polanyi: I see views changing very fast and, of course, the time that we have remaining must be used to buy more time.

Nash: Do we need more passion about this country?

Polanyi: There is a lot of passion beneath the surface, which is where we tend to keep our passion. But one thing we should have is more knowledge about our country. The pressure of recent events has caused me to learn more about Canada, and also to realize how much I still have to learn.

Nash: Why did you come to this country?

Polanyi: I felt at home here. Perhaps I had found a country which has the right size of population so that it is an extended village. You don't get lost in it, except geographically. Until recently I found that I could reach people who can affect the course of events and talk to them and be heard. With the country as obsessed and as torn as it is now, I find it more difficult to do that. I was also attracted by the fact that ours is a country whose history lies in the future; a place where one can have hope.

Nash: We began the country as a duality, but we have profoundly changed since then and have become a truly multicultural nation. Is there a clash now between duality, which Quebec is talkng about, and our formal policy of multiculturalism?

Polanyi: I don't see a clash. We should be better able to come to terms with duality if we rejoice in diversity. But I don't regard questions about nations as being answerable once and for all. In science we refer to an entity like a nation as being in a state of dynamic equilibrium. We enjoy a continued existence as a nation because the forces pushing us together are approximately able to balance the forces tearing us apart.

All we should ask is that these forces be sufficiently close to equilibrium that we evolve rather than explode. There is no standing still.

Nash: Is there a particular role for scientists like yourself to play in this constitutional crisis?

Polanyi: I doubt it. We are merely citizens. If we have something to offer, it is the fact that we have seen our understanding of the physical world turned upside down in the course of a lifetime, and then seen science move on vastly stronger than ever before. We scientists ought not to be too timorous about change.

Nash: One of the keys to resolving this is finding an acceptable way to hear each other. So often it seems that we are in a dialogue of the deaf. Do you have a sense that we are beginning to hear each other?

Polanyi: Deafness, it turns out, isn't incurable. There is a sense in which I very much welcome the present turmoil. Changes have already occurred in perception and are further sharpening our minds. To answer your question, we are being forced to listen to each other as never before.

Nash: What would you like Canada to be in the year 2000?

Polanyi: A country is, as I have said, in a constant state of flux. It continues to exist by continuing to grow, so I see an ever-changing Canada. I hope and believe that the looser association with the province of Quebec will gradually give way to a wish on their part to be integrated more fully. If we are right in believing in Canada, it should become increasingly evident that it is advantageous to be close to the centre.

Nash: Do you then envision a Quebec pulling away either totally or partially and, in time, coming back together with Canada?

Polanyi: I don't want it to pull away totally, and that's why I am pleading for a Canada that acknowledges an asymmetry – which means for the present a loosening of the ties to Quebec.

Nash: The big question is, can those who favour symmetry swallow asymmetrical federalism? Can they swallow Quebec getting something that other provinces aren't getting?

Polanyi: Equity is not the same thing as advantage. There will, as most people acknowledge, be a cost to Quebec in moving away from the centre of decision-making. Why should others insist on paying that price, just because Quebec is determined to do so?

Nash: What are the reasons that you think we need Quebec as part of Canada?

Polanyi: Quebec helped shape this entire nation. Its culture is not, therefore, only to be found in the province of Quebec. To the extent that it is there, we need to import it. For example, I notice in my travels to Quebec the relative absence of anti-intellectualism. That is something we might learn. That and a vitality and confidence which we lack. One can also turn the question around and ask why Quebec needs us. Quebec needs us, I am being a bit facetious, rather in the way Scotland needs the United Kingdom. Scotland is a country, too, with its own history, its own language, its own culture, literature, even a half-baked currency. But Scotland is acknowledged to be too small for the Scots. So the best people from Scotland are busy running things in England. I would welcome it if the very best people in Quebec were running Canada. I hope that they will want to do so.

JACK WEBSTER

Glasgow-born Jack Webster is renowned throughout Canada, but especially in British Columbia, for his joyously pugnacious style of interviewing. A journalist in Glasgow, he emigrated to Canada in 1947 and became a reporter for the Vancouver Sun. Subsequently, Webster found his métier in open-line radio, and for twenty-seven years he anchored hard-hitting, highly popular phone-in and interview programs, championing those with grievances against authority. Later he transferred his style and popularity to television, from which he retired in 1987. Since then, he has been in high demand as a speaker, has written his autobiography, and is a panelist on the CBC show "Front Page Challenge."

"Anything is better than outright separation."

Nash: How important to you is it for you to be a Canadian?
Webster: One hundred per cent totally important. I became a Canadian citizen five years to the day I came to this country. I made that a point of principle. I don't feel anything except a Canadian. I am not a British Columbian first and a Canadian second.
Nash: As a Canadian, you must get alarmed by what you see happening right now.
Webster: I think we are on the verge on disaster unless people stop quibbling and nit-picking about bits and bloody

pieces and remember that if you take Quebec out of this country, there ain't no country left.

Nash: What do you think the chances are at this point?

Webster: I hope there will be a flood of common sense. One of the biggest disadvantages at the moment is that we lack anybody in the way of a good strong political leader. That's quite serious.

Nash: You speak of yourself as a Canadian nationalist, but how do you define a Canadian?

Webster: We are a modest kind of people. We have a great international reputation, or had a great international reputation, as the honest brokers. I don't feel any less of a Canadian when I am in Winnipeg or in Toronto. I feel a little bit strange in Ottawa.

Nash: How about Quebec?

Webster: One of my faults is that I have been in Quebec only maybe a dozen times in forty-five years, to go to Expo 67 and to cover the FLQ and the 1980 Referendum.

Nash: How important do you feel it is for Quebec to be within the Canadian confederation?

Webster: Without Quebec we are a fragmented land mass, which is in danger of being further fragmented. An accommodation must be made with Quebec, even if we have to swallow a little bit.

Nash: What kind of things do you think we might swallow?

Webster: The distinct society. I think we could swallow the distinct society, providing there was no overt discrimination.

Nash: What about bilingualism? It's become a flash-point of distress for some people.

Webster: Only among the older generation as far as I am concerned. People are still very strong on the French immersion courses. Mind you, it's a Yuppie move. All the Yuppies want to be bilingual because they realize it adds to their own culture.

Nash: You do a lot of travelling, and you keep your finger on the public pulse, what's your sense of the public mood about Quebec and our future?

Webster: I think that by and large if you are speaking to a bunch of trade unionists somewhere, they don't give a damn. There is an apathy about it, and that's the biggest single danger.

Nash: Why is that? Are they just bored by the subject?

Webster: Partly it's the fault of the media. There is not much doubt about that. And the centralization of the media in Eastern Canada is another big handicap, I think.

Nash: You think we should do anything we can, short of evisceration of the nation, to keep Quebec in?

Webster: Yes. Anything is better than outright separation. We could have totally different financial formulas. They could, in effect, be independent up to a point, with a customs union and tariff union. Maybe what is needed is not a Republic of Quebec but just sovereignty for Quebec.

Nash: Whatever sovereignty may mean. It means a lot of different things to different people.

Webster: I doubt very much if there is a will to separate the country, including among the people of Quebec. It's always been my feeling that the ordinary working man in Quebec is the same as the ordinary working man in British Columbia. He wants a bloody job, that's one thing he wants. He wants decent education. He wants medicare.

Nash: You're an immigrant. What do you think of our multiculturalism policies?

Webster: I think one of the biggest mistakes we made was when, because of political expediency, we adopted the policy of multiculturalism. Without an official policy of multiculturalism, it's so much easier for people to assimilate.

Nash: We always take such pride, though, in the mosaic that makes us unlike the melting-pot of the United States.

Webster: I think the mosaic is a phoney. If you want to keep your culture, keep it, but I see no reason why any tax money should be spent to encourage the artificial maintenance of non-Canadian cultures in this country. The multiculturalism policy was begun by the Liberals for sheer political advantage and has been taken over and continued by the Tories for exactly the same reason.

Nash: We talk a lot about the problems of Canada, but what are the good things in this country?

Webster: We are a civilized nation. We are a literate nation. We have a reasonable education system. We have a great medicare system, if it survives. Somehow or other we are a more tolerant people than the Americans. We are a more charitable nation. We've got unlimited resources, if we can use them sanely.

Nash: In your heart, what do you think this country will look like when we cross into the twenty-first-century?

Webster: To me the physical separation of Quebec with artificial entrances and exits is unthinkable. We must be perfectly prepared to make some accommodations. We will have to watch for the interests of the non-French Canadians in Quebec. But I just don't see the country breaking up.

LOIS WILSON

A former moderator of the United Church of Canada, Lois Wilson has served as president of the World Council of Churches 1983–1991 and as chancellor of Lakehead University at Thunder Bay, Ontario, 1990–1991. She is trustee of the Nelson Mandela Fund, chairwoman of the Urban-Rural Mission in Canada, vice-president of the Civil Liberties Association of Canada, and councillor of the National Board of Amnesty International (Canada). Rev. Wilson was ordained as a minister of the United Church of Canada in 1965.

"[Being] a Canadian is caring for your neighbour."

Nash: What do you think are the qualities that make a Canadian?

Wilson: One clue is what other people think of us. I've spent a lot of time overseas, and a lot of people want to get into this country. We are seen as a very desirable country to live in. What I equate with that is a certain openness to diversity and, hopefully, an affirmation of those diversities within some unified structure. We have the opportunity in this country to create a place that is hospitable to a wide variety of peoples and cultures. I really hate to see that lost through a loss of imagination or lack of political will.

Nash: Do you see that loss right now?

Wilson: I see hints of it as the West pulls away. I see Quebec as really having had it, and now pulling away.

Nash: Did we romanticize too much the sense of the English and French, and the East and West, working together in a country so spread out geographically?

Wilson: Maybe we did romanticize it. Yes and no, because it seems to me that it takes a country with a strong centre to be able to look after the most vulnerable parts of a country, the most vulnerable people. You can't do that unless you've got an entity called a country.

Nash: You speak of a strong centre, and yet much of the discussion today seems to focus on dispersing power from the centre to the regions.

Wilson: That's fine so long as there isn't complete abdication. What are the guarantees then that the vulnerable economies and the vulnerable people will be cared for in our society? Part of what it is to be a Canadian is caring for your neighbour, not just as an individual thing, but through legislation, through our social policies.

Nash: Is that endangered if you diffuse power?

Wilson: It depends on the arrangement.

Nash: What arrangements would you like to see? What kinds of powers should be retained as a central function?

Wilson: Enough to guarantee that the weakest members of the society are going to be looked after. I am afraid that if the provinces all pull away and we become separate entities, there won't be enough critical mass left to do anything.

Nash: What's your sense of the mood of Canadians across the country today?

Wilson: I think people in the West are just tired out. They don't want to think about it any more. It astonishes me that many people in the West think it is a virtue to speak only English, because in my international travel I am handicapped because I can speak only two languages and I really should have four or five. But in the West, I find a fatigue. They don't want to think about it. I find the mood in Quebec is mixed, but it's not the way it was in 1980. They have been pushed a little further now.

Nash: What happened, what caused that feeling in the West and that feeling in Quebec?

Wilson: There is very little sense of the whole of Canada because of the size of the country. Not too many people have a strong sense of Canada as a whole, and the more we back off into our provinces, the more we become provincial and have a narrow view of our responsibility to each other. We go to the United Nations and sign all these declarations talking about our responsibility to the weakest people of the society, and it seems to me that we are in danger of being a pigeon at home and a parrot abroad.

Nash: How far would you go in terms of meeting the aspirations of Quebec?

Wilson: I would go a long way. I am astonished at the attitude of Anglos who just say, "Well, let Quebec go. Who cares?" We care a great deal.

Nash: What would we lose, the rest of Canada lose, if Quebec did go?

Wilson: We might lose a country. It's not just losing a province.

Nash: Why would we lose a country?

Wilson: Because geographically the Maritimes would be cut off, and I don't know what would happen to them economically. I don't know what the West would do, whether they would go south, because right now so many of the patterns are north-south. I don't know, but I have a feeling it might be the signal to other provinces to break off. Another thing that worries me about Quebec is there seems to be an opinion there of, why doesn't English Canada say what it wants? as though English Canada is an entity. We are not. I live on a street where we are the only Anglo-Saxons for some blocks. There is no entity called English Canada.

Nash: You are a minority not only on your street, but a minority in the country as a whole.

Wilson: Exactly.

Nash: In a way, that fundamentally changes the nature of Canada, and yet our institutions tend to reflect what has been rather than what is. How can you reflect the new reality, and how can you reflect the impact of cities as well as provinces, on our way of doing things?

Wilson: That's right. Cities have become so huge now that

we have become an urban population. I know politics is about power-sharing and power-grabbing and so on, but I really would hope that the politicians would not look upon the whole negotiation process as, "I'll try and get this, and you try and get that."

Nash: You would rather see people responding to a broader proposal than just how to keep Quebec in.

Wilson: Oh yes, it has to be a whole redefinition of the country, I think, not just a little "Let's fix it up" and "What do you want?"

Nash: Who does that? The politicians have been doing it in the past through a kind of executive federalism.

Wilson: The whole credibility of the political process right now in Canada is very low. People don't look to politicians to give us any lead, which is a very sad state of affairs. What I think is involved is restoring the credibility of the political process, as well as looking at some vision of what kind of country we want, and then attempting to shape the institutions to reflect that. How that's done, I am not sure, but I know it's not enough to leave it only to the politicians.

Nash: Do we have a Canadian soul?

Wilson: I think we are beginning to get one through the literature, the art, and it's not all wonderful. I went to see *Dry Lips Oughta Move to Kapuskasing* by Tomson Highway, which is a terribly searing play, but that's part of our soul. I think we are beginning to emerge from that time when the only thing we knew was that a Canadian was not an American.

Nash: What is the role of the church in such a fundamental debate as this?

Wilson: One of the things we can do is at least keep articulating the kind of quality of life that we want to see in Canada. I mentioned social equality and the care for your neighbour and the care for the most vulnerable. This is one of the things that we would want to see. It is the articulation of values, I guess. Another one is the affirmation of the cultural identity of groups of people in the country.

Nash: Where do you think Canada will be in four or five years from now?

Wilson: I wish I knew. Many, I sense, are not really taking Quebec seriously, and I think they need to be taken seriously. I think we need a total redefinition of the kind of country we want, and then figure out how the institutions are going to be shaped to do that. We've got the time to do that before Quebec drops the hatchet.

Nash: If you were prime minister, how would you go about trying to achieve that?

Wilson: I don't know how one persuades politicians to look at the country outside of their own little bailiwick. People are so confused about what's happening, and the pace of change is so fast. We've never had to face this before. We've just gone on and muddled through. So much of the country's beginnings were purely pragmatic. The railroad made Canada. That's why the cities were strung along the border. Maybe we don't have these glorious visions that other countries have of themselves, but we are a pragmatic country; we are a cooperative country, because that's how we came into existence. We need each other.

Nash: How much of a danger do you think there is if there is a split with Quebec, that the English-speaking part of Canada might be drawn into the United States?

Wilson: I think quite a large danger. We've already got free trade. It's a constant struggle within Canada to preserve our own cultural identity, to identify it, to create it, and preserve it.

Nash: Everything comes back to providing a proposal for change. Can there be a consensus?

Wilson: Yes, and it has to be a fairly radical change. Things are different now, because of the growth of cities, the huge non-Anglo-Saxon immigration, so that the demography of our country is completely changed from what it was when we became a country. Transportation and communication have changed. All those things are not yet reflected in how we operate.

Nash: Is our attitude towards this country one of the fundamentals that we need to change?

Wilson: Absolutely. When you leave Canada you hear what

people are saying. They think we are all crazy, dismantling a country, when look at what we've got. They see a country with vast resources, openness to new people, ability to assimilate a great diversity of people. They see a bilingual country. They can't understand why we are doing all this internal fighting and pulling apart, so that pretty soon we may not have a country. Let's not let it fail because we haven't got the imagination or political will to figure it out.

HAROLD HORWOOD

Well-known Canadian author Harold Horwood was a key player in bringing Newfoundland into Confederation in 1949, working intimately with Joey Smallwood. He was organizer and campaign manager of the Newfoundland Labour Party, chairman of the General Workers Union, and was elected to the Newfoundland House of Assembly in 1949. He later became editor of the St. John's Evening Telegram. *His first book was a novel published in 1966, and since then he has written extensively about Newfoundland history and has been active in various writers' organizations. He now lives in Nova Scotia, near Annapolis Royal.*

"Canada is Toronto-centred."

Nash: Since you played such a key role with Joey Smallwood in bringing Newfoundland into Confederation, looking back on that effort and all that's happened since then, has Confederation really worked out well for Newfoundland?

Horwood: There was no alternative for Newfoundland. They could have postponed Confederation for another ten or twenty years maybe, but in the long run there was nothing else for Newfoundland to do, and the reason we sought Confederation was for economic reasons. The Newfoundland people are enormously better off, financially better off, than they would have been if they were independent.

Nash: Is there a sense of Canadianism among Newfoundlanders?

Horwood: There is a certain sense among young people, the ones born since Confederation. But it's not very strong. The farther you get away from Toronto, the weaker the sense of Canadianism becomes, no matter which direction you go in.

Nash: Why is that?

Horwood: Because Canada is really an Ontario creation. Ontario is the centre of the country, and Toronto is the centre of Ontario.

Nash: Sir John A. Macdonald was from Ontario.

Horwood: That's right. Canada is Toronto-centred, always has been. This may be one of the problems for Quebec. If it wasn't Toronto-centred you would probably have less separatism. Newfoundland thought of itself as an independent, separate country for a long time, and the feeling still is that the connection with Canada is some sort of economic-political connection, but no feeling of unity.

Nash: No passionate emotion of Canadianism.

Horwood: No, not at all. Canadian nationalism just doesn't exist in the Atlantic provinces, in my opinion.

Nash: Is that part of history, a hesitancy to be part of Confederation in the first place? Joseph Howe was certainly not an ardent supporter of Macdonald in the beginning.

Horwood: Partly that, and partly the fact that the great period of prosperity in the Maritimes and in Newfoundland was pre-Confederation. There was a period in the late eighteenth century and the mid-nineteenth century when there was a big ship-building industry. The great houses throughout Nova Scotia were all built by shipyard owners and ship builders from the pre-Confederation days. We look back to the glories of the past.

Nash: In your judgement, is there such a thing as a Canadian identity, or is there a series of different identities?

Horwood: The only thing that gives Canada any sense of unity is the fact that we have this colossus next door that we have to keep defending ourselves against culturally.

Nash: At the time Newfoundland was considering its future, there was a proposal that Newfoundland join the United States rather than join Canada.

Horwood: There was a strong feeling among Newfoundlanders that they would like to do this. There was a long-standing connection between Newfoundland and New England, particularly Boston.

Nash: Is there still some of that sentiment about joning New England in Newfoundland today?

Horwood: I would say it isn't very strong any more.

Nash: Given a Quebec separation, would there be a strong sentiment of wanting to attach the Maritimes to the United States?

Horwood: Absolutely not. There is no feeling at all here that we should join the United States. All the way back to the American Revolution there was a strong feeling against it. When you think of the way Nova Scotians fought on the sea against the Americans in the American Revolution, and again in the War of 1812, it wasn't just a minor thing. The privateer war was a major business down here in both these wars. The Americans won the first one, and we won the second one.

Nash: You have seen all the things Quebec is seeking. What kind of reaction do you have to them?

Horwood: You have to remember when you say Quebec is doing this, is seeking that, that you are talking about Quebec politicians. Let's not confuse that with there being a tremendous feeling among the Quebec people for the kinds of powers the politicians are seeking. It isn't necessarily so at all. I think one of the things that has been largely overlooked is the enormous difficulties in the way of any kind of separation. When someone in Quebec City talks about sovereignty association or outright separation, it sounds like it is only a matter of signing the documents and tomorrow we are two separate countries. The entanglements with the rest of the country that have gone on for so long are not going to be easy things to get rid of. What do you do about all the federal property in the province of Quebec? Do you just give it away or do you negotiate a sale of it? What about the national debt? Do they assume their share of it or not? I think one of the great issues that almost nobody mentions is the minorities in Quebec, not just ethnic minorities, but ethnic minorities which are also geographical minorities, like the Arctic. The Quebec Arctic was given to Quebec, it was placed under trusteeship by the federal government because Quebec was a province of Canada. It would never have been done if Quebec had been a separate country in 1912, when the Northwest Territories were carved up and a chunk of it was given to Quebec. And, of course, the people of the area were not consulted.

Nash: Do you think that, if there were a separation, part of the negotiation might be to withdraw that piece of property from Quebec?

Horwood: The people of the Arctic are certainly strongly opposed to Quebec separatism. The last thing they want is to be part of a separate Quebec. The eastern Arctic is an area I have spent a lot of time in, and the feeling there is practically unanimous. Do you ignore this? Do you say Quebec is going to take these people, who have already had a certain kind of relationship with the Canadian federal government and who learned to speak English so they could deal with the federal government? Do you simply abolish all this and say we are going to give you away to a foreign country? The issues are much more complex than people seem to think.

Nash: But you were saying earlier that the people in the outer areas of Canada have less affinity for the whole nation.

Horwood: The Canadian union is still a useful thing. It's something you think of in terms of economics, of its effect on the people. It isn't an emotional thing like it might be in Ontario, where you have this strong feeling that this is my country. Nobody has any strong feelings about the Canadian flag down here one way or another.

Nash: What do you think the rest of Canada should say to Quebec, given the twenty-two demands in the Allaire report, and given what the Quebec leaders have been saying?

Horwood: I believe we need a strong federal government. I

think the federal government is too weak, not too strong. Quebec is going to have to come to terms with this. I don't believe for a minute that Quebec is going to separate. I have never believed it. The question of Quebec's identity, of Quebec being a distinct society, is not an issue. Of course they are a distinct society, why not write it down in black and white? But the separation of powers is something that has to be negotiated over a long period. This is not something that is going to be settled quickly and the idea that it is all going to be done in a referendum in 1992 is nonsense.

Nash: What happens if Quebec has the referendum and there is a decision by the voters to support a form of sovereignty?

Horwood: I don't believe there will be any such decision by the voters, but if there were, then what happens is that they begin negotiating with Canada.

Nash: Why do you feel so strongly that the people of Quebec won't vote for sovereignty?

Horwood: Because they voted against it on a sixty-forty split there before. In any election that's a landslide. Now it is closer, and after Meech Lake there seemed to be in the polls a big likelihood that if you took a vote then, sovereignty association would win. But support has been dropping steadily ever since. By the time all the issues are aired, by the time the Quebec people have looked at the economic issues and so on, and have considered the penalties involved in separation, I am convinced they will vote for the sensible thing.

Nash: There was a sense after Meech Lake, real or perceived, that English-speaking Canada, particularly Newfoundland Premier Clyde Wells, had rejected Quebec.

Horwood: That was absolutely wrong. The rejection was not of Quebec, it was of the Meech Lake accord, and you've got to realize that is quite a different thing. It was a very bad constitutional proposal.

Nash: What's your vision of Canada?

Horwood: I would like to see a strong central government for economic reasons, but not because of any vision I have. I think that the outer fringes of the country depend more on a strong central government than provinces like Ontario and Quebec do.

Nash: We don't have much flag-waving passion. Are we lacking something in that?

Horwood: This is rear-view-mirrorism, as McLuhan called it, looking back to the nineteenth century when you are talking about flag waving. This is not twentieth-century thinking. We need less of it than we have had. The United States is essentially a nineteenth-century country. Their period of flowering was the 1890s. That's when they achieved their level of greatness, which they never surpassed, except in terms of pure physical things. In terms of ethos, they belong to the 1890s, and probably always will. The period when it was, "My country right or wrong," is over and done with.

Whatever happens to Canada, I hope we are still evolving to the point where we can be an effective part of the future. We are quiet people, we are conservative, we are rather uninteresting, rather peaceful, rather law-abiding. If Canada started to fall apart, there is no possible way they'd begin murdering each other in the streets the way they are doing in the Soviet Union. You are not going to have a war between Quebec and New Brunswick,

Nash: What are your thoughts about bilingualism in the country?

Horwood: It ought to be plain to everybody that the future of French in North America really depends on the future of Canada. French exists in North America because of Canada. If Quebec separated, my view is that, in two or three generations, French would disappear in North American completely. Certainly, outside Quebec itself, there would be no more pressure for bilingualism. The Acadians would have to go back to speaking English as they did a generation ago. French inside Quebec would disappear eventually, too.

Nash: Why? A central purpose of separation would be to ensure continuation of the language.

Horwood: I am sure that is the purpose, but the practical thing is you can't have a little French-speaking enclave of 5 million people in the midst of 300 million English-speaking people, speaking the world's dominant language. They would simply have to use English in all their dealings with the rest of North America, and very quickly French would cease to be anything, except that it could be preserved in the same way that Gaelic is preserved in Ireland, as an academic exercise.

MONA GUPTA

As a McGill University biology student, Mona Gupta was a member of the McGill team that won the World University Debating Championships in 1991, held at the University of Toronto. Born and brought up in Sydney, Nova Scotia, the fluently bilingual Gupta has been a student activist and leader throughout her school years. Aside from her school work, she has acted as a language instructor, been a volunteer tutor, and was a volunteer in the Sydney Loaves and Fishes soup kitchen.

"People have to calm down."

Nash: As a university student, what do you feel about the debate on Canada's future?

Gupta: I think to a large extent the question has been blown out of proportion, to be quite honest with you. The media, unfortunately, are doing a job of stirring people's emotions up. I teach English as a second language at a high school in Montreal, a French school, and I listen to them talk. They say Quebec needs to separate. I ask why, and they say, "Well, you know it would be better," and finally when you press them enough they say, "Because my parents said so. That's what it says on televison. That's what it says in the newspapers." I understand that French people feel a need to protect their language, but you wonder how much of the adamancy and the vehemence is a result of the media. In the same way that in English Canada you wonder how much of the stomping on Quebec flags and Reform Party activism is a backlash rather than a real resentment about French.

Nash: What is your own feeling about the issue? You sound like you are a federalist.

Gupta: What makes you think that?

Nash: Just what you said.

Gupta: I can't hide it very well. I don't want to say I am this, or I am that. I think that part of the problem is that people feel a need to identify with some camp, and then from there on it becomes a battle. I have several concerns. My first one is with the fundamental idea that culture needs to be protected by law. I am not sure if it does. But if you assume that it does, then you wonder to what extent that protection needs to go. And I wonder sometimes if Quebec were to separate, what the differences would be in Quebec legislation that would protect the culture. Some people say the whole point of Quebec separating is not just to protect their culture, but to build a unique society, different from English Canada. I wonder how much different French Canadians are from English Canadians that we can't live in a country together.

Nash: Are we different?

Gupta: I think at least there is a perception that we are, and I think that's important. In other tangible ways we are, the legal system demonstrates that. I think there are definitely cultural ideas that are different. When you look at the temperament of Quebec and the temperament of English Canada, you do see differences. There was recently in the news a story about Mitsou's video, about whether Much Music should show it, and they were saying in English Canada they wouldn't show it because they are too prudish. The other point is that, as time goes on, there are going to be other issues that, to me, are more important than the need to close ourselves off culturally. Issues like the environment. Issues like that have nothing to do with countries. Pollution doesn't stop at borders.

Nash: It seems to me that pride plays a very large role in shaping attitudes among francophones. Is that fair to say?

Gupta: I think pride does play a big role, and probably with just reason. Twenty or thirty years ago in Quebec, French people who didn't speak English would have a difficult time ever being successful, either in business or in politics. If you wanted to be successful you either had to be English or you had to stop being French a little bit, whether that meant totally accepting the English language, or socializing with English people, or whatever. I also think that, for various historical reasons, the church created this situation whereby French people probably looked at themselves as less privileged than English people, and with fewer opportunities. I just worry that the pride on both the English side and the French side is being carried to an extreme.

Nash: Quebec has put forward the twenty-two points of the Allaire report. What kind of response do you think that English-speaking Canada should make to them?

Gupta: I think Quebec has made it clear that the twenty-two demands are not hard and fast. There is certainly room to negotiate and manoeuvre. The first thing that people have to do is calm down. It is pretty clear that they are willing to negotiate, so let's sit down and talk about what we can get out of this. Different people have been suggesting different things: asymmetrical federalism on the one hand, or complete separation. I think this is constructive. We have got to stop forming committees and start doing something soon, because they are serious about having a referendum, and it's getting closer. My biggest concern about responding, and this is mainly in relation to English Canada, is that the process be significantly more participatory than it was with Meech Lake. If anything has caused a real demoralization and lack of confidence in politics, it was that whole process, where people felt that decisions were being completely taken out of their hands.

Nash: How far do you think English-speaking Canada should go in meeting the Allaire requests?

Gupta: I don't know if Quebec doing something necessarily takes something away from English Canada. That is sort of the point of asymmetric federalism, that one province can go ahead and do things without undermining the ability for another province to defer to the federal government. You are dealing in faith also to the extent where you are asking provinces if they assume greater powers, to be responsible. Just because they would have more power, they would not necessarily not want to coordinate projects with the rest of Canada.

Nash: Do you worry about the consequences if Quebec did separate? What do you think would happen to the province?

Gupta: That's anybody's guess right now. Separatists are getting up and saying it is going to be great economically, we will be so successful, and English Canadians are getting up saying it will be a disaster, the whole country will fall apart. That is ridiculous. It's ominous, no one knows what is going to happen. If, in fact, the province separates at least in part to build a distinct society, to create a situation where their culture is very important, then I worry at the costs to other cultures and other groups.

Nash: Some people feel that multiculturalism is fundamentally undermining Canadianism in the sense that it puts emphasis on the individual foreign cultures and thereby lessens the sense of nationalism.

Gupta: No, I don't think so. If you went across Canada and asked people, "Do you think there is a Canadian identity and does that mean something distinct and different from being Italian? Even though you maintain your heritage, do you also identify with Canada?" then people would say yes. My mother is a good example. She never took Canadian citizenship when she came. She is still a landed immigrant, but she very much identifies with Canada now. She goes to India quite often to visit relatives, but she comes back because there is something here for her now. She has a new life here. I don't think not having a policy of official multiculturalism is going to strengthen a national identity.

Nash: Do you have much family discussion about the question of national unity?

Gupta: No, not really. I think a lot of people are a little bit fatalistic. They think that Quebec is going to leave this time, and that there is not much anybody can do about it.

Nash: What do you think?

Gupta: I am confident that if people would just sit down and be rational about this, talk about it, then it can be settled. If sitting down and negotiating a new deal with English Canada and staying in Canada means that fifteen years from now the whole thing is going to start up again because it isn't quite enough, then maybe separation or sovereignty now is the best thing. Let's deal with it in some way and move on, because this has been going on far too long. It would be nice for it to be settled and to start thinking about other things.

Nash: Is education, to some degree, at fault in our not better understanding each other?

Gupta: Yes. The biggest part of the problem is that the whole second language issue is not dealt with seriously enough in English Canada. As a result, it makes the threat feel even more real in French Canada and they say, "Well, we have to learn English to get by. Why can't you people learn French?"

Nash: What kind of Canada would you like to see by the year 2000?

Gupta: I'd like to see the language issue dealt with quickly, because there are other things that are more important. It is not that I don't think language is important, but I think that questions of the environment and the economy are more important. I'd like to see much more attention being focussed on the environment, and I'd like to see Canada create a society that has taken some global leadership in creating a healthier environment. That's what I think our main focus should be in the coming years.

Nash: What does it mean to you to be a Canadian?

Gupta: I don't think I would want to live anywhere else. I am happy here. I like the country. I am still finding out about different provinces, I lived in P.E.I. for a summer, in Ontario for a summer, and I am hoping to go out west and see what it is like there, too.

Nash: What kind of values are there that you see here?

Gupta: I was thinking about this the other day, about how

Canadians are so anxious about having no identity. I really think there is a temperament in Canadians than makes them different from Americans, different from Europeans. They are, by and large, friendly and cautious people, somewhat conservative in a social sense. I find them to be open-minded, generally accepting of things, generally willing to try things, willing to have a slow pace of life. I do not find that Canada is a country of extremes. I look to the United States and think, extremes.

Nash: How important is the monarchy to Canada?

Gupta: To me it's not that important. I personally do not feel any attachment or loyalty to the Queen. I know that there are a lot of people who do and who, in a way, view that as a very important symbol of English Canada. And that's another thing that causes problems with the French because they don't like to view any sort of loyalty towards the Queen.

Nash: In a renewed federalism, if we get such a thing, should we have the monarchy, or should we dispense with it?

Gupta: If you just get rid of it, it's going to make it look like we are giving in to Quebec. If you keep it, it looks like you are giving in to English Canada. I think ideally it will be dispensed with over time, until getting rid of it doesn't seem like an insult to anybody. I don't feel anything for it myself, and I don't think a lot of people identify very strongly with it, at least not a lot of people my own age.

KEN READ

One of Canada's great sports heroes, Ken Read was the leader of the fearless group of Canadian downhill racers who dominated the international ski world from 1975 to 1984. They were known as The Crazy Canucks. He won six World Cup titles, and was a member of two Canadian Olympic teams. In 1978 he was named Canada's Outstanding Athlete and in 1979 Canada's Outstanding Male Amateur Athlete. Since retiring in 1983, Read has launched a career in sports broadcasting and promotion. He is Chef de Mission for the Canadian Olympic Team in Barcelona in 1992. Read is fluent in English, French, and German and lives in Calgary.

"Everybody likes Canadians."

Nash: You have won awards galore for Canada, you have represented Canada in events around the world, what's your sense of what being a Canadian means?

Read: Perhaps the most important thing is that everybody likes Canadians. We have credibility. While I was on the World Cup tour, we were everybody's second favourite, the home country being the favourite. I had people saying, "If our best can't win, we would like you to win." That stems from our passion for what we did. We really enjoyed what we were doing, and we enjoyed the environment we were in, and people appreciated that. It is because we don't come across as aggressively as Americans do. I think people enjoy that, and they like doing business with us.

Nash: In what other ways are we different from the Americans?

Read: We express our passions in different ways. The common word seems to be that we are nice. I would not want to be like the U.S. in the way we express our patriotism. I have seen other examples in other countries, Austria versus Germany, for instance, and how Austrians are able to stake out their own identity without having to resort to doing it the way the Germans do. So, in that way, I don't think we have to run around waving the flag.

Nash: Within this country, there certainly are irritations between Quebec and the rest of Canada, and the question is how should English-speaking Canada respond to the demands of Quebec for a transference of powers from Ottawa to Quebec or to all the provinces?

Read: The sense I get is that we need renewed federalism.

Nash: What does that really mean?

Read: This runs a little against my grain because I tend to be a centralist. I guess I am pragmatic in the sense that if it is going to mean a breakup of the country, then we have to change. If the people feel there has to be change then that has to be respected within a democratic society. We do have to make some changes but the limit I would put on it is that we can't end up with an unworkable federal system. We should be sitting down, putting the passions aside if we can, and saying we have to make a country that is going to work internationally and that also recognizes the fact that we are a very diverse nation.

Nash: At what point does the federal government lose viability and become a fairly empty shell?

Read: I would think if certain powers are devolved to the provinces, that, in turn, the provinces should be willing to say, okay, then, the federal government has to retain control over certain things, such as interprovincial trade, environment, transportation, and other national issues. In culture, I am sympathetic to Quebec's notion that it is a small enclave in a teeming sea of English within North America, which I think the West doesn't really fully appreciate.

Nash: We hear a lot about western alienation, in Alberta particularly, as the province seeks some of the powers Quebec is seeking. How real is that western alienation?

Read: Western alienation is real, but not in a separatist sense of the word. It's alienation in that there is a lack of control over one's destiny.

Nash: It is not really a western separation then, but rather a western desire for greater participation in the centre of federalism.

Read: We have a voice, but that voice can be overwhelmed very easily.

Nash: Should that western voice become a part of the decision-making process on such things as appointments to the Supreme Court or regulatory agencies?

Read: I would be sympathetic to a restructuring of Parliament, which would have a House of Commons being "rep. by pop." and the Senate being changed to being representative of the regions.

Nash: Equally representative?

Read: Equally.

Nash: How do you answer the Ontario argument, or Quebec's, that this would be unfair because of the size of Ontario's or Quebec's population?

Read: That is a tough argument. Again, we are dealing with the massive size of our country and the diversity of our country. And then, the other part of the debate is the fact that, with immigration, the largest group within Canada now are those who are neither English nor French. That to me has changed the debate dramatically. In addition, we have a country that was a coming together of English and French, but we also can't forget the aboriginal issues which must be resolved.

Nash: If Canada were to split, would English-speaking Canada become more vulnerable to the United States?

Read: It is something that really bothers me. I would not want to become an American. But we would be more vulnerable.

Hopefully, there are enough people out there who would stand up and say no. Too many times I see within the debate people saying, "Well, we are really no different than the Americans." I really enjoy going to the U.S. and working with the Americans, which I do quite a bit. But one of the reasons why I enjoy going to the U.S. is because it's so different from Canada.

Nash: President Bush has clearly said he prefers a united Canada.

Read: Yes, and we do have much to offer to each other. I have seen tiny countries, Switzerland is an example, where there is far more diversity within the country than there is within Canada, and yet we talk about our differences. Switzerland has four official languages.

Nash: You have colleagues in Quebec, did you ever discuss some of these things with them?

Read: In general I can say the majority that I spoke with wanted to remain part of the Canadian experience. If we were to split, we would lose far more than we would gain. But there is no question in my mind that Quebec's pride has been wounded.

Nash: Many English-speaking Canadians look to Estonia, Latvia, Lithuania, and other regions in the U.S.S.R. and support their separation from the Soviet Union but feel quite differently about Quebec separating. Are we being slightly hypocritical?

Read: I think there are fundamental differences. In many cases, the regions of the Soviet Union that are looking for independence were brought within the Soviet Union by force. There was conquest. Canadian Confederation was a mutual agreement. They were colonies and they got together. That to me makes a very strong difference. The other side of this is that we have lived together for well over a hundred years. It is not a paradise, but we have a common experience.

Nash: What do you think will happen by the turn of the century?

Read: My vision is that we will come together. This should be done in a sensible way, with some powers perhaps being transferred to the regions, balanced by maintaining national standards so that a Canadian in Vancouver is not dramatically different from a Canadian in Halifax. But let's all agree that we want to continue this national experience.

GEORGES ERASMUS

Georges Erasmus served as national chief of the Assembly of First Nations from 1985 to 1991. An articulate and vigorous spokesman for native rights, Erasmus began his career as a field worker for the Company of Young Canadians in 1970. In 1976, he became president of the Indian Brotherhood of the Northwest Territories, later known as the Dene Nation, and was instrumental in organizing opposition to the Mackenzie Valley pipeline proposal. Erasmus left his post as national chief of the Assembly of First Nations in the summer of 1991.

"It's very hard for me to consider myself a Canadian."

Nash: What's your broad sense of Canada? What does it mean to you personally?

Erasmus: Well, as a Native person I have never been fully satisfied with Canada because it's never done justice by Native people. So it's very hard for me to consider myself a Canadian. I consider myself a Dene, an aboriginal person, a citizen of an aboriginal nation. I could see a time when Native people could fully embrace the concept of Canada, and that would be when the question of Native sovereignty has been fully addressed. When Native people say we have never extinguished our sovereignty, what they are saying to Canada is that there is a way to accommodate us and that is to recognize us similarly to the way in which the United

States has recognized Native sovereignty. Under those circumstances, I think you would have everyone of Native descent across the country far more willing to look at a different type of Canada, so that the majority, I think, would then be able to say, "Yes, I am a citizen of an aboriginal tribe, but I am also a citizen of Canada."

Nash: From your perspective, what's the single most important element in this new Canada that we are trying to build?

Erasmus: There has to be some kind of equality between the respective communities of Canada. A better balance of powers and respect for each other than we have ever had in the past. And this time Native people must be part of the overall scheme so they have some kind of jurisdiction over themselves.

Nash: How, specifically, would power be shared?

Erasmus: I think that some of the requests that are being made in the Allaire report can be accommodated without endangering Canada. But I think if you gave Quebec all that it is seeking, you would weaken the centre of Canada to the point where it wouldn't be a benefit to Quebec, either. But there are central powers that could be provided to the regions without endangering Canada. For instance, it would never endanger Canada for Newfoundland to have offshore rights and for fisheries to be within their jurisdiction. So, likewise, give Quebec powers that would provide them with cultural and language and community security and recognition of their distinctiveness. I could live with terminology like Quebec is a "nation" in the Constitution. I don't have any problems with that at all.

For the West, it's not so much that it is seeking more powers, it is more to have a bigger effect on the country as a whole. So for them it's far more important that reform happens to the larger national institutions: Parliament, the Senate, the Supreme Court, and so on. And it is important that individual members in Parliament have more freedom so that they can, for instance, vote against their party when their constituencies absolutely require them to. Committees in Parliament have very little authority. It would be very useful for the regions for committees to have more autonomy and jurisdiction. The concept of the Senate also may need to change so that you have equal numbers for everyone.

Nash: Everyone meaning every province, every region?

Erasmus: Every province, every region, plus you must go beyond that to accommodate Native people.

Nash: How do you do that?

Erasmus: There are the obvious ways, such as having a number of seats in Parliament that Native people would be guaranteed.

Nash: Something like New Zealand's arrangement with the Maoris?

Erasmus: Something like that. The Senate also possibly could have the same arrangement. The Supreme Court could have a judge, perhaps, who is absolutely required to have had experience and knowledge and awareness in First Nations' law and law-making and aboriginal and treaty rights. But for Native people, just changing the national institutions is not going to be anywhere near enough. Even if you went to the point of making sure that you had guaranteed seats even in the provinces, this would not be sufficient because the primary thing that is required for Native people to be fully accommodated is for them to have their own autonomy.

Nash: What does that mean in practical terms?

Erasmus: In practical terms it would mean that you would have the equivalent of provinces that are Native, that are not contiguous in geographic boundary, but have governments that are similar perhaps to the present provincial structures, with one or two extra powers. One of the powers I would think that Native people everywhere in this country would want to have under their control is fisheries, which is now a federal power.

Nash: What are the areas that you think should be exclusively or primarily federal in jurisdiction?

Erasmus: I think the powers we now have federally, by and large, serve reasonably well. But there are a number of areas where it might be argued that provinces should have more control. One, for instance, is the area of family law. Divorce is federal, marriage is provincial. That seems to me to be a bit of an anomaly. It doesn't make too much sense to separate family law in that way. I would think that many provinces also would want to control fisheries, particularly if you are bordering on the Atlantic or the Pacific. Also the offshore. Communications is important to some provinces. The environment also, but I suspect that the environment is one area in which we should all share jurisdiction. There are no boundaries that can stop pollution.

Nash: Given all the pressures, and given the time demands, are you an optimist or a pessimist in relation to whether there can be a unified Canada?

Erasmus: I think the makings of a deal are there. But there is going to have to be a willingness to arrive at agreements that will provide some balance. The reason we fought so hard for change in Meech was that we were going to be worse off with Meech. It was never an attempt on the part of the First Nations to drive Quebec out of Canada, and it certainly was never an attempt to do damage to Quebec or put Quebec in its place.

Nash: Just for a moment, look at the possibility of Quebec splitting away. What would be the position of the Native people, particularly the Cree in northern Quebec? Would they then seek to split away from Quebec itself?

Erasmus: If past positions indicate what they are going to do, I would expect them to decide to stay with Canada, one way or another.

Nash: How would they do that?

Erasmus: We are already hearing indications from different parts of Quebec that, if Quebec leaves, then one questions the territory they are leaving with. What right do they have to take all that land that they call Quebec with people in there, people who were there before the French?

Nash: Basically, you are talking about the northern part.

Erasmus: Northern parts, and who knows what other parts. When Quebec entered Confederation it was a very small province. Legally, for the Native people there, their land was never given to Quebec to take out of Confederation. So at the very least the Native people should have the same right as Quebeckers. If Quebec wants to leave Canada, then aboriginal people within the territory should have the right to leave Quebec with their territory intact.

Nash: It's hard to know what a sovereigntist really is, but in a way, you're a sovereigntist too, only from a Native point of view.

Erasmus: That's right. You will remember that in the Oka incident, the Mohawks were saying that they were sovereign, that they had never extinguished their sovereignty. The permeating thought among indigenous people is that to have non-Native people come amongst them does not mean they have extinguished their sovereignty. Perhaps if there was to be a difference drawn between ourselves and some of the Quebec sovereigntists, it would be that, while we want it very clear that Native sovereignty is our source for jurisdiction, we can accommodate ourselves within Confederation. It would be a stronger Canada because Canada could then look to the world and say we have accommodated our Native people, and they are comfortable to be within Confederation. Their sovereignty is our sovereignty. Their sovereignty is Canadian sovereignty. Canada's sovereignty didn't start a couple of hundred years ago, it started when Native people first were here.

Nash: If there were a split, what would be the repercussions for Canada in general and for Native people in particular?

Erasmus: For us in some ways it would be a win-win situation because our proportionate population would jump by quite a lot. Within the Prairie provinces the demographics are that non-Native people are leaving the Prairies at the same time as the Native population is increasing tremendously. So we would have a situation a few years down the road, particularly if the North becomes provinces, where a number of provinces will be dominated by Native people. So we will have a bigger impact on the country in the future than we have now.

Nash: What's your personal preference for Quebec?

Erasmus: Quebec undoubtedly can survive on its own. But I also think it is going to be very traumatic for both Canada and Quebec if a split occurs. Anybody who says you can just smooth this over and it is going to be clear sailing is wrong. I think that equity markets both within Quebec and outside of Quebec are going to be drastically affected. Psychologically we are going to be affected for a long time.

Nash: In what way?

Erasmus: What we are going to find out is that we are much more emotionally attached to Quebec than we realize. It is going to be like a very major breakup in the family, and there is going to be animosity. In Quebec, I think that they are going to have second thoughts eventually, and they are going to have a psychological loss. They will have emotional scars. There will be some regrets, there will be some pain, and it will never go away.

Nash: The confrontation between Ottawa and the provinces has led to a souring in the land about institutions and politicians. How did that come about? How did we get that sourness?

Erasmus: What's happened since 1967 is that not only has Quebec continued to portray the problems first quietly and then loudly, but so have Native people. You must remember that it was only in 1960 that we were legally allowed off the reserves without a pass, and allowed to vote and run for office. It was only in 1969, I think, that we were allowed to vote in Quebec. So when the Centennial was happening in 1967, we couldn't even vote in all parts of the country yet.

Nash: How do you enhance a sense of Canadianism? Do we need more Pierre Bertons writing our history? Are there other ways in which we can reflect on our past as well as our present?

Erasmus: We need to do things which bring out our own people in this country. We need our own film industry. We need our own music industry. We need our own culture portrayed. We need our history to be told by ourselves. You can go to just about any part of this country and you will have people there who will be able to culturally portray their community or their region, but they might not necessarily have access to national institutions like television or radio. We need to encourage local people to tell their own stories locally and regionally.

Nash: You need vehicles to do that. And again you come back to the question: Is that achieved primarily through federal encouragement or can each individual region or province be strong enough to provide vehicles for articulation?

Erasmus: Federally, I think you want to portray what we are nationally as a single state. Provincially and regionally, you want to encourage what we have locally and in our own provinces. We don't do that very well at the moment. Nationally, we seem to be trying to compete too much with Hollywood. It gobbles up a tremendous amount of money and energy to try and compete on the world stage. If you are really seriously talking about bringing out the national character you virtually need a revolution to occur out there that involves a lot of people, rather than one or two or even half a dozen superstars. I think it is far more important to encourage small local community activities that bring out the local story-tellers, the local musicians, the local cultural leaders.

Nash: In your own sense of Canada, your own dream of Canada, what do you think the country is going to be like? What would you like to see by the year 2000?

Erasmus: I would like it to be a country that has dealt with all the outstanding issues for Native people and to have accommodated Quebec fully and adequately and fairly, and still have a federal government that makes sense. But on the other hand, I don't think it is necessary for each province to be uniform. I would also hope that during the next ten years we have resolved how we are going to deal with the environment. To do that we also need to address how we are dealing with resources in Canada. We have continued to have the mentality that we are living in a big storehouse of resources that is never going to be depleted and we can use them any way we want, irresponsibly or foolishly or whatever. I think we should change that mentality to one of stewardship and responsibility. That is similar to what Native people believe, that they have a responsibility to make sure that future generations are going to be able to live in plenty, and that they are also going to be able to have good lives.

SHIRLEY CARR

Shirley Carr has served as president of the Canadian Labour Congress since 1986. She first became active in the labour movement in 1960 working with the Canadian Union of Public Employees. She served as a member of the governing body of the International Labour Organization between 1980 and 1985, and she is vice president of the International Confederation of Free Trade Unions and chairwoman of the Commonwealth Trade Union Council.

"We are an unhappy people right now."

Nash: What would you like to see Canada look like as we enter the twenty-first century?

Carr: My hope is that we stay together as a nation. Not only will Quebec have to be recognized as a distinct society, but I also have a very grave concern about the Native community. I think we are going to have to deal with the three questions: the nation itself, the province of Quebec, and also the whole question of the Native community.

Nash: There seems to be such a tremendous gap between the Allaire report, and other proposals coming from Quebec, and the rest of Canada in terms of what is viewed as a future.

Carr: Perhaps we should have somebody take all of those reports and take the good and put it on one side, and then take the bad and put it on the other side, and see if there is some middle ground. I say that because, right now, with the mood of the people in Canada, it would be very difficult to come up with something that is going to be acceptable all across the nation. We are an unhappy people right now, and until we deal with the economics of the country, I am not sure we can get people away from a hostile attitude and a hostile mood. Until we can shift that attitude a little bit, I think the real constitution of this country will not be put into place the way it should be.

Nash: How did we get into that mood of sourness? During the 1967 centenary celebrations, we were fairly alive with a sense of enthusiasm about being Canadian. Yet we've lost that.

Carr: Canada is a nation of different people, different groups. We have tended to say "I am Irish Canadian," or "I am French Canadian," or "I am Italian Canadian" instead of being a Canadian, period. I think that's one of the mistakes we have made. The second mistake that I find unacceptable as a private person is the whole question of signing the constitutional accord and not having Quebec in there. Nothing should have been done until that was all put together. It might have taken a little longer, but I think in the end it would have proven to have been the safeguarding and safekeeping of the nation.

Nash: Is that when the momentum really began to build for a sovereign Quebec?

Carr: Yes, I think so, because you just don't keep a unique province, in its cultural sense and in its language sense, you do not keep them on the outside and expect them to say, "Okay, now I am ready to come back in." They just won't do that.

Nash: We've got a proposed deadline now of a referendum in October 1992. Can English-speaking Canada get its act together in time?

Carr: I think the framework can be there. I certainly don't think that every *i* can be dotted. I just don't see that. It is too important a question, and again, you have the other group of Canadians, the Native people, who have not been listened to yet properly on this question.

Nash: In the constitutional arguments you hear about the future, most of them seem to centre on a movement of federal power to the provinces, to a larger or lesser degree. Is it inevitable that there has to be a weakened federal centre and stronger provincial centres?

Carr: I would not want the federal centre to be weakened.

Nash: But then how to you achieve a deal?

Carr: Obviously something has to be rearranged for the rest of the country, and the majority of provinces are mature enough now to be responsible enough to carry some of the load. And there can be some movement.

Nash: What kind of movement? We have the specifics of Quebec's ideas, but we are still developing ideas in other parts of Canada. What kind of movement would be possible that would still meet some of Quebec's concerns?

Carr: Culture is one. I think culture is a national question, and we have to be very sure that we accept and recognize that. But there has to be the opportunity for culture to grow, and in Quebec there is great opportunity there. Every single province is different in its own way. On health care, I would think there could be some movement there, too.

Nash: And still be able to maintain the standards?

Carr: We would have to maintain national standards, and the provinces could add to them but not take away from them. The federal government has to be realistic and understand there are going to be powers it's going to have to come to terms with regarding the role of the provinces. I do not think the federal government should give up any of its power regarding natural resources. It should not give up its national energy program. It should not give up those things that we know belong to the whole nation.

Nash: Would there be a danger, with a sovereign Quebec, of the rest of Canada being pulled to the south?

Carr: There is a danger, but I would hope that that never happens. I think Canadians do not want to be Americans. Canadians are very distressed with the close relationship this government has with the government of the United States.

Nash: It's been said that we are having a debate on the death of Canada. Is that too extreme a description?

Carr: It is not going to be the death of the country. I am one of the lucky ones who travels the country. I know there is some unhappiness out there, but it will be overcome when the economy and the country are better. I am sure that the majority of Canadians want this country to stay together.

Nash: In your travels in the West, do you sense a stronger anti-Quebec feeling than you might have anticipated, or do you think it is again a passing phase?

Carr: Well, it's just starting to come out, and I think it is because of the economic situation. When we deal with this at our union executive council, my colleagues from the West say to Quebec, "Please, please help us. What we have to try to do is understand what you want so that we can understand what's required."

Nash: Quebec has said what it requires, but is that yet understood by other Canadians?

Carr: It's very emotional. People are totally confused because one day they hear this and the next day they hear something else. They are saying to themselves, "I am not sure whether I should be mad at Quebec or whether I should be mad at the whole world out there, which is trying to tell me what Quebec wants without giving Quebec an opportunity to tell us themselves."

Nash: That calls for political leadership, but we haven't seen a lot of cooperation among the provincial and federal leaders over the last few years.

Carr: That is the sad thing about it. If people could only rise above their position and talk about the nation instead of thinking about whether they will get elected next time around. That is the price the politician has to pay. That's the message I would like to give to the politicians. If you really are interested, you've got to leave at home what you are in your province and bring everything that you can think of that your province can do to keep the country together. But don't base your actions on the fact that you are looking toward the next election. I am not sure they are courageous enough to do that.

Nash: What should they be looking for?

Carr: Elections come and go, and politicians come and go. If they want to contribute something to the nation they have to forget about the fact that they are going to get elected or not. I am not even sure the politicians are the ones who should be handling this. At this stage of the game the politicians have not done very well. I don't know where you would find politicians in this country who are prepared to say, "Okay, while I am in these meetings, I am not going to be worried whether I am going to get re-elected."

Nash: That presupposes a lot of public influence, non-political influence, on the political people who will be making the judgements and decisions.

Carr: That's true. I guess I'm living in a dream world when I talk like this, but I can't see it any other way. It is worth the price to keep this country together. It is worth the price to go and try to be a free spirit and talk about the nature of this country. When you are looking at the life of a nation, you have to take that chance.

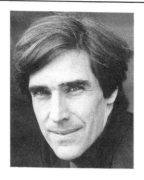

MICHAEL IGNATIEFF

Writer, broadcaster, and historian Michael Ignatieff was born in Toronto, educated at the University of Toronto, and at Harvard and Cambridge, and now lives in England. He writes for The Observer *in London and hosts* BBC2's "The Late Show." *He is the author of several books and won a Governor General's Award for non-fiction in 1987. His first novel,* Asya, *was published in 1991.*

"This dialogue of the deaf."

Nash: What's changed between the Canada you grew up in and the Canada to which you come back from London?
Ignatieff: I am Rip Van Winkle. I haven't lived in this country since 1969. I grew up in a Presbyterian, Anglican, deeply English Toronto. I have distinct memories of standing up when the national anthem was playing at the end of movies. My grandmother was deeply tied to a vanished part of Canadian history, which was imperial federation – a strong connection to the British Empire. That was mother's milk to me, that very British sense of a Canadian identity. In the early sixties, when I went to university, I could sense the ground shifting under my feet. Toronto was becoming an Italian town, a Portuguese town, a black town. When I left, the beginning of that radical transformation of old Tory Toronto was occurring.

I also grew up in a milieu of intellectuals. My grandfather was a schoolmaster, my dad was a public official of the Pearson generation. That generation of people had a very fierce, strong sense of what the country was. An intensely British character was at its core. They knew a thousand reasons why they weren't Americans. They also knew that they were part of a particularly internationalist Canada. When you were north of the border, you were in one of those little parts of the world that was coloured red on the maps. Through my own lifetime, that was becoming a more and more mythic Canada; it had less and less relation to reality. I left at a moment when that old British identity was disappearing.

Nash: What do you come back to now?

Ignatieff: A very different Toronto. Just in twenty-five, thirty years there has been a blurring of what once seemed to me to be a small, provincial, small-minded, small town, but in a curious way very sure of what it was. I now look at a much more dynamic, much more with-it, city. It is a light year away from 1965. I am not so sure we know as clearly who we are as a result.

Nash: You believe the multicultural mosaic has had the effect of blurring our identity?

Ignatieff: The immigration that came to Canada in the sixties transformed the place, certainly Metro Toronto, and the consequences have been largely good. But I think it has become very difficult for the political class. People who care about the country, who care about politics and are high-minded, slightly humourless, Canadian do-gooders, suddenly were confronted with a population they couldn't reach. How exactly does the political class reach and invoke and connect to the Dundas Street Chinese? Immigration has made Toronto an infinitely richer place, but it has made the business of political brokerage and political leadership much more complicated than it was in the fifties and the sixties, when you could simply play a certain symbolic game and assume that everybody understood. But people don't understand the symbolic game any more.

Nash: Because they don't understand the symbols?

Ignatieff: Yes. I think that is a good thing, but it makes for difficult times.

Nash: You talk about that period, and our history prior to that, being British. It was also French, of course; it was a duality. The question being asked today is whether the duality has validity in the kind of ethnicity that has occurred in Canada in the last twenty, thirty years.

Ignatieff: Certainly the Québécois, paradoxically, are using the two-founding-races mythology at a time when the rest of the country realizes how jarring that is and how incoherent that is. I have always felt the founding-races line didn't have a resonance. French Canada has also changed out of recognition. We have deep roots in Quebec, in the Eastern Townships, the core of English-speaking Quebec, but that world has changed. In my childhood Montreal was pretty well competely unilingual, and the world I knew was unilingual, and now it is, rather like Toronto, polyglot, tremendously cosmopolitian and, rather unlike Toronto, very much more sure of itself. I have a lot of contacts within the Québécois cultural community, and I have watched their state of mind evolve over ten years. Separation and national identity has ceased to be a religious cause. It has become much more pragmatic.

Nash: Based on economics rather than emotions.

Ignatieff: Yes. It is the politics of pride, but curiously, it was a religious cause. Personal identity and the political cause were one. When I talked to people in the early seventies who were separatists, it was clear this political goal was meeting deep personal needs, and that's what I mean by religious. It was a really intense and burning thing, and it was powered by a memory of grievance. Flash forward to 1991, I was in Montreal in January, and you have a much cooler, more sober, even bored sense of it all. They say, "It's going to happen."

Nash: What's your sense? Is it going to happen coming out of this current crisis?

Ignatieff: In 1960 or 1959, I could understand the deeply felt grievances. I can't quite see the grievance now. A politics of grievance has now been replaced by a politics of pride, in which sovereignty becomes a kind of affirmation of pride. But I keep feeling some of the drive of that original grievance has been lost and a kind of calm certainty has come. You ask me what is going to happen, and I am deeply puzzled because I don't see that any split needs to happen. I can see all kinds of accommodations, constitution-makings, that would avoid it happening, and I can also see the sense of grievance evaporating. But on the other hand, the thing that is so incredibly puzzling, if you live outside this country, is that the cultural difference between London and Paris is considerably less than the cultural difference between Montreal and Toronto. And that cultural difference has grown. The Québécois go to Florida, or New York, or Paris more often than they go to Toronto. They don't have a sense of hostility toward Toronto, but a total indifference, a sense that there is nothing to be taken from there that is of any interest.

Nash: Is the gap between English-speaking Canadians and French-speaking Canadians living in Quebec unbridgeable?

Ignatieff: It shouldn't be. I think some of it has to do with the fact that there has been this dialogue of the deaf between the two cultural communities. English Canada says crudely to Quebec, "We need you because otherwise there is no real reason why we shouldn't become Americans. You are the difference that makes us all different." The Québécois look at that statement and say, "That's patronizing. We don't want to be in a federation simply to make you feel different from the Americans." There is a part of me that sometimes thinks let's separate. Let's chop this thing up. We have a 124-year-old document that was written for colonial society and doesn't correspond to current realities. All that's kept us together is a kind of typical liberal Canadian goodwill of a vague sort that never really dealt with fact.

Nash: You think we should separate, then. Get it over with?

Ignatieff: That's the rational part, the cold part, of me. The warm, hot part of me is very attached to a sentimental idea of federalism from coast to coast. Federal states are very noble experiments in the modern world, but federalism is, in fact, having a lot of difficulty everywhere – India, Ethiopia, and the Soviet Union, where there is a kind of bastard coercive federalism – all of these states are having a terribly difficult time. A Muslim says only Muslims can understand

Muslims. Only whites can understand whites; only blacks can understand blacks; only Québécois can understand Québécois. That epistemology of the modern world, it seems to me, is fantastically dangerous. In a way, the emotional side of me thinks that federalism stands for a different epistemology. It says, "We can understand each other. We don't have to love each other, but we are talking about understanding and there can be understanding across difference."

Nash: Your heart is for maintaining the federalism and your mind wonders whether that is a valid thing to do in this country.

Ignatieff: My mind wonders simply because I think we have such an accumulation of bitterness. We have a thirty-years' war going on in this country, a constitutional debate that is now as old as many of the people alive in this country. Thirty years of this, the best minds in the country, the entire political class, concentrating hard. It's not for want of trying that nobody has been able to solve it over thirty years. That's why the rational side of me is saying it's divorce time, because it will cut through this thing, and English Canadians will have to find a principle of difference other than having a French-speaking minority, and the Québécois will have to find someone else to blame for their problems.

Nash: Is there anything that English-speaking Canadians could offer that would satisfy Quebec's thirst for being master in its own house? English Canadians are probably prepared to think about culture and language, but when you get into others areas such as economic areas, it becomes trickier.

Ignatieff: To be master in your own house is much more than a question of constitutions. It is a question of feeling a personal identity and national identity that are fused and reinforce each other. That's not a matter of constitutions. When I think of a Québécois nationalist, I don't think of a rabid, intolerant, parochial, provincial kind of person. I don't think of someone who is indifferent to minority language rights. I just think of someone who will tell you with tears in his eyes, which again is new terrain for an English Canadian, that, "I know where I was when I heard that René Lévesque died." English Canadians couldn't tell you where they were. They might tell you where they were when Jack Kennedy was shot.

Nash: You have referred to it as the politics of pride. How could English-speaking Canada respond specifically to that? You can respond specifically to a request to transfer this bit of power or that bit of power, but that's not addressing the question of pride and emotion.

Ignatieff: Pierre Trudeau did have a vision and, at heart, a very emotional vision of federalism that says we can understand each other. The premise was that differences can be understood, and he got up across the country and said that, and it was a much more powerful rallying cry than people realized. I hesitate to say that it has died because it still has a claim on my heart and, I think, a claim on the heart of millions of English Canadians. But you go to Quebec and the malice for Trudeau is so deep, it is another fact in this divide. The degree of active dislike for him in Quebec is another fact that makes me pessimistic.

Nash: Is there a sense that he was primarily concerned with the nation, whereas the people to whom you are referring essentially are concerned with what goes on within Quebec? They say, "We really don't care whether you speak French in Manitoba or Vancouver, we want to have control of our interest here." In other words, they are inward-looking rather than outward-looking as Trudeau was.

Ignatieff: Yes I think that's true. There is a high degree of indifference in Quebec to the question of minority language rights across the country. It was important emotionally, but I think that vision of federalism never really washed in Quebec. It's such a big country. St. Boniface is a hell of a long way from Chicoutimi. Everybody has ignored the reality of our politics coming against our land. The emotional part of me says what is fantastic about this country is the sheer impossibility of the political project faced by our geography. When people say it is the most boring country on earth, I want to scream because the political challenge of making a nation out of this amount of land was an epic historic achievement, and the epic quality has been caught by only a few people. Pierre Berton caught part of the resonance.

Nash: What would you like to see Canada be?

Ignatieff: It could exist in two forms: either in a renewed federal form, or in a kind of odd bi-national state, the kind we haven't seen, in which there would be two sovereignties, but they would have many ties in sense of currencies, common approach, and so on. There are certain aspects of the Canadian character I would like to see continue. I think our self-deprecation and our diffidence are absolutely excellent qualities in a world where everybody is baring his soul. But the key things about a nation are what kind of politics it stands for in the world and, I think, a sense of a public-enterprise culture in the very pragmatic sense that you've got to have strong marketers, and you've got to have a strong state, and they have to work together. You have to work out this very particular mix of state and market solutions to social and economic problems.

Nash: Whether it is one or two countries north of the forty-ninth parallel?

Ignatieff: That's another curious similarity between English and French Canada that has never been stated. Look at René Lévesque's nationalization of Hydro. That's a very Canadian thing to have done. We don't talk about about that; that, in fact, the ways in which the state and the market get together to develop their societies is curiously similar in both Quebec and English-speaking Canada, and there is no reason we can't hang on to these similarities. I just feel that Canadians, when pushed hard about their social programs, about the role of state, will care about these things because they come right down to where they live, right down to their guts. There is still the basis for that kind of public-enterprise culture. In saying that's what I hope for in the year 2000, I hope I am not indulging in a kind of fond, despairing hope, but something that is anchored in our experience in a way that we can count on in the next century.

V. Tony Hauser

J. ROBERT S. PRICHARD

Professor Robert Prichard is President of the University of Toronto and a highly respected legal scholar and university administrator. He was dean of the Faculty of Law at the University of Toronto from 1984 to 1990, having joined the faculty in 1976 as an assistant professor. Born in the United Kingdom, Professor Prichard is a graduate of Upper Canada College in Toronto, and attended Swarthmore College, the Graduate School of Business at the University of Chicago, and the Yale Law School. He has served as chairman of the Council of Canadian Law Deans and chairman of the Committee of Ontario Law Deans, and had been a member of the Ontario Law Reform Commission.

"I think we will stay a single country."

Nash: What does it really matter to the average person if Quebec leaves? How would a person see any difference if we were split apart?

Prichard: I ask myself the same question with some frequency because, for as long as I can remember thinking about Canada, I have always felt very strongly about the centrality of Quebec and the presence of Quebec and French language and French culture to Canada. It's part of my own conception of the country, even though I speak French very poorly. I think it is more than just emotion, though, as I look at those things that make this a distinctively attractive country to be part of, to claim citizenship in. I am an immigrant from England, and I say without hesitation that this is the finest place I can imagine. This is a country that has struggled in a way that few have, building a genuinely bicultural, bilingual, bijuridical reality that's now becoming multicultural, multilingual, multiracial, bijuridical in a way that most places aren't. This is a highly worthy, exciting possibility, and I think if you break us down into our constituent parts, sure there are terrific communities and terrific local parts of Canada, but it is not nearly as rewarding as the possibilities of the whole.

Nash: I share that sense of the possibilities of the whole and so do millions of others, so how did we collectively get into this constitutional confrontation?

Prichard: Because we are a deeply democratic society which permits us to talk about secession, breaking up the country, without ever talking of violence, without ever talking of force. There are very few countries in the world that permit that degree of genuine, free self-exploration. It's a wonderful example to the rest of the world that we are genuinely working our way through this question, and we fully accept that one possible outcome may be that we cannot maintain the current integrity of Canada. It's not an outcome I have any sympathy for, but I respect it as an outcome which I would come to accept. People ask why is Canada doing this to itself, and if Canada has it so good relative to the rest of the world, why would we consider taking it apart? It's a strength, not a weakness. It is an exercise born of a confidence about ourselves and our commitment to working problems through in a peaceful, free way.

Nash: In broad terms, what would be the best choice for Canada of the various options that have been talked about?

Prichard: I think we will stay a single country, that the national government will be a lot more than a post office. I think at the end, Canadians in all parts of Canada will be of the view that their lives are richer for a united Canada than they would be for a dismembered Canada. Canadians want government as close to them as possible, as local, as regional as possible, consistent with a set of political institutions and political commitments, constitutionalized as appropriate, that define a nation that is more than the sum of its parts. So I can imagine a significant simplication of the federal government. I think the federal government has done a considerable harm to itself through its undue reluctance to accept withdrawal from various fields and an undue reluctance to accept a government that is closer to the people. I start with a strong presumption in favour of decentralization, subject to trying to articulate those things that must be done nationally in order to realize the broader vision.

Nash: What are those things that must be done nationally?

Prichard: I start with the Charter of Rights. I think our commitment to social justice, which is best expressed through our health system, but which is also expressed through a variety of programs of social justice, from workers' compensation to health to unemployment insurance. I think these programs are symptoms of a genuine commitment to social justice that is distinctively Canadian. Somehow we must have national expression of that commitment, whether this is through social and economic rights in the Charter, whether this is through national objectives for certain social programs, or whether this is exclusively through national income redistribution.

Nash: Do you think that Quebec would accept this approach given the current mood?

Prichard: There is no doubt that Quebec has been highly hostile, has been deeply concerned that the Charter could lead to undermining the distinctive nature of Quebec. But the people of Quebec are no less committed to their rights in the Charter than anybody else.

Nash: How do you give Quebeckers a sense of the value of working within the federation?

Prichard: I think you have a genuine willingness to review the distribution and exercise of government power in Canada so as to realize the whole benefits of great decentralization. A genuine willingness for the federal government to consider withdrawal from fields where what we have is over-lapping levels of government, which is counter-productive and ineffective. You must have in place a set of principles that compel our allegiance to something broader, and I start with the Charter. I start with a commitment to social justice. We must have respect for the bicultural, bilingual in our country. And there is the question of the aboriginal peoples. It is common ground to all Canadians that we must commit ourselves nationally to respecting these people.

Nash: How would you do that? What mechanisms would you provide to give the aboriginal presence in the federal system a boost?

Prichard: I think that proposals for the aboriginal peoples of Canada to be granted powers equivalent to that of a province, although recognizing the absence of a contiguous geographic presence, would readily play themselves out in Senate reform, readily play themselves out in replacing the Indian Act with a new version, readily play themselves out in nego-tiations for self-government.

Nash: What does your instinct tell you about the ultimate outcome of our national debate on the shape of Canada? Will we be able to find the formula in the rest of Canada that will be acceptable to Quebec?

Prichard: I think we will succeed because I think most Cana-dians can find common ground. It would be particularly intense if we break up. I think it is extremely risky for all parts of Canada. The economic costs are significant, but that in some ways is the least of the threat. Canada has been able to hold on to a status as one of the major powers of the earth, despite our modest population and relatively modest eco-nomic circumstances. We've got an enormously enviable rep-utation internationally. But if we separate, over time we will lose much of that. I would like to think of Ontario as a strong, important place, and it commands my loyalty as a community, but it's a mere shadow of Canada. And I must say I feel the same about the Atlantic provinces, and the same about the West. Anyone who spends time around the globe knows it is still the best calling-card in the world to say that you are a Canadian. I don't think you can be born with a greater opportunity than to be born Canadian.

Nash: If we become less than we now are, what would be our influence on the world?

Prichard: I think we would drop to secondary status.

Nash: What danger is there, too, that we may become more drawn to the United States?

Prichard: My own prediction is not that we would become parts of the United States in a formal constitutional sense, but rather that each part of Canada would lose dimensions of their distinctiveness as a result of not being part of a greater whole. I think what would happen is not constitutional amalgamation with the United States of British Columbia or of Alberta or of other parts of Canada, but rather a loss of strength and a loss of distinctiveness, a loss of capacity to create a community for ourselves that is genuinely distinctive. Provincial governments in Canada already have significantly greater powers than the state governments in the United States.

Nash: A deadline has been proposed of October 1992. Can we develop a consensus in areas of Canada outside Quebec in time to meet that deadline, and in time to have an agreed-upon constitutional approach for a new Canada?

Prichard: I don't see this as something that will be completed and put to bed in a short period of time. We are a country unlike many in that, in a free and open way, we are prepared to continue to talk about our relationships among ourselves. We will continue to do so through this decade and into the next and the next.

Nash: Well into the twenty-first century?

Prichard: Yes. So the trick is never to let the amplitude of our conversation reach such a point where we let go of a united Canada. If we do at some point step over that boundary, I will count myself among those who will devote a chunk of the rest of my life to trying to bring it back together.

Carlos Cocola

TOM KENT

Born in England, Tom Kent worked with the Manchester Guardian *and* The Economist *before coming to Canada where, in 1954, he became editor of the* Winnipeg Free Press. *In 1963, Kent was named Prime Minister Pearson's principal policy adviser and later served as deputy minister in the departments of Manpower and Immigration and Regional Economic Expansion. He went to Nova Scotia in 1971 to head the crown corporation Devco and, later, Sydney Steel. He subsequently chaired a royal commission on the media and became dean at Dalhousie University in Halifax. He lives in Mabou, Nova Scotia.*

"We've got to restore and deepen the social contract."

Nash: Is the current constitutional confrontation an inevitable product of our history, inevitably flowing out of conflicting national objectives and regional desires?

Kent: I think it was inevitable. I don't think, for example, that Meech Lake would have done more than postpone the conflict and make it even more difficult. It is an issue that is best faced now one way or the other.

Nash: Do you sense in the country a will to survive?

Kent: I think there is a desire to survive. How strong the will is, is very hard to tell. But yes, I think it is there. It is strong enough, if only we can overcome what I call the atrophy of the political process.

Nash: Are we thirsting for some sort of political saviour? Is that what is needed?

Kent: Certainly better leadership than what we have, but I don't like the man-on-a-white-horse idea. What we've got to do fundamentally, in my view, is restore and deepen what I would call the social contract, which I think is the essence of any satisfactory nation. It's a feeling on the part of the community that the institutions of the community, the public ones above all, genuinely exist in order to lean against the unfairness, the arbitrariness, the inequalities of society. I think we had that in Canada, particularly in the post-war period, but I am afraid that in the seventies and eighties it faded quite a lot.

Nash: Is there any one particular reason why that happened that stands out?

Kent: The one that for me was the start of the process was the position adopted by the Trudeau government early in the seventies on the issue of employment. The most fundamental expression of a social contract is a high level of employment. Now it isn't always easy to have a high level of employment, but there should never be any doubt about it as the objective. Trudeau, in his unsympathetic style, very early on when unemployment had gone to 6 per cent, which at that time was a horrifying level, said, "Oh well, it has to be, and we are quite prepared to have it go higher." That was to my mind a denial of the essential objectives that are embodied in the idea of the social contract. And then there was also the business that it was "not my job to sell your wheat." By his style and by the very inconsistent attention that he gave to many issues, and especially economic issues, Trudeau really did quite a lot to upset that consensus. And ironically, the man who did deeply care about national unity and a strong federal government, in fact, undermined it by some of the things he did. I have every respect for his Charter of Rights and Freedoms, but most of the things that he did or failed to do, I think helped lessen the sense of the contract and, of course, made so many of his policies ineffective.

Nash: Do you have a vision of what Canada should be like?

Kent: To me, the fundamental thing is the sense of social contract, which is democratic, egalitarian. What it has to have is institutions that people can feel are trying move steadily in the direction of a better society. Obviously that has to be expressed through all kinds of national institutions, such as the railways and the CBC, which is the most important one. I don't say that to please you, Knowlton, I feel it very strongly. Particularly, I would have to say, CBC Radio.

Nash: I get the sense from you that you want a strong central, federalist government, and not that much devolution of power to the provinces.

Kent: The federal government has to have four fundamental powers. It may be that the federal government has too few rather than too many powers in respect to the economy. The position of maintaining some sort of economic union through a vague association is, in my opinion, absolutely unacceptable. You can have a satisfactory economic union only with a strong federal government; a federal government responsible for not just the monetary policy, for managing the currency, but for overall fiscal policy. By that I mean that policies of the provinces have to be harmonized with it more effectively than they are now. One of the most muddled areas of jurisdiction is the regulation of financial institutions, which should be purely federal. Foreign affairs, defence, are other areas. And we have to have a federal government which has cultural responsibility, at least in terms of the CBC. I am not so sure that the Canada Council, and so on, is as important, but certainly the CBC, the main channel of public communication across the nation, has to be a federal matter. The CBC and the regulation of other broadcasting activities. Now if those four areas are clearly federal, then I would be prepared to live with a great deal of devolution to the provinces in almost everything else. Perhaps devolution is the wrong word, more powers to the provinces, though. There have to be flexible arrangements so that some provinces, smaller provinces, can have things run by Ottawa. But the larger provinces can run themselves quite satisfactorily. But again, on those fundamentals of external affairs, which is so crucial to economic policy in the globalized economy, external affairs and therefore defence, on all the main instruments of economic policy, and on the most fundamental communication instruments, those, in my view, have got to be federal. If Quebec would not agree to that, I would say sadly that it is better to have separation than to dilute federalism to the point at which it becomes ineffective.

Nash: Do you judge that it is likely Quebec would agree to those four areas?

Kent: If it is properly put, there is still quite a decent chance that it would. I think opinion in Quebec is not accurately reflected by the power ambitions of Quebec politicians. That is particularly true in external affairs, where from the early sixties Quebec politicians had a great desire to operate on the international stage. But I don't think that goes down to the popular will. And I think the desire not to disturb the economy is strong enough that there is a very reasonable chance that a properly articulated proposal on behalf of the rest of Canada to Quebec, on the sort of lines I have talked about, would, in fact, get a majority in Quebec. It is what we have got to try, and if it doesn't work, too bad. Then it is still better to build the rest of the country and accept a separate Quebec.

Nash: If Quebec said no to those proposals, do you think there is enough cohesion in the rest of the country to proceed as a unit? Or is there a danger of some areas beginning to think in terms of also splitting away?

Kent: I think the provincial governments would take the opportunity to demand more power, but I don't think that would reflect the popular will. No, I think there is enough sense of cohesion in the rest of the country that they would want to rebuild a country under federal leadership with a strong federal government in the areas I have been talking about. I think the country would cohere without Quebec. I hope it won't have to, but if need be, it would.

Nash: If need be, with a separation by Quebec, how do you divide up things like the national debt and the assets, and so on?

Kent: That would be a very tough negotiation, and that's why I think it is so important that the rest of the country should produce a proposal that, even if it doesn't turn out to be a majority, quite a lot of Quebeckers would be prepared to accept, so that the atmosphere of that pretty difficult negotiation could be conducted in a not too unfriendly atmosphere; that it could be a reasonably cheerful divorce by consent rather than a nasty battle. There are very difficult issues. The most difficult of all is the position of the aboriginal people in Quebec. A clear obligation of the federal government in its arrangement with Quebec, if it comes to separation, has got to be one in which we don't shuffle off our responsibility for those people. We have to ensure that the terms of the separation are such that aboriginal rights, as they have become in the rest of the country, are also implemented in Quebec.

Nash: Do you think that sovereignty asssociation is possible?

Kent: No. Not as it seems to be defined. Sovereignty association, as everyone talks about it, is really a device for maintaining an economic union, in which the partner that has only one-quarter of the population would have as much say as the partner that has three-quarters. That clearly is not going to be acceptable to English Canada. It just can't be acceptable.

Nash: So in your judgement, Quebec would have to be totally separate?

Kent: No. What I am talking about is what people are now talking about as asymmetrical federalism; what we used to call special status. Special status is a bad name because it gave the idea that Quebec was having special privileges. Asymmetrical federalism means Quebec running many things that elsewhere in the country are run by the federal government. It means Quebec members of Parliament not participating in those activities which in the rest of the country are federal, but are not in Quebec. You could build a political structure of that kind. It would be a somewhat difficult one in some ways, but it could be done, and we should be willing to try it if Quebec will accept it and if the central economic powers, and the others I have talked about, remain federal.

Nash: Aside from what your preference is, what do you think Canada is likely to look like in the year 2000?

Kent: Well, perhaps I am a perpetual optimist, but I think something like the kind of thing I have been talking about is perfectly possible. I think there is enough will for it lying there, provided we can get a process into some sort of shape. The danger is that, on the one hand, there will be no amicable deal with Quebec, but a nasty separation. The danger on the other hand is that the federal political parties and the provincial premiers will accept a dilution of federalism in order to keep Quebec in – a dilution of federalism to an extent that will destroy the possibility of the sort of country we have been talking about. But you ask me what I think is most likely, and perhaps rather optimistically, I think what I have been talking about is desirable and is still most likely.

Nash: You differentiate between what the politicians may do or are thinking of doing, and the people. You seem to feel there is more flexibility among the people than there is among the politicians. Am I right?

Kent: I think that among the people there is more will to pursue the kind of Canada that we have been talking about. But the political process has become so fundamentally weak and, in the general sense of the word, corrupt, that the politicians are not hearing the wishes of the public. Getting the political process into better shape is a fundamental condition. That's what people want. They have completely lost faith in the political process. Clearly it has got to be restored.

Nash: Talking about politics, in relations to the aboriginal people, would you set aside a number of seats in which only an aboriginal person could be elected?

Kent: Yes. I think that could very probably be a part of the structure. But one of my theses would be that we should elect the House of Commons by proportional representation and have a Senate elected from single-member constituencies. The Senate could play a very useful role, not only in the conventional idea that it strengthens the regional voice, but in making those regional voices even more real by the senators being the spokesmen for their constituencies.

Nash: Are you a Triple-E supporter – a Senate elected, equal, and effective?

Kent: I am not in the sense that I think it is practical to have an equal number from each province. Certainly the Senate should be heavily biased towards regions rather than one man one vote. But I don't think that Ontario can be expected to have the same number of senators as Prince Edward Island.

Nash: Which the Americans do.

Kent: Yes, but that's a different history. Our history has always been in terms of regions rather than individual provinces. The other reason why I don't agree on the Triple-E is that I don't think the Senate can or should be effective in the sense of being as powerful as the House of Commons. The government can answer only to the House of Commons. The Senate could have very considerable powers. But in the last analysis, after a delaying period and so on, legislation passed by the House of Commons has to become law.

Nash: Threaded all the way through our conversation, we have been talking about what Canada means to you. Could you sum up what you think of when you think of Canada?

Kent: It's a country which has succeeded in being an extremely free, tolerant society, with a good deal of concern about equality. A society that has a degree of equality of opportunity through its educational system, through its human resource policies, its training, and so on, and a society that provides medicare, an essential ingredient in the concept of the sort of society we are. Above all, what's important is the diversity of its people. One must never, in my view, talk about English Canada. It's not English Canada, it's the highly interesting conglomeration of people of many kinds. Sure it's important that we have a common language across most of the country. As French is in the language of Quebec, English has to be the language of the rest of the country, but with a great deal of diversity of origin, and so on. I hope it's a country that will continue to be tolerant in its acceptance of new people, though I have a strong view that the main criterion for immigrants should be how young they are. The ideal immigrant is an orphan. Not that immigrants should be only orphans, but the younger the better. Still, a society that is, above all, free, and relatively equal.

CONCLUSION

I began my search for a Vision of Canada as a saddened pessimist. I end it as a cautious optimist.

At the start of my travels and conversations I was oppressed by the negative rigidity that lay behind the "T'hell with them!" attitude that I sensed in both Quebec and English-speaking Canada. It is still there, but I've found it is not as pervasive as I feared, nor as ingrained. In spite of the cacophony of the constitutional debate, as reflected in my conversations across Canada, I found a deep, if quiet, pool of affection for and pride in our country. Unlike our southern neighbours, we are introverts in articulating our patriotism, but it's there just beneath that protective outer layer of professed indifference.

The first hint that my pessimism was a misreading of the mood came, of all places, at the Montreal Expos opening home game of the 1991 baseball season. Jostling through the fans down to my seat along the first base line just before the game began, I muttered apprehensively to my companion Mordecai Richler, "I hope to God the boos aren't too bad when they play 'O Canada.'" The spit-and-polish Canadian military band, with drums and trumpets poised under cloudy skies, stood just back from the pitcher's mound. As the first notes sounded scattered boos arose, and my heart sank. "God, here it comes," I moaned to Mordecai. But, at first almost imperceptibly, and then slowly growing louder, there were cheers in the upper part of the left-field bleachers, then in centre-field, and then 35,000 voices in Olympic Stadium drowned out the booing, surging into an almost defiant roar as "O Canada" ended and Oil Can Boyd took the mound for

Montreal. It was an astonishing, revealing, and, for me, awakening moment of anecdotal evidence that there is a strong residue of Canadianism even among these mostly French-speaking Montreal baseball fans. Alas, it didn't do the Expos much good, for they blew a lead and lost their opener to the St. Louis Cardinals 5-4, but it did rattle my pessimism about the attitude of Quebec and the future of Canada.

As I sought to explore the Quebec soul outside the baseball stadium, I found three distinct groups: separatists, federalists, and sovereigntists. There may be quarrels over how many Quebeckers are in each group, and while there probably are more separatists than federalists, the sovereigntists dominate, representing perhaps as much as one-half of all Quebeckers. For separatists, the only issue is power. They may exploit the issue of pride, but they have a new-found, cocksure confidence about their own economic entrepreneurial ability and cultural creativity and a contempt for the way Ottawa has managed the Canadian economy. But the sovereigntists are the deciding swing group, the focus of the battle for Quebec's soul. To each of them, sovereignty means something a little different, a kind of soothing Linus blanket covering a multitude of have-your-cake-and-eat-it-too options. It is a comfort for those who, to paraphrase Dalton Camp, wear a separatist heart on a federalist sleeve. For some, it means power; for most, it means pride.

Today's brand of Quebec nationalism began with Honoré Mercier in the 1880s, was nourished by Henri Bourassa in the early years of this century, was inflamed by the Quiet Revolution of three decades ago, was electrified by De-Gaulle's "Vive le Quebec Libre," emboldened by René Lévesque, and propelled by the collapse of the Meech Lake accord. As Allan Blakeney says, "something snapped" in Canada over Meech, and Quebeckers, cherishing their nationalist history, recoiled in wounded pride at what they perceived as a slap in the face from The Rest of Canada. But something has been happening to all those highly charged particles of separatism. A kind of ennui is spreading among some Quebec sovereigntists, eating into the exuberance, eroding the force. There is now a weariness with the debate, spawned in part by a desire to get on with other things and in part by nagging worries about jobs, health care, the future. Dedicated separatist activists may retain their determination, but the outcome of any vote will be decided by sovereigntists concerned with pocketbook issues and pride, and by the attitude they see in The Rest of Canada. There is, however, a danger that The Rest of Canada may misread this creeping weariness and become lethargic in developing a renewed federalism. The Quebec mood is volatile and will readily switch about if Quebeckers see any real or perceived sign of rejection.

That large, decisive bloc of soft sovereigntists wants a message from The Rest of Canada that recognizes their pride, recognizes in tangible terms the historical bargain of duality that Sir John A. Macdonald and George-Étienne Cartier made in 1867, and recognizes the need for a new, functional, pragmatic federalism, shifting powers both up and down to make Canada work more effectively. As Premier Bourassa has said, "We need a new Canada. The old one no longer works."

Most of the rest of the country wants changes, too, and so there is an opportune confluence of Quebec desires and Canadian needs. To oversimplify the attitudes of the nation, Quebec wants more power within the province; Atlantic Canada and the West want more effective representation at the centre; Ontario wants only a few changes; and Native people want recognition of their founding-nation status and a form of self-government.

Bourassa's vision of a new Canada as outlined in Quebec's power-demanding proposals shocked The Rest of Canada out of its wits. Alarms bells of defiance rang out across the country as many snapped that separation was better than evisceration, that Quebec wanted Ottawa turned into a post office and nothing more. But evisceration or separation doesn't have to be the only choice. There is every indication that the message the people of Quebec want to hear, especially the swing voters, is acceptance of the partnership of duality; power adjustments to recognize that reality in areas of language, culture, immigration, communications, and a few others; and acknowledgement of Quebec's distinct society.

But the central question is, what will be the response to that desire? The Rest of Canada has geological fault lines that ideologically separate the nation. There are those who say, "Peace at any price!"; those who want Quebec to stay, but not at any price; and those who say, "Let them go!" Indeed there is an odd-couple alliance between Quebec separatists and the "Let them go'ers" in their mutual disdain for duality.

Quebeckers have thought about all this for years, but The Rest of Canada has not, and thus Quebeckers have a much better developed idea of what they are and what they want than people in the other provinces. There is, in fact, no English Canada as such, but rather a kaleidoscopic society still mostly ruled by white Anglos on the last legs of their societal dominance, who find soul-searching uncomfortable and articulating emotions a bit embarrassing. But this is a defining moment and the very nature of the constitutional crisis is forcing them and all of English-speaking Canada to look inward and examine their souls to decide what kind of a society and nation they want. We are not going to follow the precedent of the American Civil War to prevent part of our country breaking away, and, besides, there is no Lincoln around. There also is a gnawing self-reproach as we reflect on our indifference toward the Native peoples from Batoche to Oka. In recent years we have developed a bitchy, waspish, self-absorption and a contempt for established authority that has warped our ability to understand our country and has brought a dangerous fragmentation to the nation. The inability to get our act together has encouraged the separatists in Quebec, as we in so-called English Canada have watched our political undertakers sleepwalk their way to separation.

But, as Quebec's mood may be modifying, ever so slightly, so, too, is that of The Rest of Canada. The ill-humour may be easing as we think the unthinkable and stare at the abyss of separation and its implications of international irrelevance, financial instability, and Americanization. Even more persuasive, however, is the growing awareness that there are unique Canadian qualities, that this country may indeed already be that "kinder, gentler" land that George Bush hopes the United States might one day become.

One of the problems for English-speaking Canadians is that they are forever searching for their identity. There used to be a clear-cut identity in The Rest of Canada and it was British. "A British subject I was born. A British subject I will die," said Sir John A. "Ready. Aye ready!" said another prime minister, anglophile Arthur Meighen. But there are new realities overriding our old values. Our Britishness has been diminished by immigration and our increasing aping of America. New Canadians from Europe, Africa, the Far East, and elsewhere now dominate our city streets, if not yet our levers of power, and their values are not the values of the founding British, let alone the founding French.

Another old value succumbing to a new reality is the constitutional pendulum of power. Centralism bestrode the nation from the Second World War to recent years, but the battle cry of decentalization and "Power to the Provinces!" has swung the pendulum back toward the provinces. Through the televised executive federalism of First Ministers' meetings, we saw the clash of nation-building versus province-building, with an apparent provincial goal of "*dix* nations not *deux* nations" in a phrase used by Professor Edward McWhinney. The provincial power drive radiated from the irreconcilable conflict of two visions of Canada: duality and equality. Surely, duality is historically correct; it is the bargain made in 1867. The British may have been victorious in that fifteen-minute battle on the Plains of Abraham, and Lord Durham may have urged assimilation of the French, as he warned of "two nations warring in the bosom of a single state," but Macdonald and Cartier chose another way; they chose English-French partnership.

History changed Canada, however, into a nation at cross-purposes, as we spread west and north, as immigrants flooded in bringing new ideas and cultures, as we became more Americanized, as provincial barons confronted federal lords in a paralyzing combat over national objectives and regional demands, and as Native people began demanding constitutional recognition of their rights.

So the confrontation between the vision of Canada as a duality and burgeoning demands for equality is the essence of the question for English-speaking Canadians. If duality is rejected, Quebec will almost surely go on the grounds that The Rest of Canada is welshing on history. The challenge now is to devise language that will both accept history and recognize contemporary reality, and that points to asymmetric federalism. For that matter, asymmetry already exists, for instance, in the different legal systems in Quebec and The Rest of Canada, and in other matters. From my conversations around the country, it seems to me most Canadians are prepared to accept Quebec as a distinct society for, of course, it is in language, culture, and style, and most Canadians also appear willing to accept Quebec authority over language, culture, manpower-training, immigration, and some other areas. I also sense a willingness in The Rest of Canada to use the constitutional crisis as an opportunity not just to address Quebec concerns, but to reinvent the whole of Canada through a new federalism that is less ideological and more functional and pragmatic; a nation that has equality but not necessarily uniformity.

In my search for my Vision of Canada, I was sobered by the almost unrelenting pessimism of the constitutional experts to whom I talked. Having sat around the negotiating tables for so many frustrating years, they reflect on past rigidities and shudder at the huge gap between stated positions, feeling that only a miracle can bridge it. But this time, I believe, it's different; this time the deadline is real; this time it's the last chance for Canada; this time, if we fail, we won't be throwing away an opportunity, we'll be throwing away a country. That realization concentrates the mind as nothing ever has in our history. And this time, too, the public has imposed itself as never before. Politicians will ignore public attitudes at their peril, because what Canadians want is an answer, not a posture.

Aside from reaffirming the duality, the partnership with

Quebec and its distinct society, that answer also means functional pragmatism in our federal-provincial power structure. It means a serious look at the ending of provincial trade barriers, which currently make Canada's economic union less free than the European Community's and costs Canadians an estimated $6.5 billion a year; at ending the duplication of and competition between provincial and federal services; at the need for strengthened national standards or objectives in such areas as education, health, welfare – the social contract as Tom Kent describes it; at more regional power in central institutions, including an elected, effective, and if not fully equal, at least nearly equal, Senate; at a loosening of the rigidities in constitutional amending formulas; and, of critical importance, a serious look at a new, fair deal with aboriginal peoples, so they have more control over their land and their destiny, and more representation at the centre.

Without a vision people shrivel, so, apart from what Lise Bissonnette has called "the plumbing" of nation-building, we also need to articulate a chest-swelling evocation of a national vision of Canada, some poetry in our constitution enshrining the values, principles, and spirit of this country. We need something more emotional than "Peace, Order, and Good Government," although perhaps a little less provocative than "Life, Liberty, and the Pursuit of Happiness," or "Liberté! Égalité! Fraternité!" Our history has been less bloody than the nations that gave birth to those stirring mottoes, but that has made us less bloody-minded and has led to our genius for compromise.

Despite some sharply conflicting rhetoric, most of the nation, my cross-country soundings indicated, is ready to accept the bulk of these conditions of a virtual revolution in federalism. All revolutions are the kicking-in of a rotten door, and Canada's constitutional door is ready for kicking. There is an almost desperate need for persuasive political voices organizing, stimulating, and articulating consensus-driven ideas, which can dissolve the visceral frustrations on the surface of our body politic. For years we have suffered constitutional constipation, and what we need now is action and political leadership less motivated by power-grabbing and more sensitive to the people who really do want this country to work.

We may not be a nation of flag-waving, Yankee Doodle Dandies, but through this debate we are discovering deep within the Canadian spirit a surging awareness that we have something unique and precious in this land in the northern half of North America. If we fail, a spark of hope, of humanity, will have sputtered out.

Printed in Canada